TELEVISION 1955 MONTAGE BY CECIL MADDEN

CECIL MADDEN, 1944.

STARLIGHT DAYS

THE MEMOIRS OF

CECIL MADDEN

THE WORLD'S FIRST TELEVISION PRODUCER

Television in the 1930s
and Wartime Radio

EDITED BY
HIS GRAND-DAUGHTER

JENNIFER LEWIS

TREVOR SQUARE PUBLICATIONS
LONDON

STARLIGHT DAYS

First published in 2007 by
TREVOR SQUARE PUBLICATIONS
31 Trevor Square, London SW7 1DY
Email: starlightdays@gmail.com

ISBN 978-0-9556645-0-2

Photographs courtesy of the BBC,
except for those credited from other sources

Produced and printed by members of
THE GUILD OF MASTER CRAFTSMEN

Cover Design by RPM Print & Design
Book Design and Typesetting by Cecil Charles Smith
Typeset in Garamond Book

Printed and bound in Great Britain by
RPM PRINT & DESIGN
2-3 Spur Road, Quarry Lane, Chichester, West Sussex PO19 8PR

CONTENTS

The Alexandra Palace, North London.

1

BEGINNINGS

HERE'S LOOKING AT YOU

"Experiment, make it your model day and night,
Experiment and it will lead you to the light.
If this advice you'll only employ
The future can offer you infinite joy and merriment.
Experiment and you'll see."

COLE PORTER

VICTOR HUGO said, "Nothing in the world is so powerful as an idea whose time has come." In the summer of 1936, our time had come. One August day my staff and I were all summoned to the Council Chamber at Broadcasting House by Director of Television Gerald Cock and told our new jobs. I was to be producer and planner for the new television service. We were told, as was obvious, that no one knew anything about television production and that we would all have to learn. However we were also told we would have four months to prepare and that nothing would be expected of us until November. Fair enough. Then we all piled into cars and went out to see our offices at Alexandra Palace in North London.

My office was on the third floor of the Tower, communicating with Gerald Cock's own office through a secretaries' room. When I got there my room had my name on the door but was entirely bare of furniture, except for a telephone on the floor in a corner, which was shrilly ringing. It was Gerald Cock. "Wash out all I've been saying", he said, "I've had Alex Moody on about the Radio Show at Radiolympia. They can't sell the stands, they don't want it to be a failure and they want us to rescue them with television. He also said he had agreed, no demur would be accepted and we must get on with it.

He said, "You are the senior man. Get the staff together, think out what you're going to do, and let me know by six o'clock. You open in nine days."

So I was thrown in at the deep end. As it turned out, it was providential. It gave us no time to think and become self-conscious. I got the staff together immediately and told them that this was how it was going to be, and I asked, "Now who wants to produce the first programme?" Nobody wanted to. So I said, "Now, I am in charge, there's not going to be any argument, I am going to produce this programme." George More O'Ferrall asked to assist me. Peter Bax and Harry Pringle requested to be studio managers. In the excitement we little realised it would be part of television history, and that television would really change the world.

August 26 was the date we would open. I decided to put on a variety show, and there was no time to waste. I phoned a songwriter, Ronald Hill, and commissioned a new song. He came up at once with '*Here's Looking at You!*' a title that was an inspiration. Titles are very important and I decided our whole show should be called '*Here's Looking at You*'. This move intrigued the press and cheered the radio industry. From now on they expected miracles.

Putting together that first programme was teamwork. We all scoured the current shows and quickly engaged redheaded singer Helen McKay. The Three Admirals were a

Gerald Cock,
first director of
BBC Television.

Cecil Madden,
Programme Planner and
producer of *Picture Page.*

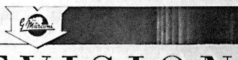

This Marconi set was advertised in *Radio Times* in February 1937.
The picture on the set on the left was viewed as a reflection in a mirror.

piano act who had just finished in '*Anything Goes*', the Cole Porter musical show at the Palace Theatre. We booked the Griffith Brothers 'Pogo the performing horse' with Miss Lutie, and Carol Chilton and Mateo Thomas, two Chilean dancers whose dates had gone wrong. Chilton and Thomas were a first class act based on balancing on plates on rising pedestals. The horse was to please children of all ages and contained Fred Griffith and Ronnie Tate, son of the celebrated Harry Tate. They worked with 'Miss Lutie.' It was a good bill and they all liked each other, despite the appalling lack of communications to North London. Artists kept getting lost in the grounds while walking up the hill. Leslie Mitchell, Jasmine Bligh and Elizabeth Cowell had been secretly hired some months earlier, but as Bligh and Cowell were both taken ill at the last minute, Leslie Mitchell did the announcing alone for the first few days.

The next problem was that we had been ordered to do the show twice a day for ten days, alternating between the Marconi System in Studio A one day and the Baird System in Studio B the next. Studio A had a control room at one end, perched high up at the top of a ladder, B had a low control room jutting out into the studio and set in the middle like a turret. We concentrated on A as the system was more satisfying. In fact the Baird System really didn't work, it was like using morse code when you knew that next door you could telephone.

The only technique I knew was of the stage, so I divided up the studio into three stages behind one another, separated by curtains. The three cameras were placed roughly in line but at different heights. They were light and could be lifted off the stands and held in the arms, but the image in the viewfinders was upside down and focusing could only be done by hand. For a close-up the camera had to go in close. You don't miss what you never had.

The Radio Times with programmes for the first official week at
Alexandra Palace. The billing for the opening was incorrect because the
revised arrangements for the inauguration by the two television
systems, Baird and Marconi-E.M.I. were too late for inclusion.

THE RADIO TIMES, ISSUE DATED OCTOBER 30

PROGRAMMES

9.15 Tempo and Taps
ROSALIND WADE
in a demonstration of Tap Dancing

Rosalind Wade, as well as being a brilliant dancer herself, has an extraordinary flair as a teacher. She has appeared in Variety and has organised dancing scenes in several Hollywood films. This, then, is a great chance for would-be tap-dancers to pick up a point or two from an expert.
Altogether, she runs eight dancing troupes. Radio listeners will remember the regular broadcasts of her Dancing Daughters.

9.35 Interval
Time, Weather

9.40 MARTIN TAUBMAN
with his Electronde
A Demonstration of its Music and Effects

10.0 CLOSE

Thursday

3.0 PROGRAMME SUMMARY

3.5 BRITISH MOVIETONE NEWS

3.15 Interval
Time, Weather

3.20 THE MERCURY BALLET
Marie Rambert's Company
in
Pavane and Tordion from Capriol Suite
(*Warlock*. Choreography by Frederick Ashton)
Solo from Swan Lake } (*Tchaikovsky*)
Sugar Plum Fairy
Shepherd's Wooing
(*Handel*, arr. Beecham)
Solo from Forge de Dance (*Berners*)
Columbine (*Tchaikovsky*)
La Guirlande } (*Hugh Bradford*)
Pompette
Pas de Trois from Alcina (*Handel*)
with
MAUDE LLOYD
WALTER GORE
ANDRÉE HOWARD
FRANK STAFF
HUGH LAING
THE BBC TELEVISION ORCHESTRA
Leader, Boris Pecker
Conductor, HYAM GREENBAUM

Marie Rambert was trained by Maestro Enrico Cecchetti, maître de ballet of the Diaghileff company. She appeared with that company in 1913, and later in London in the ballet Pomme d'Or. After her marriage to Ashley Dukes, she opened a school of ballet and founded the Ballet Club in her own little theatre now known as the Mercury. Here regular performances of ballet are given and a repertoire of over twenty-five original works has been produced. The company of young English choreographers and dancers trained by her includes Pearl Argyle, Maude Lloyd, Andrée Howard, Frederick Ashton, Harold Turner, Antony Tudor, William Chappell, and many others whose work has created an English tradition in ballet.

3.45 'Television Comes to London'
A BBC Film

4.0 CLOSE
At the close of this afternoon's programme a chart arranged in co-operation with the Air Ministry will forecast the weather

9.0 PROGRAMME SUMMARY

9.5 BRITISH MOVIETONE NEWS

9.15 Autumn Glory
Prize Chrysanthemums
from the National Chrysanthemum Society's Show
Described by W. WARDMAN and E. F. HAWES

9.30 Interval
Time, Weather

9.35 THE MERCURY BALLET
(Details as at 3.20)

10.0 CLOSE

Friday

3.0 PROGRAMME SUMMARY

3.5 Silver Fox Breeding
Four foxes will be exhibited by a representative of the Silver Fox Breeders' Association of Great Britain and Northern Ireland

3.20 BRITISH MOVIETONE NEWS

3.30 Interval
Time, Weather

3.35 From the London Theatre
SOPHIE STEWART
(*By permission of London Film Production, Ltd.*)
in scenes from
The Royalty Theatre production
'Marigold'
a Scottish Comedy
by L. ALLEN HARKER and F. R. PRYOR
Stage Production by J. Graham Pockett and Lance Lister
with
Jean Clyde, Walter Roy, John Bailey, Brenda Harvey, Violet Moffat
Presentation by G. More O'Ferrall

Sophie Stewart, a Scot, made her first appearance in London in the title role of Marigold in 1929. She has played this part nearly a thousand times in England, Canada, and the United States since then, but this play had such a rare charm that it is once again revived in the West End.

Here you see Sophie Stewart (left) in the title rôle of *Marigold*, scenes from which will be broadcast on Friday afternoon at 3.35. With her are Jean Clyde as Mrs. Pringle and John Bailey as Forsyth.

4.0 CLOSE
At the close of this afternoon's programme a chart arranged in co-operation with the Air Ministry will forecast the weather

9.0 PROGRAMME SUMMARY

9.5 BRITISH MOVIETONE NEWS

9.15 Boxing
A Demonstration of Training by Members of the
ALEXANDRA AMATEUR BOXING CLUB

9.35 Interval
Time, Weather

9.40 'Television Comes to London'
A BBC Film

10.0 CLOSE

Saturday

3.0 PROGRAMME SUMMARY

3.5 The Zoo Today
Some animals with their keepers
Introduced by DAVID SETH-SMITH

3.20 BRITISH MOVIETONE NEWS

3.30 Interval
Time, Weather

3.35 Cabaret
MABEL SCOTT
Singer of Modern Songs
HORACE KENNEY
Comedian
MOLLY PICON
In songs and impressions
THE BBC TELEVISION ORCHESTRA
Leader, Boris Pecker
Conductor, HYAM GREENBAUM
Production by DALLAS BOWER

4.0 CLOSE
At the close of this afternoon's programme a chart arranged in co-operation with the Air Ministry will forecast the weather

9.0 PROGRAMME SUMMARY

9.5 The Autumn Galleries
Pictures and Sculpture from Forthcoming Exhibitions
Described by JOHN PIPER

9.20 BRITISH MOVIETONE NEWS

9.30 Interval
Time, Weather

9.35 Cabaret
(Details as at 3.35)

10.0 CLOSE

N, in the studio that made this transmission possible.

9.20   ' Picture Page '

N, A Magazine of Topical and General Interest

Devised and Edited by CECIL MADDEN
Produced by G. MORE O'FERRALL

The Switchboard Girl . . . . JOAN MILLER

This is the first of a series in which people of interest will be introduced. In the recent test transmissions, Squadron-Leader Swain, who broke the aeroplane altitude record, was one of the subjects. In every way the technique is novel. For instance, Joan Miller, who links the show together, introduces each person by plugging in a telephone switchboard after a few preliminary words of description. She is a young Canadian actress who was recently leading lady in the Clemenceau play *The Tiger*, and last December she played in the radio version of *On the Spot*. Curiously enough, when she was in Vancouver she used to train telephone girls.

9.50   BRITISH MOVIETONE NEWS

The Radio Times
with the programme
for the first official week
at Alexandra Palace.

Studio B,
The Baird System:
showing the
'Intermediate Film Camera'
behind the glass window
at Alexandra Palace.

We played an act on stage one, then the curtains parted and cameras moved on to stage two, and then again to stage three. It worked quite well, saved time, was continuous, since cameras could not cut as in films and as television can cut today. Only fades could take one camera picture to another. It was affectionately known as the Madden processional technique.

Hyam Greenbaum, married to harpist Sidonie Goossens, conducted the newly formed and oddly instrumented Television Orchestra. He was mad about French horns. My curtain system enabled the orchestra to start in one place and move round to be set up in rostrums in a circle at the back of the studio for the dancers and the finale.

One problem with filming a fast paced variety show was timing, when to fade from one camera to another. The fade took a minimum of eight seconds, so as we rehearsed I had to estimate the right moment to tell the camera to "turn over" and hope that the fade would be completed before a performance climax was reached. For Chilton and Thomas's act *Tapping in Rhythm* the camera had to follow Maceo Thomas's feet as he tapped up a staircase. He would then do a spectacular leap, and land on the floor, still tapping. From the close up on his feet I had to mix to another camera to get the jump and the landing. The difficulty was to make sure the mix was complete before he took off. Sometimes it was, and sometimes it wasn't and you would see two confusing images superimposed on each other, not the dramatic leap and landing we intended.

We somehow did the twenty performances, twice a day for the ten days, for some 300 enthusiastic viewers in homes and the visitors to the Radiolympia Exhibition in booths, really the object of the enterprise. It improved daily and by the end was reasonable.

The annual Radiolympia exhibition 1936.

"The music hall show was appropriately entitled "Here's Looking at You" and came over with perfect synchronization of sound and vision and with complete continuity of movement."

THE TIMES, AUGUST 28, 1936

Twenty performances later, on Saturday September 5, we all heaved a sigh of relief. Everyone signed my copy of my own original script which I kept for Museum purposes. The Observer echoed the whole press and wrote, "The BBC is on the right lines. The miniature variety show they put on with the aid of the Emitron cameras was a gem." And that was the beginning of broadcast television in Britain. No doubt it's still the only show that has been done live twenty times.

The annual Radiolympia exhibition gave an opportunity for trial transmissions in the summer of 1936. The highlight was a revue, *Here's Looking at You.*

Singer, HelenMcKay, performed the title song. With her, (left to right) were The Three Admirals (songs); Carol Chilton (Creole singer and dancer); Leslie Mitchell; Elizabeth Cowell; Maceo Thomas (with Carol Chilton); Helen McKay; The Griffiths Brothers (comedy horse) with 'Miss Lutie'.

Here's Looking At You!

Here's looking at you
From out of the blue.
Don't make a fuss
But settle down and look at us.

Here's looking at you
It seems hardly true
That radio
Can let you sit and watch the show.
This wonderful age
Goes to show that all the world is a stage.
First you heard, now you see
And you wonder what the next thing on the list will be?

What a hullabaloo!
We are just peeping through
To say "How do?"
Here's looking at you!

In the olden days the belle of every ball
Used to be the toast of fellows one and all.
Now that television's at our beck and call,
I'll play host.
Here's my toast:

What a hullabaloo!
We are just peeping through
To say "How do?"
Here's looking at you!

2

EARLY DAYS

MY BEGINNINGS

The Maddens have a motto, *Fortior qui se Vincit* and trace a very ancient main line in Ireland. Maine O'Mor, after successfully slaying the Firbolg King, formed the province of Hy-Many. About 700 AD Hy-Many was divided between two brothers, the younger being Eoghan Buac. A Celtic poem of about 1347 in the Library of Trinity College, Dublin, says *"The progeny of Eoghan Buac, the Hero, are the great race of O'Madden."*

Eoghan Buac retained one sixth of Hy-Many, which became the homeland of the O'Maddens and was called Sil Anmchadha, latinised as Silanchia, about 160 square miles. The Book of Lecan in the Library of the Royal Irish Academy gives the Sept's title as Ui Madadhain. The West Gate of Galway Town had written on it: *"From the murderous O'Maddens, Good Lord, Preserve us."*

Moving down the years much more could be written, but among many distinguished later Maddens from whom we stem was a milder character altogether, the Rev. Samuel

Madden (1686-1765). He was a philanthropist and writer, one of the founders of the Dublin Society and became known as "Premium Madden" from generous endowments to Trinity College. His play *Themistocles: A Tragedy* was successfully produced in London. He was a contemporary and friend of Swift and Johnson, and Johnson said of him, "His was a name Ireland ought to honour."

Among Madden ancestors is Oliver Goldsmith, the playwright (1728-1784) whose comedy *She Stoops to Conquer* is still played regularly.

My father, Archibald Maclean Madden, was a Foreign Service man all his life. Educated at Cheltenham and Trinity College, Cambridge, after a time as a clerk in the House of Lords he joined the Foreign Office. In 1886 he was appointed clerk to the British Legation at Tangier under Sir Herbert White and Sir Arthur Nicholson, later Lord Carnock.

My father married in Gibraltar Cathedral in 1902. My mother was Cecilia Catherine Moor, eldest daughter of Canon Allen Page Moor of St. Clement and of Truro Cathedral.

My father was asked to change services in 1902 and take over H.B.M.'s Vice Consulate in Mogador, in South Morocco. Mogador derives its name from the Saint Sidi Mogdul. A mythical derivation is that Mogdul was a Scotsman named McDougal whom the natives 'canonised'. It is now called by its Arabic name of Essaouira or Picture City. There is a Mogador Theatre in Paris, home of spectacular musicals.

I was born on November 29, 1902 and my father filled in and signed my birth certificate in his own hand. My brother Humphrey Page Madden was born three years later. In 1907 my father transferred to Casablanca as HBM's Consul.

In our household it seemed to be always the Sabbath.

Cecil Maden in Morocco circa 1905.

Casablanca 1906.
Right to left: Cecilia Madden with sons Cecil,
Colin and Humhrey, and servant Maati.

Muslims, Jews and Christians worship, or rather holiday, on Fridays, Saturdays and Sundays respectively, so some members of the staff were always missing. It came down to a four-day week. However from our three Moorish menservants, Omar, Elarbi and Maati, I soon learned to speak Arabic, followed by French and English. Spanish came later.

Morocco was primitive then in matters of sanitation, and dirt was usually slung into the middle of the cobblestone streets. Not surprising that the smells were awful and epidemics were rife, with camps outside the towns for those dying of typhus.

Life was violent, with stabbings and murders to go with almost every cry in the night. My mother woke up to find a huge snake sitting on her bed: she remained motionless until a servant came in and killed it from behind. We had an enormous pet chameleon who spent his entire day going up and down the banisters, nonchalantly changing colour when it was time to go into the garden at night.

It was a time of tribal unrest, culminating in the French bombardment of Casablanca from the cruisers *Galilee*, *Du Chayla* and *Gloire* after the massacres and siege of the town by tribal Arabs on August 5, 6, 7 and 8 1907, and the subsequent Franco-Spanish military occupation. To quote the *DAILY MIRROR* of August 21, 1907: "But for Mr Madden's heroic conduct the British Consulate would have been captured and many Europeans massacred by the Moors." Or *THE TIMES*: "French marines landed and protected the British Consulate with their guns on the flat roof, Mrs Madden's pillows being used against the recoil. One of her napkins tied to a bayonet was used for the actual surrender."

My father negotiated this surrender for Mulai Amin and sent the party to the French Consulate. But by then the destruction of the town had been great, with a carnage of 3,000 Moors killed, many Jews and many French.

Sir Gerard Lowther thanked my father for his action in persuading the French to postpone bombarding the town from the sea, and for remaining in the British Consulate when urged by the French to evacuate, and my father was appointed CMG.

My father also took a leading part in what is known as the 'Agadir Incident' in 1911, with the German gunboat *Panther* despatched. This was diplomacy as it used to be practised. The 'Incident' grew out of Germany's ambition for Colonial expansion in Morocco. Lloyd George was carefully watching this incipient situation and it was cleverly frustrated by getting the whole German party lost in the interior of Morocco at a critical moment, and so out of touch. It could have started a European war but it fizzled out, one of the great bluffs of history. The Germans were given a small strip of French Equatorial Africa to settle the matter.

Offered a move to Bilbao in Spain in 1914 as HM Consul, my father's credentials then were signed by "Yo el Rey" (Alfonso XIII). The British Ambassador in Madrid at the time was Sir Arthur Hardinge. The district takes in all the Basque Provinces and reaches as far south as Avila, roughly on a parallel with Madrid. The burden of World War I, with Spain neutral, riddled with Germans, spies everywhere, enemy submarines merrily refuelling at night, ruined his health, ending in an emergency tracheotomy in a Spanish hospital without anaesthetics. From then on breathing was only possible through a tube. He returned to the Foreign Office and died in 1928.

My father was a skilful artist and keen organist. He was organist of Kew Church even when a young man in the Foreign Office. Everywhere he went he took a large portable organ to play Bach daily. This organ was lost at sea on his final return to England in a cargo vessel, S.S. "Moneyspinner", abandoned by its crew in heavy seas in the Bay of Biscay. But it was found, salvaged, and the organ was subsequently delivered at Clapham Common, damp but still willing. After more constant use during my father's last days it is now at St. Mary of the Angels Song School.

My father was not the first member of the family to make his career in North Africa and beyond. His father (my grandfather) Surgeon Major General Charles Dodgson Madden A. B., K.H.S., was born in Kilkenny and educated at Trinity College, Dublin. He joined the Army in 1854 and served in the 39 Regiment during the Crimean War and in India with the 43rd Light Infantry at the time of the Mutiny. In the Abyssinian Campaign he was medical officer in charge of the First Field Hospital at the Capture of Magdala. Here is a snatch of a letter to his wife on April 14, 1868:

> "The fortress is an extremely strong place but the smell of dead men and animals is so fearful that it would be impossible to live in it for some time to come. There is a steep cliff where Theodore had thrown over a hundred and fifty unfortunate Abyssinians. Theodore's crown of gold and jewels is in the Chief's tent and will, I suppose, be sent home to the Queen."

My grandfather was later with the Madras Army and with the Government of India, in Malta, and in charge of the Royal Victoria Hospital, Netley. I inherited his military chest of drawers, which was immensely heavy and was obviously carried in two sections through mountains and ravines in the Crimea, India and Africa.

My grandmother was Miss Alice Lilias Maclean of Drimnin. She died in the Clock Tower Apartment in Hampton Court Palace. One of her brothers, my most colourful great-uncle, and also my Godfather, was Kaid Sir Harry Aubrey de Vere Maclean, K.A.M.G., known as 'Maclean of Morocco'. A double of King Edward VII, he was in the 69

Foot Regiment. When at Gibraltar he left the Army and entered the service of the Sultan of Morocco as Instructor to the Moorish Army. He was a confidant of Mulai el Hassan, the Sultan, and Abd-el-Aziz, his son. He was known in Morocco as *El Koroui* (the Colonel). Every day he put on full Scottish dress with kilt to play the bagpipes up and down the lines of his Moorish troops under the blazing sun. In 1901 he accompanied as "guide, philosopher and friend" a mission from the Sultan to Great Britain. Twelve years later he received the Freedom of the City of London.

In 1905, when I was two years old, he was lured into a trap and fell into the hands of the bandit leader Raisuli. For seven months he was kept a prisoner in the mountains.

British Legation, Tangier. July 5, 1907.

Dear Mr Madden,
If I am more distressed than I can say over the Kaid's capture. He went entirely against the warning of myself, the Sultan and Carleton, so he has only himself to blame and I am surprised that after thirty years experience he would believe in the word of a Moor. I warned him that his capture would have grave political consequences, but I had no power to stop him.

However it is no use crying over spilt milk and we must do our best to get him out. I am in daily correspondence with him but Raisuli has not yet formulated his demands. I shudder to think what they will be. They may be nothing. They may be almost unacceptable. In any case it will be a tough job.

Yours sincerely,
(Sir) Gerard Lowther.

KAID "DAUNTLESS AS EVER".
(From our Special Correspondent, William Maxwell)
ALCAZAR, JULY 30, 1907.
El Bagdadi destroyed four villages on Saturday and three on Monday. He killed Kmass Tribesmen and is now camped two hours from the Kaid's place of detention. Raisuli declares that victory lay with him. Raisuli came to the tent of his captive and threatened to shoot him instantly unless he wrote to Sir Gerard Lowther urging withdrawal of the soldiers and asking what terms the British Government proposed. Kaid Maclean is treated with indignity and the ruffians who guard him constantly threaten to cut him to pieces. The Kaid, dauntless as ever, told Raisuli he would never extract a penny of ransom. 'You may do with me what you please', he said. 'I look upon myself already as a dead man.'

Here is the story of Kaid Maclean's release as quoted by Reuters' agency on February 7, 1908.

KAID MACLEAN FREE –
DRAMATIC ENTRY INTO TANGIER.
Kaid Sir Harry Maclean is in exceedingly good spirits. His entry into Tangier on Thursday night was quite dramatic in its circumstances. It was a terribly stormy night and was pouring with rain. The procession was headed by twenty mountaineers on foot, each armed with a Mauser. Then came a mounted escort, all the men manifestly full of suspicion. The Kaid rode in the centre, heavily hooded, with Raisuli riding behind him... "It is authoritatively stated that Kaid Sir Harry Maclean will proceed to Rabat as soon as possible, and that he will remain in the service of the Sultan Abd-el-Aziz should his assistance be required.

Raisuli has received protection papers for himself and family. He will not take the £5,000 ransom money in cash, but as a guarantee of good faith with the British Government has banked the money, receiving interest at a slightly higher rate than on the £15,000 which is already banked at 4%.

Kaid Maclean states that although he is well he is feeling the effects of his bad treatment and bad food, and he will need a short time to recoup. He is in his usual spirits and bears no resentment towards Raisuli, but he says Raisuli's followers behaved in an extremely offensive manner.

Soon after Mulai Hafid became Sultan, deposing Abd-el-Aziz, his half-brother. Maclean of Morocco died at 72 at Drimnin House in Tangier, in 1920.

My grandfather's brother, Major General Samuel Alexander Madden C.B. (1824-1887) entered the Army as an Ensign and saw service in Burma with the 51st Light Infantry. He was at the storming of Rangoon, at the storming of the White House Redoubt, the capture of Bassein and the repulse at Prome. He was at Pegu and in the Umbeyla expedition in 1863. He commanded his Regiment in the Yowaki Campaign in 1877. He again commanded the 51st through the Afghan War. He was in Lord Robert's famous march on Kabul.

Another brother was a distinguished sailor, Captain Edward Madden RN (1827-1877) who commanded HMS *Endymion* in the days of sail and HMS *Hector*, a warship which had both sails and steam.

A distinguished cousin of my grandmother's, who was a great help to my father, was Donald Crawford, K.G. and Liberal H.P., who died in 1919. He was Sheriff of Banff, Fellow of Lincoln College, staunch Gladstonian and a friend of Lord Rosebery. He was married twice, divorcing his first wife and citing Sir Charles Dilke, a notorious case at the time. Donald Crawford figures as a character in the play *The Right Honourable Gentleman,* the part being created in London by the actor Richard Leech and the first Mrs Crawford being played by Anna Massey.

My mother having an immense Consulate with very large rooms, had a kind of salon in Casablanca and her parties were highly popular with the Resident General Marshal Lyautey and the other French Generals Moinier, Drude, Franchet d'Esperey, Giraud and d'Amade, who all played vital parts in France's destiny. A regular visitor was the popular Manual Fernandez Silvestre, Commandant of the Spanish 'Moorish Police Force' in Casablanca, sent under the act of Algeciras to raise a native police force. He came to a tragic end in battle in the Rif.

Among other regular visitors to our Consulate came two French military aviators, Max van den Vaero, of Dutch extraction, and Do Hu Vi who was Annamite. Both suggested that I should be taken flying and, surprisingly, my parents agreed. The Bleriot planes then were held together with what seemed like string, were quite open and I remember being weighed, then a sack of sand being dumped in with me to make up the weight of a man. The Arabs, who were very fond of ambushing French Foreign Legion troops marching to the distant Forts, hated the plane, which could spot and swoop on them from the skies, so woe betide any that accidentally fell or got shot down.

In the further process of toughening Cecil for life to come, it was proposed that I should cross the Sahara to Timbuktoo on a camel in caravan. It took many weeks, and if you can survive such a form of hell, in a panier, in the heat, with the flies, dirty fingers, dirty figs, no water, you can survive anything. I recommend it to no one.

I was sent to a French girls' school where I was

Cecil Madden at Dover College, aged 15.

considered *un petit chou*, then, growing up, to a French Lycee where they vivisected small animals, then later to an English Prep School at Aldeburg Lodge in Suffolk, making all journeys out and home alone with a label on my jacket. All this helped to conquer my natural nervousness and make me fairly resilient for the challenges to come.

The Great War caught up with us and the school, with its remarkable joint Headmasters Wilkinson and Spurgeon, moved from the sea coast inland to Rushbrook Hall with its fine collection of paintings. I left Prep School with a scholarship to Dover College, which was a help to my harassed father, who was by then working as HBM's Consul in Bilbao Spain, his salary cut in half by the exchange rate, and living at the sea in Las Juenas, where my youngest brother, Colin, was born, thirteen years younger than myself. The family later moved to a smaller house in the Barrio Sant'Ana.

Undoubtedly, along with many cousins, including many Admirals, I was destined for the Navy. However, short sight made a visit to the Board of Admiralty a waste of time. Cricket balls kept hitting me in the face when I dived to catch the wrong one. My brother Humphrey, younger by three years, did indeed join the navy, becoming a Fleet Air Arm flyer and a Navigator, before being invalided out after WWII. He was followed into the Navy by Colin, Rear Admiral, C. B. E., M. V. O., D. S. C, A. D. C.

Through World War I, I always struggled out to Spain for holidays, usually on tramp steamers of great age. My worst experience was trying to reach Spain via France, being caught in Paris, a quite small boy alone with heavy suitcases, when Paris was nearly surrounded. I spent three days and nights in a disgustingly overcrowded railway carriage in complete darkness, in a tunnel underneath Paris. Incidentally I was accidentally wounded in the First World War. It sounds very grand but it was actually from a shell fired from a submarine near Dover, which fell on a corner of the School House, Dover College, during prep. My bunk, being a corner, jutted out furthest and I was covered in blood and splinters, though relatively undamaged. Immediately the whole school was evacuated to a freezing, disused convent at Leamington Spa, where on the night of our arrival all the frozen pipes burst in arctic weather and a Zeppelin raid happened simultaneously.

Dover College's great headmaster, W.S. Lee was always a great character and an inspiration.

School never interested me at all, except as a means to an end. Luckily both schools had excellent Shakespeare theatricals. One could have wished for instruction on current affairs, less on the Classics. I was never any good at cricket or rugger. I hated puffed-up prefects, the fagging, the initiation rags. Impatient of the time, I filled it with endless reading on the theatre and the cinema (Max Linder was my idol as a film comedian). Having worked hard I was glad to get out into the world and live.

The war was still just on and I did some Kings Messenger work. Chased by German agents, changing trains with packets that were too big to conceal, it was like all the more sordid spy novels and really exciting while it lasted.

It was then I decided to study theatre at first hand. I presented myself at the stage door of the Arriaga Theatre where there was a touring company with an immense repertoire, including Bernard Shaw's *Pygmalion*. I was soon understudying and ultimately playing Freddie. My Spanish was good and I looked an English youth – indeed, I was one. I must be the only Englishman ever to play Shaw in Spanish in Spain. Luckily it is a very small part in translation. When I met G.B.S. years later this anecdote amused him hugely.

I helped back stage, studied lighting, went on in endless

pieces, some musicals. Companies had a repertory of up to sixty shows. No-one knew them all properly, but the old prompting system three lines ahead operated. It was torture to master but when you are young you can get used to anything. The dressing rooms were dreadful, the lavatories disgraceful, the theatres huge, and built on five-tier opera house lines. They could take an immense amount of money, particularly as they all played twice nightly, at 6.30 and 10.30, often an entirely different show, with three performances on Sundays and no day off. There I was concerned in French farces, English translations, Spanish zarsuelas (traditional operettas) and revue. A sensational success at the time was *Santa Isabel De Ceres*, a straight play set in a brothel. It had a cast of 34 and was sometimes played for sixteen performances a week. What would Equity say today?

RIO TINTO

I was urged towards Shipping by my father, and for a time I joined the Spanish Chartering and Insurance Agency under Guy Meyler. I was not cut out for it but I learned all about coal bunkering of ships.

Sir Arthur Steel-Maitland, who had done much to urge reform of the Foreign Service, knew my father and I applied to him for work in the Rio Tinto Company, where he was a Director. After various tests in Spain I was engaged to work in London at 3 Lombard Street, next to the Mansion House. I used to watch Lord Mayors shaving from my desk. I had taught myself shorthand and typewriting and being put on the Shipping and Copper desks I had endless duties, one of which was to insure cargoes leaving the piers at Huelva with pyrites and iron ore from the mines in Spain. Imperfectly briefed, on my first Saturday I found myself entirely alone and, having no clue as to what was expected of me, I failed to insure an £8,000 cargo in SS *Teti*, which sank immediately with the ship. I fully expected to be sacked, but was saved by a General cover which was invoked.

I hated the City life, the overcrowded buses and tube trains, the stifling, crowded, cheap restaurants with indifferent food abominably presented and slowly served which was all the harassed clerks, typists and secretaries could afford. My only consolation at that time was meeting Frederick Ashton for lunch every day in an ABC restaurant. He had been at school at Dover College with me and we both agreed the desk life was not for us. He escaped to Diaghilev and the ballet world and became a choreographic Knight. I tried taking sandwiches and eating in churchyards, or listening to organ recitals when it was raining, but the rush hours were continually trying and I was glad to be sent out to the mines in South Spain. This would remove the temptation of seeing every play and show in London, which I used to do nightly in the gallery, and forced me to do some writing myself.

Rio Tinto is fairly near Seville and fifty miles from Huelva, the port for the mines. Huelva was a dull town, with a good theatre even then, and was the home of a celebrated Matador. The Rio Tinto, or coloured river, runs blood red from the soil full of iron ore and is certainly spectacular, if sluggish.

The mines were Pyrites Mines. Any lump of it is greenish in colour and contains about half iron, half sulphur, with small percentages of impurities such as copper, lead, zinc, arsenic, selenium, cobalt, etc. Some was shipped out as crude cupreous ore for the manufacture of sulphuric acid, some dumped on huge heaps and sprinkled with water which emerged as copper liquor, and was precipitated over scrap iron, the precipitate being shipped to other countries for smelting into copper.

I shared a house in the British Colony area at Rio Tinto, called *Bella Vista*, with two young charming Cornish mining engineers. We suffered from a lusty young Spanish woman housekeeper who was perfunctory in everything. She gave us no choice of food which was endlessly (1) soup, (2) fried brains and (3) goat's meat, with local white wine to drink. When you were confronted with this, first thing and four times a day, it got monotonous, and athletic mountain goats taste like leather. Nor could my mining colleagues understand the gradual disappearance of the wine. This worried them obsessively. They were certain she drank it. Ostentatiously marking the bottles did no good and it still went down. They resolved to settle the matter, so they pissed into a bottle and waited for the resulting explosion. The wine still went down. Truculently the Cornishmen sent for the woman and asked her where the wine went. She simply answered, "I always put some in your soup to improve the taste."

My work was in the mine offices, mostly invoicing, but as extracurricular activities I saw to it that the local theatre engaged good touring companies. The performances were extremely dangerous in a wooden building, since its stage was lit by acetylene footlights, with sweeping costumes, such as period crinolines in musicals. I encouraged making a film of the mines, drawing the maps myself, besides organising cinema shows for all the outlying villages. The films obtainable, mostly French, were shown in the open air and so could have audiences on both sides of the screen. If anyone brought a mouth organ or accordion everyone started dancing. I wrote for the Company what I called "The Child's Guide to Pyrites", no doubt a standard work by now.

Late at night the sombre figures of the miners could be seen trudging to work from villages miles away. Day and night the mining went on, deep in the earth, in conditions of great heat, walls of pyrites reeking of sulphur and moisture in the tunnels with copper liquor on the floors, which corroded everything. Opencast mines, huge holes in the ground, were spectacular but largely mined out even then.

One day I was asked to go to a distant village to check the stores of explosives there. I was told to go and get a horse. I had done absolutely no riding so I went to the stables with some alarm. Choose any horse you like, smiled the boys, they are all the same. The one I chose took an instant dislike to me. Every time I was hoisted on he turned and galloped back into the stable, the idea being to make me smash my head against the top of the door. At last we got going, amidst shouts or laughter, and to keep up the silent protest good old Rosinante literally walked sideways like a crab, for hour after hour, in blazing August sunshine, going through every village in this way and refusing to respond to any reins or conversation. At last we got to the distant hut, I duly tallied the dynamite sticks and powder, and the time came for the hideous homeward trip. This time the horse decided to try different tactics. He did the whole journey at top speed, up and down mountains, exactly as in a chase in cowboy films. The idea was, of course, to shed me somewhere, preferably miles away, and gallop home alone. However I was determined this should not happen and we somehow made it back together, battered but triumphant. I knew then I would never qualify as a Mountie.

Although my work was in the offices, working out the cost of the percentages as assayed in each sample, it was mostly mathematics and I had had great trouble to obtain School Certificate or Matriculation in the terrible three, arithmetic, algebra and geometry. Everything took me longer than anyone else and I had to take home masses of work at night. This took valuable time when I was trying to study the construction of famous plays and writing revue sketches.

The iron in the soil meant that the open air staff swimming bath was so thick and red it was like diving into tomato soup. Sometimes it filled with frogs but one got used to them, though their concerted croaking at night could keep everyone awake for miles.

One day I was invited to a drink by a Mr Harrison to celebrate the birth of his daughter, christened Valerie. Some twenty years or so later a temporary secretary looked up from her typewriter at Alexandra Palace and told me she was this same girl. She had artistic ambitions. She moved on to Ealing Studios, married Michael Pertwee, changed her name to Valerie French, acted in revue, divorced and went to Hollywood for films.

Being of an enquiring nature I asked one of the Cornish engineers to let me accompany him one day on his job in the mine. He agreed, so it was up at 4.00 a.m., and then a rocky walk for miles to the entrance of the underground shaft. There all our clothes were left in lockers and we donned a kind of thick vest and combinations like pyjamas, with a black jacket and trousers and thick boots. All these were boiled daily, so they got pretty shapeless. The heavy felt hat, too, was grotesque. Then down the cage and we were soon below in the sulphur fumes. Everything went up one's nose. I was given a lamp with a flame and learned to hook it round my left hand so as not to burn my wrist going down perpendicular ladders, which we descended all the time going deeper and deeper down. I quickly regretted my enthusiasm. The roof of every floor dripped, you looked down, never upwards, as the copper liquor in your eyes could blind you for life. Our feet slushed in copper water, the boots had no nails or they would have dropped out. Every now and then a horde of rats would go past, the size of small dogs. They had a use, for if the pyrites mass shifted and caught fire the rats left quickly and so the fire could be located. Also they got so hungry that if a miner opened a basket his food would be snatched almost instantly. Laid down the tunnels were rails, so trucks of ore would come rolling past by gravity. They were be so quiet they were on you before you knew it, when it was essential to flatten against the side to avoid having your face taken off. This jump backwards either made the flame of the lamp go out or burn your hand.

My guide suggested I tie a handkerchief round my face as I was getting full of iron dust and sulphur through mouth and nose. It was a glimpse of hell, like a Doré drawing. But worse was yet to come and it was still only about 6.00 am. Suddenly my guide said he would have to go back to see an overseer about something: he turned and left me, telling me not to move on any account. He then forgot about me and continued on his rounds.

My lamp went out, I had no way to relight it, my handkerchief fell off into the copper liquid, I was nearly blinded by the copper dripping through my hat, and suffocated by the fumes. I decided not to walk as trucks would rush past and I might never be located again. At least I did one thing I was told – I was still in the same place.

My guide only remembered me about 6.00 pm when he was back at our house taking a bath. My God, Cecil's in the mine! He had to go back then and try to find me. By then I was in a very poor state and saw no humour in the situation!

I was writing sketches and sold some to various revues. Later, back in England and back in the City, I also wrote some plays and was lucky enough to find Managers and get my work produced, better still with excellent casts.

My great friend Hugh Tennant, who was Secretary to the Chairman, Sir Auckland Geddes, suddenly died at the Rio Tinto itself. This was very sad and involved some staff changes: I was offered the post of Secretary to the Hon. Richard Martin Preston, the Managing Director, and later to Sir Auckland Geddes.

Sir Auckland was big and heavy, a very simple man despite his great wartime reputation, also a former British ambassador in Washington, but he suffered from high blood pressure and failing sight. What seemed a trick of coming to big meetings without a single paper always unnerved the other side. Geddes absorbed the facts, listened silently all day and always gave a decision, usually a masterly one.

Twice a year he would visit the mines in Spain with a board deputation and their wives. The mountains of luggage in three currencies were agony to me. Then twice a year he did the same to America, to contact interests in Wilmington and Baltimore. He always travelled in the old "Mauritania" where the Royal suite could be studied in advance and the walls and room sizes adjusted to suit the special needs of his party. In New York he always stayed at the Ambassador Hotel.

In October 1930, we were leaving New York on the tide at 7.00 pm on a Saturday and George Gershwin's great show "Girl Crazy" had opened at the Alvin Theatre two nights before. It was a smash hit, seats were selling at a hundred pounds each, tickets were quite unobtainable and I wanted to catch the matinee. So I timidly phoned George Gershwin, whom I had met in Paris and who lived at Riverside Drive where I much admired his own paintings. He answered the phone and I told him I could not get in at any price. "Think nothing of it, dear boy" he said, he was in a British phase at that time, "Meet me at the stage door at two-twenty." So, with some trepidation, I arrived at the stage door at two-twenty and there was this extraordinary figure with a huge black hat and a great overcoat, looking rather like Fagin. "Dear boy, follow me," he said and without wasting time he led me down into the darkness and to my horror we emerged in the orchestra pit.

"Sit in my chair," he said, "I shall be standing anyway." I was covered in confusion, but I sat down in the conductor's seat, with the score laid out in front of me. He took off his paraphernalia, tapped his conductor's baton, the overture started and up went the curtain on this marvellous show. And what a show it was! Songs like *I Got Rhythm*, *Embraceable You*, *They're Singing Songs of Love but Not for Me*. And the cast - Ethel Merman, Willie and Eugene Howard and Ginger Rogers, making her stage debut in a white cowgirl outfit. At half-time George said, "I leave you now, dear boy, Red will look after you."

So I sat still and a man appeared from below, with red hair. He didn't even use a baton, which Gershwin had used, and at the end of the show he said "Hi," or something like that, and disappeared down with the orchestra. I didn't know what to do so I just climbed out of the orchestra pit and left with the public. It was in fact Red Nichols and the famous Five Pennies with no less than Benny Goodman, Gene Krupa, some say both Dorseys, Jack Teagarden and Glenn Miller - they were the pit orchestra. George later sent me a copy of the one most neglected song from this score, *Sam and Delilah*, a kind of send-up of *Frankie and Johnny*.

Everyone knows the Gershwin smash hit shows *Funny Face*, *Oh Kay!*, *Tiptoes*, *Lady Be Good*, *Primrose* and *Jig Saw*. Few remember he wrote the whole score for a London revue, *The Rainbow*, a failure with thirteen Gershwin numbers, or his other shows, *Treasure Girl*, *La, La Lucille*, *Show Girl*, *Song of the Flame* and his film *Delicious*. He had so much to give, so little time, only 38 years.

When I returned to London via Paris I assisted in staging some of my material in two revues. The backstage conditions in Paris were dreadful, worse than Spain, the whole pervaded by inadequate sanitation. It always surprised me that stars put up with it. The talent was excellent but I was sorry for "Les Nues", rather large girls undressed on their top half and overdressed below. They suffered terribly from the draughts. All the shows were too long. The typically French sketches were usually Army Caserne or Barrack humour. The Paris revues were always ingeniously lit, set and staged, with clever use made of levels owing to the restricted depth of the stage.

Maud Loty was a most amusing comedienne at the Concert Mayol and Gina Palerme a formidable leading lady there. Two most attractive dancers were the Irvin Sisters. There were some fine low comedians at the time, Dandy, Dranem, Dorville, Bach, Boucot, Saint Granier all teeth and smiles, Fernandel, and Bourvil.

I got to know the lovely Spanish singer Raquel Meller, who sang José Padilla's *La Violetera* while throwing out bunches of violets, and her hit *Seranillo*. Padilla was himself doing a piano act on the stage, featuring his own great numbers, especially *El Relicario* and *Ca C'est Paris*, two of the greatest show atmosphere numbers ever written. Earl Leslie danced with Mistinguett, who made a hit with *Mon Homme*. In Mistinguett's revues, such as *En Douce*, there was nearly always a concealed tank representing the River Seine, and Mistinguett invariably ended her sketch and leggy Apache dance by being thrown into it, emerging later with a wonderful headdress down the steep staircase for the finale.

I went to the theatre nightly and thus saw Elenora Duse at the New Oxford and Sarah Bernhardt at the Coliseum, last glimpses of legendary greats.

THE LONDON STAGE

South London, where I have often lived, has never

supported its theatres. Even in Elizabethan times Burbage left Shakespeare and the Globe to cross the River Thames to the North Bank. South London's many fine old Playhouses have slowly petered out into other purposes. The Elephant and Castle, home of Tod Slaughter and melodrama like 'Maria Marten', the Clapham Junction Grand, the South London, the Surrey, the Camberwell Metropole and Palace, the Penge Empire, the Brixton, The Kennington Princess of Wales, the Balham Duchess, the Rotherhithe Terriss and more are no longer the same.

The Shakespeare, Lavender Hill, where Macqueen Pope told me he had once acted, was damaged by a bomb. It had a street sign on its side street, 'THEATRE STREET SW11'. When I saw this beautiful theatre being demolished I applied to the breakers for this to be saved from the rubble. A long time passed, then one day, sitting in my office in the Scenery Block of the Television Centre, the door opened and an enormous workman, covered in honest dust, walked in holding the vast and heavy iron sign, saying "This is for you." And surprisingly added, "And how right you were." It is now in the possession of the British Theatre Museum, a memento of South London's eternal shame.

My own introduction to drama came on our own doorstep in Casablanca, where the Arab gate-keeper improvised dramas of Sultans, Pashas, and Kaids with innumerable wives, all probably quite unsuitable for a child, each differentiated by headgear made out of handkerchiefs and anything that came in handy. This was my first encounter with what I have since learned were 'glove puppets'. One day I went into a bazaar where boxes of the real thing could be bought. I learnt to improvise dialogue in French as well as Arabic, and a few years later in English and Spanish. Spain saw my greatest thespian triumphs when I used to set my stage in a window and bore bewildered Basques for hours on end with entire plays by Molière.

My parents used to send me to French families in the school holidays to improve my French and broaden my outlook. I actually spent most of my time in cinemas watching such serials as *Judex*, *Fantomas*, and *The Broken Coin*. I was fascinated by the fairs and travelling shows, my first kind of entertainments. One holiday I was sent to Salies de Bearn, near Pau, another to Bordeaux, and so on. The French puppet plays in the fairs were vaguely religious in origin but actually concealed bawdiness, such as "Le Pauvre Père Antoine" which was in fact a series of temptations of St. Anthony. So it is not surprising that I became an honorary Vice President of the British Puppet Guild. Puppeteers are the salt of the earth, they never grow up, they are simply grown up children in any language.

When very young indeed, I wrote a short play called "*In the Bled*" about murder and lust in Morocco. I posted it to Horace Hodges, the old star of *Grumpy*, *Lightnin'* and other plays, whom I did not know at all. He wrote such a charming reply urging me to keep at it; as a result I really did so.

The French playwright H.R. Lenormand let me do an English version of his *A L'Ombre du Mal* about French Equatorial Africa. I called it *The Equator*. William Foss staged it with George Zucco, Dorothy Dunkels, Alan Napier, Bruno Barnabe, Osmund Willson and Leonard Brett. I subsequently adapted more Lenormand plays, including one about primitive Alpine folk in 1860 which I called *Crevasse*.

Then I wrote a play myself, about flying the Atlantic solo. It was called *The Hero*. This was put on by the de Leons, staged by Norman MacDermott and played by Betty Carter, Frederick Cooper, Marie Ault, Corlton Brough, Fred Rivenhall and Dan F. Roe. The Assistant Stage Manager was called Patricia Burke. Among a reasonably good series of press notices came this: "Author unknown, but 'Cecil

Madden' is supposed to be the nom-de-plume of a minor film actress."The Era described it as "Nothing if not topical."

A dear friend of mine, Mrs Emily Cobham, invited me to dinner to meet the famous Mrs Patrick G. Campbell, then elderly and very formidable. The idea was to take her to see the play. After an excellent meal Mrs Pat selected a cigar, took an entire bunch of bananas from a bowl in the hall and devoured these in the taxi, handing me the skins to throw out of the window into the face of a passing cyclist. She sat motionless throughout the play and the intervals, then suddenly rose like the Lady from the Sea and, before the panatrope could play the customary 'God Save The King,' she looked straight at me, before a startled audience, and said "I shall never forgive you for that mother!"

I became interested in a play called *The Twin*, on the subject of spiritualism. Sir Auckland Geddes, who had backed an American play he fancied, encouraged me to acquire the rights and, helped by him, I rewrote it. Gordon Harbord presented it as *Through the Veil* at the Embassy Theatre in Swiss Cottage with Helen Haye, C.M. Hallard, Lucy Sibley, John H. McCormick, Alfred Clark, Alisa Grahame, Margaret Delamere, H. Brough Robertson and Rosalind Atkinson. Rosalind's comedy as a maid was so effective it almost upset the balance of the play and showed her potential, which everyone has since admired at Stratford and elsewhere.

As I had not written the whole play, to acknowledge Sir Auckland's part he thought of the name Guilbert for some reason of his own, and Stone from Stone Buildings where he had chambers. It looked so odd he was persuaded to alter it to Gilbert Stone, which was where the trouble started. This caused embarrassment to a barrister who had exactly this name and who accused us both of involving him in a play about psychic matters. So when it was transferred to the Duchess Theatre, restaged by Norman

Loring and after a newspaper disclaimer of Gilbert Stone, the credit was revised as 'By Cecil Madden and X.Y. Stone'. This was an error of judgement made in a fit of pique and unfortunately amused the press who sensed there was a story behind it and who then never left any of us alone. Hannen Swaffer wrote his notice without seeing the play at all, though he came just in time to see the artists taking calls. There were nightly scenes in the audience when spiritualists who had legitimately bought seats demonstrated noisily. This did no-one any good and audiences dwindled. I felt after a few weeks that our audiences must be people who had failed to get in to *Rose Marie* at Drury Lane, opposite. Sir Auckland Geddes and I also wrote a political play, *The Red Horseman*, but though due for production at the Embassy Theatre, he withdrew it as it dealt with politicians like Balfour and others more or less as themselves.

At the Vaudeville Theatre the Gatti Brothers and Archibald de Bear put on a play I adapted from the Spanish by José Lopez Rubio and Eduardo Ugarte, *De La Noche A La Manana*. It came on called 'Max and Mr Max'. It was about a man, Max, and his conscience. His conscience, Mr Max, was visible as a person and talked to Max, anticipating his actions and reproaching him for his baser thoughts, when a lost and provocative girl came to his lonely cottage asking for a room for the night and he installed her in the best bedroom. She is followed by her husband. He also has to be put up for the night but is told that no woman has come at all. Nicholas Hannen staged it and played Max impeccably, D.A. Clarke Smith played Mr Max, Kathleen O'Hagen played the woman and Edmund Gwenn her husband. Aubrey Hammond designed the setting. It was done much later at Alexandra Palace in television, produced by George More O'Ferrall as *One Night, One Day*, with lovely Lilli Palmer and Barry Jones, D.A Clarke

Smith, Finlay Currie and Ivor Barnard. A version was staged in America as *A Touch of Magic* with Signe Hasso.

Other minor achievements included a small film, *The Great Conway*, written by S. E. Reynolds and myself with Jerrold Robertshaw as an old actor, Hubert Gregg as an announcer, Jackson Wilcox as a dresser and Norman Hackforth, the composer, as a pianist. We also wrote a film of London's Chinese dockland, *The Secret Dragon*, starring the celebrated Lai Founs jugglers. I contributed to a revue, *All's Well*, which starred the great little comedian Billy Merson. My sketch *Clown's Entree* gave him a character study he enjoyed playing with Babs Valerie.

Then came *Saturday's Children*. Maxwell Anderson wrote the original American play and it could have been done as it was, but Anmer Hall felt it could be anglicised as it was a simple story of office life, much the same anywhere. I adapted it and it was staged at the Westminster Theatre by Henry Oscar with Dorothy Hyssop making her debut, stunningly beautiful. HCG Stevens was the Press Representative; I had produced some of his own short plays myself. The first night was glittering: Noel Coward was there, Dorothy Dickson, Dodie Smith, Ian Hay and such critical giants as Charles Morgan and James Agate. There was also an undressing scene, fairly new in those days.

Then a funny thing happened on the way to the theatre. It was the last night of the run. I ran into Robert Newton, that endearing character who was then running the Grand Theatre Fulham, renamed the Shilling, mostly because the stalls seemed to be half a crown. He was in a pub and decided he would come in to the very last night. At the end he bulldozed round the dressing rooms, having fortified himself in the intervals at the adjoining pub, saying he intended to reopen the play at his theatre in a week's time and could he have the rights. This was a novelty for him, as he had already put on *The Greeks Had a Word For It*, then a Broadway hit, without any permission. The owners decided to join him since they were unlikely to gain anything by beating him into the ground. Then he wanted all the cast he could persuade to go there with him, as he intended to play the boy himself. Which he duly did, which must have been torture to Dorothy Hyson as he only knew some of the lines in a long part. Marguerite Cellier joined the cast, all the others carried on, and this extraordinary engagement was a success, extending week after week.

The next excitement was that Robert Newton decided he liked the play and would take it on tour. He persuaded Hermione Baddeley, who was quite gloriously miscast but a good name star, to play opposite him. The play somehow changed character and these two had personal laughs all over. At the time Hermione was very social, staying in many stately homes, so she often arrived at the theatre at the very last moment, to the panic of the Stage Manager, in party dresses and picture hats to the surprise of the audience who expected a typist.

Another play I adapted was a Spanish play called *Quien Soy Yo?* by Juan Ignacio Luca de Tena, a Marquis and owner of the daily newspaper *A.B.C. de Madrid*. I called it *The President's Double* when it was done at the Birmingham Repertory Theatre in a production by Herbert Prentice.

Prestige was a short satirical work by Theodora Benson and myself at the Arts Theatre. It was staged by Athole Stewart and acted by a star cast of Adele Dixon, Ellis Powell, Reginald Gardner, Ronald Simpson, Eileen Peel, Guy Martineau and Bernard Gordon. It got a lot of upper class laughs and was ahead of its time.

Everyone who writes plays, or writes anything for that matter, knows what rejection slips do to one and the despair they engender. How about this Japanese rejection slip:

We read your manuscript with boundless delight. By the sacred ashes of our ancestors we swear that we have never dipped into a story of such overwhelming mastery. If we were to print this story it would be impossible in the future to print any story of a lower standard. So we are, to our great regret, compelled to return this divine work and beg you a thousand times to forgive our action.

'The Gloomy Dean', W. R. Inge, at that time a columnist, refused an invitation to a play of mine, "I never go to theatres." He once made the profound remark, "Nothing fails like success."

I have cupboards full of unacted plays which missed their moment in time. There is little point in bothering about them. I have always felt that nearly every play that does get staged is a year out of date, at the very least. By the time it has been written, which takes time anyway, then gone to an agent and managements, and then to actors, three years may easily have elapsed, at a fair estimate, so when it confronts a first night public it has imperceptibly gone off the boil.

I have also collaborated and this presents problems of its own. Does one have the idea and plot and the other do all the writing? There are snags to every combination. Does the order on a billing matter at all? A line, once written, is apt to become sacred to the writer, then his collaborator may alter it or cut it out altogether. Anyone who gets pompous about the value of his name or ideas should remember P.G. Wodehouse's note about his twenty collaborations with Guy Bolton. Guy was a good friend of mine and often visited me in later years with his wife:

I don't know how Beaumont and Fletcher and Massinger and Ford did it, but with us what usually happens is that Guy comes to me and says he has a corking idea for a show. I say, "Ah, yes?" and we sit down and work out a plot. This done, Guy starts writing and goes on writing until the thing is finished. Twice or thrice a day - sometimes oftener - I look in and say, "How's it getting on?" and he says "All right," and I say, "Good, good." And so, little by little, the work gets done. I suppose all collaborations are more or less like this. Fletcher used to look in on Beaumont and say, "How goeth it, my heart of gold?" but what is so remarkable about ours is not the excellence of the work it has produced, though this is considerable, but the fact that after forty years of churning out theatre joy for a discriminating public we are not merely speaking to one another but are the closest of friends. If Guy saw me drowning he would dive in to the rescue without a moment's hesitation and if I saw Guy drowning I would be the first to call for assistance. How different from most collaborators who in similar circumstances would merely throw their partner an anvil.

For practically all theatrical collaborations blow up with a loud report on the morning after the first failure, Dramatist A blaming Dramatist B for being the sole cause of it, and Dramatist B coming right back at him. Shaftesbury Avenue and Broadway are congested with collaborators whom a single flop has turned from pals together to relentless foes. Indeed whenever the body of a playwright is found with its head bashed in by a blunt instrument, the first thing the big four at Scotland Yard do, I believe, is to inquire into the movements of his former collaborators. "Didn't the deceased write a stinker with George Robinson a couple of years ago which came off after the second night?" asks the Assistant Commissioner. "I thought so. Detain Robinson for questioning. If he hasn't a cast-iron alibi he's for it."

This has not been so with Guy and me. Forty years have passed since we first came together, but our mutual esteem still persists. Any time he has a good idea for a play, I am always willing to help him out. He knows that he can count on my moral support. It is not always convenient for me to go over to his house and say "How are you getting on?" but I never fail him.

George Beardmore, the novelist, and I worked out a comedy about a gang of jewel thieves. We called it *Chatterbox*. Frederick Piffard was foolish enough to try it for a whole week in his Aldershot Rep. and John Citroen directed it. It called for a small child to play a star part, full of moods and comedy. I was told they had found one, a greengrocer's daughter who had then only carried on a lily in a Nativity Play, and my heart sank. She rehearsed a few days then got ill and was sent to bed. A minor part actress was then told to wear the clothes, try to act young and rehearse for dear life. All the actresses changed round, as is the way in Rep. Then the child recovered, insisted on trying to play and everyone reverted to her original role. The first night was remarkable and a star was born. She was Shani Wallis, then aged 13. "Shani Wallis put up a really clever and loveable performance in the title part. Miss Wallis capitalised every opportunity, created many and failed in none. More may well be heard of this clever young player." (*THE STAGE*, March 4, 1948.) Together George Beardmore and I fashioned two more plays, *Pa Morton's Place* about a holiday camp and *Concert Pitch* about a great conductor. They still await production.

Loophole was the second title of a thriller originally fashioned by my friend MacGregor Urquhart, which I revised. It is powerful stuff and it opened as *Emergency Exit* at Dundee Rep., directed by A. R. Whatmore with Yvonne Hills, John Warner and Adrian Waller. It had a good

Cecil and Muriel's wedding,1932

Cecil and Muriel at Mardie's Christening.

Cecil and Muriel with Mardie aged 4. 1941.

Muriel, Mardie and Cecil at
Charles Madden's wedding. 1942.

press. Joan Riley directed it at Windsor, and it went onto play in many repertory theatres up and down the country. Here is a selection from about fifty casts: Rosemary Harris, Mary Peach, Yootha Joyce, June Barry, Jill Fenson, Maria Charles, Daniel Massey, Hugh Paddick, Leonard Rossiter, Alan Maxwell, Geoffrey Lumsden, Clifford Williams.

The Silent Witness was another thriller we tried, then *Investigation* which Melville Gillam gave its first performance at the Connaught Theatre, Worthing, with Patrick Allen, Jill Melford, Gladys Henson and Philip Ashley. It was set by Robert Weaver and directed by Guy Vaesen.

Chelsea Reach was a collaboration with American Vincent McConnor, novelist, radio and tv writer. We both love Chelsea, its artists, its pensioners, its River Thames. All three are in this comedy of an old artist everyone thinks is dead. At Leicester it had, among others, Ray Mort and a production by John de Lannoy. Kenneth Connor starred at Watford, and Sheila Hancock at Bromley. It also had a run at the New Scala Theatre, Copenhagen, with three great Danish stars, Henrik Bentzon, Ellen Gottschalch and Marguerite Viby, the comedienne.

In 1932 I married Muriel Cochrane at St. George's Church, Hanover Square. Despite my playwriting she felt that I was not expanding in the City atmosphere and urged me not to worry about the salary and to seek a fuller artistic life. The BBC seemed to combine many subjects, and my plays were getting me known, so I applied for a job. After interviews with Sir Charles Carpendale and Sir John Reith at the top I was offered a job at the very bottom and at far less than I had been earning. I never regretted the decision. The tide in my case never led on to fortune but it was a change, and we moved to Bywater Street, Chelsea.

3

PRE WAR

BROADCASTING HOUSE

When I arrived at the BBC I was told to report to the Talks Department. The group then were Charles Siepmann and Lionel Fielden, clever and wildly contrasted men. They took an instant dislike to me.

My first job was to carry out an idea, not my own, to be called *Stars In Their Courses*, to illustrate a series by James Agate, the critic. How this happened was hardly helpful to say the least. James Agate had been broadcasting theatre talks for seven years and it never occurred to him that it could ever end. He did them well, always started by deafening millions with his cough, and might well have been left to go on indefinitely. But Broadcasting House always detested anyone getting too powerful and had secretly decided to end his reign. So they furtively approached St. John Ervine, the playwright. St. John Ervine tactlessly spoke to Agate as they were getting seated for a first night where Agate was reporting the play for both his

Sunday paper and the BBC. Ervine not only mentioned the BBC's nudge but also enquired what fee he should ask. He mentioned that 25 guineas had been suggested, and was it enough? Agate never answered him. He was so purple with anger, having been doing these so long for 17 guineas, that he rushed out of the theatre then and there, stormed to Broadcasting House, battered on the Reception Desk and demanded to see the Director General in person.

By now the BBC Talks Department was committed to Ervine so, as a sop to Agate, they came up with the idea of talks on the great stage stars, illustrated by scenes from their greatest successes. These scenes I was to produce. So I was sent off to visit Dame Madge Kendal, who was 85 and in retirement. She told me stories of her brother, Tom Robertson, who wrote *Caste* and who was really the father of modern comedy as we know it. Anyway, she elected to play Juliet. I tried to alter this choice but she was adamant: it was her favourite part. I had some trouble as her sight was failing and her large magnifying glass in front of the microphone deflected her voice, while the script shook alarmingly.

On I went. Sir Seymour Hicks was a tonic. He enjoyed being *The Man in Dress Clothes*, originally a French play. He also loved playing *Scrooge*. Matheson Lang did *Mr Wu* and *The Wandering Jew*. I was shocked to find the greatest Bensonion of them all, Sir Frank Benson himself, living unhappily in a bedsitter in Bayswater. He chose his *Richard I* and *Marc Antony*. Fay Compton played *Ophelia*, Sybil Thorndike *Lady Macbeth*. Sir John Martin Harvey recreated his *Burgomaster of Stilemonde* with his wife, Nina de Silva, and also *The Only Way*. He was extremely affecting in the famous final lines at the guillotine. Marie Tempest played *The Marriage of Kitty*, her greatest success, and Noel Coward's *Hay Fever* which she had created more recently. Irene Vanbrugh recreated her Rose in *Trelawny of the Wells* and. Hilda Trevelyan *A Kiss For Cinderella*. It was all deeply nostalgic. Henry Oscar and Barbara Couper supported many of the old stars.

In order to confound Agate's introductory cough, I created a signature tune, using a theme from Gershwin's *Rhapsody in Blue*. This was in fact the first signature tune ever used in a radio broadcast, but it infuriated Agate, as the signature tune got more letters than he did. He refused to rehearse for timing purposes, would arrive late, hide in the lavatory and only emerge at the last moment, cough, making my life unendurable. One minute he was moody and depressed, the next bubbling with enthusiasm, sipping champagne. I kept the precious records, which I had made on wax, during the war in a cellar in my mother's old house, so they are now preserved for all time in both the BBC and the British Theatre Museum.

I proposed a series by journalists of renown to be called *Anywhere for a News Story*. These great characters had endured difficult journeys with bad communications for the newspapers and had real stories to tell. The Morning Post had been attacking the BBC almost daily and the Talks chiefs seemed unduly self conscious about this. So, without saying anything, I went to call on the Editor, H.A Gwynne. I found him charming and co¬operative, and he did a fine talk in the series. He dealt with the British expedition to suppress the cruelties of King Prempeh of Ashanti in 1895 and with Kitchener against the Dervishes. It taught me the value of personal contact. These were journalistic scoops of their time: Ralph D. Blumenfeld, Sir John Foster Fraser on Manchuria, Bernard Grant on the Messina earthquake, Colonel Lionel James of *THE TIMES*, J. L. Hodson, Henry Nevinson on the Relief of Ladysmith, W.T. Massey on the Fall of Jerusalem and Thomas Grant on the sinking of the *Sontay*. Captain Mages, his ship sinking and tilting pushed his officers off the bridge, struggled towards the stern and there, holding on, waved his cap shouting *Vive La France* as the waters engulfed him. These reminiscences were published in a book by Allen Lane, then at The Bodley Head.

Joe Ackerley, a charming playwright, was in charge of General and Topical Talks. He had been putting on a five-minute talk after the News about once a week. When he went on leave and incautiously handed over to me I decided to hot things up by putting in two different talks a night, mostly exciting stuff. I rushed survivors from a wreck in thick fog in the Scheldt to the microphone and experimented on Radio News Reel lines. This caused me to leave the Department instantly and I was transferred to Outside Broadcasts.

There the Head was Gerald Cock, full of charm. Leonard Schuster, the administrator, had earlier managed a theatrical company with his wife starring and understood stage people. My co-assistant was John Snagge, the popular Boat Race commentator. *In Town Tonight* usually needed a closing Outside Broadcast in some outlandish spot such at the top of Nelson's Column or the bottom of London's sewers. On Saturday nights I found myself out on a raft in the docks or perched on the dome of St. Paul's and various other equally unlikely places. It was stimulating anyway and almost any bright idea was accepted. I particularly remember one programme I handled with the Gravesend Pilots cutting a microphone cable with shears as the pilot tug pulled away to sea.

About then I must have caught the eye of Cecil Graves who was about to start the Empire Service, all round the clock, under programme director J.B. Clark, to be broadcast on short waves. He offered me the post of producer in charge, which included the planning. My assistants, who came later, were William McClurg and a former dancer Frederick Piffard. My secretary was Anne Devine: together we had many adventures for the sake of the far-flung imperialists.

All day and all night we broadcast. The stimulation of the long days and nights, strange hours, for it was always evening and 'peak time' somewhere ('The sun never sets on the British Empire' and all that.) It never did set with us. We broadcast everything. I even dramatised the mail in *Empire Mail Bag*, linked with appropriate music which amused people more than the words. I called a series *What They Say* or *With and Without Prejudice*, in which we dramatised sayings of the week divorced from their context. *Looking Backwards* dramatised news, both vital and unimportant. We went *Round London at Night* with spots at airports, cabarets, panto rehearsals, hotel kitchens, railway signal boxes, or high spots with a view, like the top of the Albert Hall. Howard Marshall did topical talks.

I believe in stars because they have invariably come up the hard way, know their jobs thoroughly and are professional in outlook, so I created the programme title *Starlight*. As all artists and performers were recorded and repeated up to four or five times, this title came into its own with a vengeance and I took it with me to television too, where it meant rather more.

I had a kind of resident radio repertory company with such strong artists as Madeleine Carroll, Robert Newton, George Benson, Carol Goodner, Howard Marion Crawford, Patricia Burke and Joan Miller. S.E. Reynolds wrote *Finegan's Night Club* and *At the Black Dog*. Joan Luxton brought her children's' theatre company.

I devised a magazine, *The Gossip Hour*. We did this monthly. It usually ended with a sketch. One such, *There is One S.O.S.* was played by Wendy Hiller and Cecil Parker.

Calling a series *Nightmares*, I thought of the idea of asking comedy writers to create a thriller each. It turned out to be their secret ambition. I went to Lady Cynthia

Asquith, Sir James Barrie's secretary, J.B. Morton (Beachcomber), Marjorie Bowen, H de Vere Stacpoole, Inez Holden, James Laver, Theodora Benson, Noel Langley and others. This collection was published in a book under the title, *My Grimmest Nightmare* by Allen and Unwin and also in America as *Not Long For This World* by the Telegraph Press.

As I simply could not cope with all the entertainment programmes at all hours, I called on a number of lively outside personalities, told them how much (or how little would be more accurate) money we had to spend and asked them to present revues. These four were Robert Nesbitt, Effie Atherton, Dennis van Thal and Reggie Smith. In this way alone came Edward Cooper, Queenie Leonard, composer Ord Hamilton, Vera Lynn then at Casani's Club, Hermione Baddeley, Hermione Gingold, Adele Dixon, Donald and Billie Burn (two American stars), Syd Walker, Phyllis Robins, Harold French, Morris Harvey and John Tilley. Frances Day and Stanley Holloway would often perform in a show for me with Harry Leader's band in Broadcasting House at 2.00 am.

Living Dangerously, a series I edited, brought in a man I admired greatly, Herbert G. Ponting, who was with Scott as a photographer in the Antarctic, and J.E. Williamson who invented the Williamson tube, a photosphere to photograph sharks under the sea. We had windjamming round the Horn, the voyage of the Tai-mo-shan and such personalities as Freya Stark, Cherry Kearton, Robert Flaherty, Jean Betten, Eric Shipton, Sir Malcolm Campbell and others, names to conjure with at the time. These adventures were compiled in a book by Allen & Unwin.

One of my best ideas then was a series I called *Meet the Detective*. Here is the start of what I wrote in the introduction motivating the series:

Who killed Cock Robin? For all you know your genial host may have done it himself. In the old days of the drama and novels the criminal was obvious to everyone. With time and technique come the least-suspected murderer. Nowadays it may be anyone. It may even be you.

I persuaded the great writers to tell in person how they came to create their detectives of fiction. They were all so different, so unexpected, and many travelled miles for an absurdly small fee to broadcast in person.

After the author had spoken we materialised the character by dramatising a scene from his novel with actors. Basically the idea came from Sir Arthur Conan Doyle himself, as I found a record of him speaking of his own master mind of Baker Street. Here it is:

With regard to Sherlock Homes, I was when I wrote it a young doctor and had been educated in a very severe and critical medical school of thought - especially coming under the influence of Dr. Bell of Edinburgh, who had most remarkable powers of observation. He prided himself that when he looked at a patient he could tell not only their disease but very often their occupation and powers of resilience.

"Reading some detective stories I was struck by the fact that their results were obtained in nearly every case by chance - I except, of course, Edgar Allen Poe's splendid stories which, though only three in number, are a model for all time. I thought I would try my hand at writing a story where the hero would treat crime as Dr. Bell treated disease and where science would take the place of chance. The result was Sherlock Holmes and I confess that the result has surprised me very much, for I learn that many schools of detection working in France, in Egypt, in China and elsewhere have admittedly founded their systems upon that of Holmes.

Sherlock and Holmes were both county cricketers. It was said that Conan Doyle nearly called him Sherrington Holmes, when he remembered Mordecai Sherlock, a Yorkshire cricketer, and so Sherlock Holmes came into the world.

My greatest scoop then was to get the grand old lady the Baroness Orczy from Monte Carlo to talk about the Scarlet Pimpernel. She was then Mrs Montagu Barstow. Next came "Sapper" in person to talk about Bulldog Drummond. A.E.W. Mason, a supreme story teller, talked of Hanaud, and Sax Rohmer about Dr. Fu Manchu. The detailed collection was published in a book by Allen and Unwin and in America by the Telegraph Press.

As a second series was demanded I persuaded G.K. Chesterton to present Father Brown. As a result he come to see me, at the same time as I was asked if I would show the Emil Faisal and his Suite over Broadcasting House. G.K. decided to go on the tour too and between them they took up so much of a lift there was no room for me.

G.K. Chesterton wrote to me:

I find I have committed 53 murders, alas only in the form of murder stories, lacking the manlier qualities which lead the murderer to pass from mere drama to action. Now among the virtues of the murderer we may note first his modesty. He is the one artist who does not brag of his masterpieces. Nobody can say he seeks the limelight. He has even been known to allow others the credit of his most perfect crimes.

"About the personality of my own very private detective, called Father Brown, there seems to be only one fact stated at all: that he was an Essex man and came from a totally imaginary place called Cobhole.

"Those who despise detective stories are so stupid they do not even see what is wrong with detective stories. There is no reason why a shocker should not deal with the highest spiritual problem; where it will always, perhaps, fall short of the first rank is in this, that in a great story the characters make the story: in a detective story the story makes the characters. It is made up backwards. Many police novels are quite good, the characters real, the conversation convincing. But the characters have been created to do something, preferably something atrocious, and the convincing talk leads up to a conviction.

I dramatised far too many stories myself as we had little money available for adapters. I liked particularly E.W. Hornung's stories of the gentleman bushranger 'Stingaree'. Another story among many I dramatised was what I think is the most frightening story ever written, F. Marion Crawford's *The Upper Berth*.

One morning very early I was auditioning artists and a plump girl was sitting around. She never responded to a call to come up to the microphone and start her act; and gradually it transpired that she had only come to chaperone another girl, Madge Mullen, a pianist. However she decided to sing and we were all so impressed she has never looked back as a very fine character actress, Joan Young.

We went to Armoury House, Finsbury, for an evening with the H.A.C., and to the Royal Hospital, Chelsea for the Pensioners who still toast their benefactor, Charles II. These were a prelude to a super broadcasting idea of mine, using 19 microphone points, at Hampton Court Palace with its thousand rooms, once Cardinal Wolsey's pride. The Empire Orchestra, conducted by Eric Fogg, played in the Great Hall.

We visited the Haunted Gallery, Wolsey's Closet, the Chapel Royal, the Tudor kitchens, the Royal tennis court and the Clock Tower, besides reconstructing history in the very rooms where the real scenes had actually taken place. We did this with words written by Shakespeare and Clifford Bax. Where no lighting existed we rigged pilot lights. The actors, led by Maurice Colbourne and Joan Miller, were quite unnerved by the experience. It was a thrilling night. Strange facts came out, one being the first Queen Elizabeth's capacity for drinking beer.

Just then I received this splendid letter from the American humorist Robert Benchley, author of *My Ten Years in a Quandary* and *After 1903, What?*:

To have The Thunderer devote a column to a serious discussion of a book of mine was a bit staggering. I am still trying to work out a way I can flash the cutting on people in a casual manner without looking like an actor.

"Your letter made me feel so good I sat down and wrote my first fan letter to an author, hoping to pass the warmth on. I was so successful that he called me up at two o'clock this morning from Baltimore, very drunk and crying into the mouthpiece, asking me to tell him for God's sake what life is all about and what we are going to do about it. 'Kind words never die.'

"My books have been getting steadily worse and have now reached a point where I cannot even read proof on my own books. I had rather hoped to do something different one day, a fairly scholarly history of Queen Anne's reign but I see that Trevelyan has beaten me to it. So my next book is to be called *From Bed to Worse*. My Publisher's idea of course.

One day I was walking along a corridor at Broadcasting

House when, at an open doorway of an empty room (in fact J.B. Clark's) I heard the phone ring in a sort of code ring. It was, though unknown to me, Sir John Reith's special ring, his direct call to save wasting time, and usually struck terror to all. He was a very alarming character. Irrationally, my feet gravitated to that phone and I lifted the receiver. It was, of course, the formidable Director General. "Have we ever used Gypsy Smith?" came the question. At that moment my mind could only switch to the only Gipsy I knew well, an American girl accordion player called Gypsy Nina. As we understood the great man liked quick, direct answers I replied, "Yes sir, often." It transpired that on a voyage coming back from America he had met and talked to Gypsy Smith the Evangelist, and was checking up. Since my information was quite inaccurate he is probably still gunning for the anonymous voice.

At the time of Charles B. Cochran's show *Nymph Errant*, starring Gertrude Lawrence, based on James Laver's amusing novel, and with dances by and with Agnes de Mille, I was asked to produce a broadcast for Cole Porter, mostly for the benefit of America. As the Adelphi Theatre, where the show was to be staged, was occupied with rehearsals we had to go over to His Majesty's Theatre. I remember asking Dan O'Neil to hammer nails in the background of a perfectly good stage to make it sound like a rehearsal at the Adelphi. Dan enjoyed this and did it with a will. It was a pretty distinguished trio round that microphone, Charles B. Cochran, Gertrude Lawrence, and Cole Porter at the piano. The featured song was *But He Says He Loves Me*. In the show it was retitled *The Physician*. When he got up from the piano the composer of *Samantha* and *Kiss Me Kate* said to me, "You have been most courteous. Would you like my copy?" and he handed me the song.

HOW TELEVISION WORKS

So what is television? The word is part Greek and part Latin, an agreeable compromise with the classics, and means seeing at a distance. I was asked to write a piece for a dictionary, and this was part of it:

In April 1925, John Logie Baird first demonstrated that moving images could be transmitted from room to room, but the foundation of television goes back to 1817, to the discovery by Berzelius of the element selenium. Only 56 years later it was accidentally discovered at the Valencia Cable Station that some selenium rods used as resistances altered in value under strong sunlight and this led to the discovery that the resistance of selenium became lower when it was exposed to a bright light. This opened up the possibility of converting light waves into electric impulses. Nipkow in 1884 invented his famous scanning disc. Meanwhile Faraday in 1845 and Kerr in 1877 had demonstrated the effect of a magnetic field on polarised light, but television was still not possible as no means existed of amplifying the extremely small currents available. A.A. Campbell Swinton in 1908 described a device, the forerunner of the modern television camera, in which comparatively larger currents can be obtained owing to its cumulative storing effect. He set out also an idea for the use of cathode ray beams at both transmitter and receiver, synchronously deflected by the varying fields of two electromagnets placed at right angles to one another and energised by two alternating currents of different frequencies, so that the moving extremities of the two beams would be caused to swing synchronously over the whole of the required surface within the period necessary to take advantage of persistence of vision.

In 1923 Baird in Britain and Jenkins in America were both carrying out experiments using mechanical methods of scanning which led, in 1925, to the transmission of shadows. In 1926 real images were transmitted short distances and in 1927 the American Telephone and Telegraph Company demonstrated transmission of a picture by wire over a distance of 250 miles and later repeated this by wireless.

A step forward was made in 1929 when the BBC gave Baird facilities for experimental transmissions at 30 scanning lines and 12.5 pictures per second, known as low definition programmes, originating in Baird's Long Acre studio. In 1930 the BBC equipped a studio in Broadcasting House with Baird apparatus.

In May 1934 the Postmaster General appointed a Committee under Lord Selsdon. This decided to make the BBC responsible for Television as well as Sound Broadcasting and that two selected systems, Baird and Marconi-EMI, Marconi's Wireless Telegraph Company, provided the transmitter.

Well, Lord Selsdon's Television Advisory Committee had recommended a start should be made as a Public Service. The BBC should run Television and two studios identical in size be built to transmit the picture on 405 lines, the Marconi-EMI system in Studio A and the Baird system in Studio B. Marconi-EMI worked on an electronic system, much as it is today, Baird on an intermediate film system. This photographed the scene onto celluloid, which rolled, developed and printed the result in just under 60 seconds. It was therefore not instantaneous and did not work well either.

There was besides a 'mechanical scanning studio'. This had a revolving light playing onto the character in the dark and needed special make-up, whereas for the Marconi-EMI system ordinary street make-up would often do. This Baird mechanical scanner often failed too, and broke John Logie Baird's heart after doing so much pioneering. The public was confused, as the Marconi-EMI combines had American interests in development, even though British in origin, and the Baird system was wholly British with shares on the market.

Gerald Cock, my boss at Outside Broadcasts, had been appointed Director of Television in 1935 and had been getting together his BBC team to start high definition television in studios built in a corner of the old Alexandra Palace. Alexandra Palace was on high ground in North London, and half an hour in a fast car from the West End, a disadvantage in itself, but it was to house TV for practical purposes until the end of 1954.

ALEXANDRA PALACE

When "high definition" television opened at Alexandra Palace there may have been 300 sets in homes.

The Alexandra Palace, largely domed glass, was built out of materials from the second International Exhibition of 1862 in South Kensington, opened in 1862 and burned down a fortnight later. Rebuilt, it was opened on May Day 1875 and named in honour of Princess Alexandra. It stands on a hill in North London, near Wood Green and Hornsey, and is something of a baroque monstrosity. It was a reasonable journey in a car from Central London but being a non-driver, I have suffered much in the long Underground route via Wood Green.

Blondin, dressed as a Roman gladiator, soon after

The Alexandra Palace,
North London.

crossing Niagara Falls, walked the 300-foot length of the Great hall on a tightrope 70 feet up, pushing his Manager in a wheelbarrow. It was then lit by gas jets and he complained of the stifling heat. There was a 3,000 seat theatre where the Great Vance, George Leybourne and Herbert Campbell starred, also George Conquest's Pantomime and Hengler's Circus.

The Palace housed German Prisoners in World War I and refugees from Gibraltar in World War II. It was the venue of the annual Rochdale Outing, when a horde of hungry and thirsty men and women from Rochdale would descend in coaches, drink freely at the 18 fully licensed bars, be entertained by Gracie Fields and go home happy. On one of these alarming occasions the Spanish ventriloquist Wences was to appear in a TV programme and was sunning himself on the steps of the BBC front hall when the Rochdale outing arrived. Smiling broadly he must have signed literally thousands of autograph books; with queues stretching for miles leading to him: they had not the slightest idea who he was, nor he them. Oh well, that's show business, as they say.

The building abounded with nude statues with tremendous bottoms sticking out prominently. These were plentifully used by visitors for striking matches.

To compress my story, I was to be Planner and a producer too. Others engaged were Peter Bax, designer and George More O'Ferrall to be a play producer, Stephen Thomas who had been with Nigel Playfair in his great days at Hammersmith to be music producer, Harry Pringle, an Australian, for variety, and Dallas Bower for opera and films. Leslie Mitchell was to be the male announcer and two lovely girls chosen by Gerald Cock himself, Jasmine Bligh and Elizabeth Cowell. Nearly all of these were engaged too soon and had been sent to me for training in the Overseas Service, as it latterly began to be called. They all enjoyed a gruelling time and were soon conditioned for anything. Two others were due, Cecil Lewis, a former BBC man to run the talks, and D. H. Munro, already in the BBC, who had taught me a lot about Control Room panel operation. Major L. Barbrook was the entire film unit and Mary Allen, with Jeanne Bradnock, was in charge of make-up. On the engineering side were Douglas Birkinshaw as Engineer-in-Charge and Tony Bridgewater: both had been concerned with 30-line television experiments, besides Tinker and lighting expert Desmond Campbell, all characters with great individuality.

Chapter One tells the story of our rush to put together the first television broadcast for the 1936 Radiolympia exhibition. Once this initial series of broadcasts ended, our blood was up and we wanted to go on. The difficulty was to get any money from Broadcasting House, who were all for remaining inactive until November for an official opening. They reckoned without us.

I wanted to try a magazine programme, and on October 8 we did. Gerald Cock supplied the title, *Picture Page*. I devised the method of continuity, a telephone switchboard with an electronic screen and Joan Miller, the Canadian actress, as the switchboard girl. I was also the Editor, as indeed I remained for 262 editions, and George More O'Ferrall was its first producer. Later we threw the directing open to the whole staff, who took it in turn each week. Not only did everyone try to improve on everyone else but it brought endless new ideas and trained everybody.

The whole crew and the personalities in the first *Picture Page* posed afterwards for a photograph. This magazine programme was put together by a system of scouts who were paid three guineas per item. The scouts were S.E. Reynolds, later a popular producer, Mary Benedetta Sharpe, a journalist, Leslie Baily, a journalist, Jack G. Cannell, a journalist, Dorothy Cannell, his wife, and John

Gardner. I would suggest ideas to them, as we had good lists of celebrity arrivals, or they suggested items to me. It worked admirably. That first programme is worth mentioning. There was Dinah Sheridan, then a sixteen-year-old poster model, later a popular film star of "Genevieve", Ras Prince Monolulu the racing tipster, Mrs Flora Drummond a famous suffragette, Squadron Leader F.R. Swain holder of the world's altitude record, John Snuggs a busker, and "Prestwick Pertana" a Siamese cat. Leslie Mitchell interviewed everyone.

Picture Page hit the headlines and we were in. The Observer said: "*Picture Page* is good and is sure to be popular." The Daily Telegraph went further: "*Picture Page* is a brilliant success. Production approached cinema standards of efficiency." We firmly numbered this Number One. We still had not officially opened the Service.

Then came the official opening on November 2nd. Frankly it was pretty dull. Speeches usually are, especially formal ones. The Baird system won the toss, so from the Baird studio spoke the Hon. Major G.C. Tryon, Postmaster General, Mr R.C. Norman, Chairman of the BBC, Lord Selsdon and Sir Harry Greer of Baird Television. Then they all moved down the corridor to the Marconi-EMI studio except that there Mr Alfred Clark also spoke, representing the Marconi-EMI Television Company. Then Adele Dixon sang, two American comedians Buck and Bubbles performed, the Television Orchestra played and everyone had tea. John W. Bubbles became better known later as the first *Sportin' Life* in Gershwin's opera *Porgy and Bess*. Now the place had been blessed and we were a legitimate concern.

THE OBSERVER wrote: "We are so used to being told that this country is behindhand in every form of endeavour, it is worth emphasising that the new service is the first of its kind in the world."

Picture Page, episode 1, October 1936

Joan Miller is at the switchboard,
guests included
Prince Monolulu, racing tipster;
Dinah Sheridan, poster model;
Leslie Mitchell, interviewer;
Cecil Madden is sixth from right in back row.

The great moment was to be the evening programme. I had been told that it had better be good. At that point the best thing we could think of was undoubtedly *Picture Page*. So we solemnly did Number Two on opening day. It was the turn for it to be done on the Baird system. We had Jim Mollison the great flying ace; Kay Stammers the Wimbledon tennis champion; Bossy Phelps the Thames river character with John Snagge; Jasmine Bligh and Elizabeth Cowell, the girl announcers introduced for the first time to their public; George Whitelaw writer and cartoonist; Alexander Shaw the film producer; Mrs Donisthorpe; the Tinsleys, the Pearly King and Queen of Blackfriars, and Algernon Blackwood who told two of the shortest ghost stories in the world.

THE OBSERVER, who seemed to have adopted us, said: "Television in the home is a very pleasant form of amusement and instruction." *THE TIMES* came out with: "The cameraman's task is not easy, for the image he is televising appears in the viewfinder upside down and of course in colour. It is a pleasant shock to us to see the image in colour but, as the result has to be in black and white, things are not made easier for him and as the picture is reversed he has to learn to wheel right to follow an actor who appears to be going left and to point his camera up in order to get an image lower on the screen."

Daily afternoon programming started at 3:00 pm Evening programmes started at 9:00 pm and ran until 11:00 or midnight. The problem as a planner was what to put in the programmes.

The budget for talent, copyright, costumes and scenery was £1,000 a week, which could be budgeted at about £100 a day for afternoon and evening programmes with a bit extra for major events. Shortly after our run at Radiolympia, a call came to me from a man who said to me, "My name is William Streaton, I am your new booking manager,

I have dealt with people like Caruso and there is nothing I don't know about how to handle artists. You can book no one except through me. When I told him our program budget he said, "You can't pay anyone over 25 guineas, that's your maximum figure." I said "I don't think they'll like it very much," and he said "That's how it's going to be." I got a call from Sophie Tucker, who at that time was a very big star, playing two houses at the Palladium and playing at Grosvenor House, earning a fortune. And she said "Cecil, we've known each other for many years, I fancy being the first American star on your new television when programmes start." And I said, "Right Sophie, it's agreed, you shall be number 1." "Ah, she said, but what's all this nonsense about 25 guineas,?" I said, "Well, that's not really my fault, this is how it's got to be. She replied, "I want to be the first, so I'll tell you what we'll do. Ted Shapiro and I have talked this over, and as we're two people we'll take 40." And thus "The Last of the Red Hot Mamas" was the first American chanteuse on British television.

Planning the television schedule there was never any doubt in my mind that the emphasis should be on drama. To my mind there was no limit to the writing you could dramatise, the world's books, the world's plays, the classical theatre, the current theatre, new writing. The writer would be the trend-setter, the taste maker. 'A play a day' was our aim and the Radio Times said so in print, so plays formed our backbone. Every play was repeated to save effort, and if the first performance were done in the afternoon, by our shift system, it could be polished up for the night's show.

With no news department of our own we approached the cinema interests and hired cinema newsreels which we showed in agreed rotation; British Movietone News and Gaumont British News mainly. We also were able to get a number of cartoon films made by Walt Disney in the early days of Mickey Mouse, and these were highly acceptable.

Picture Page, February 23, 1949.

Special episode to celebrate the sale of 100,000 television licences.
Presenters Joan Gilbert, Cecil Madden and Leslie Mitchell tell viewers
about the first television broadcast from Alexandra Palace in 1936.

Since both news and cartoons, indeed any films, came from separate telecine rooms, and this enabled the studios to be cleared and reset safely. With only two studios we cut them in half, placing the cameras in the centre facing both ends, and thus created four studio working areas. In this way we could easily put on five or six substantial items per transmission. Afternoon programmes started at 3:00 pm, evening programmes at 9:00 pm. They usually ran to 11:00 pm or midnight.

A tedious form of thinking that had to be combated was the start-small-build-up-gradually school. I was determined that we should start big and go on better. Luckily we were able to carry out a sensational first week.

We put on a play, a ballet and an opera. This sounds ambitious and it was. For the play we went to the Royalty Theatre and obtained their production of *Marigold*, so the first drama stars were Sophie Stewart and John Bailey, in a production by George More O'Ferrall. Marie Rambert's Mercury Ballet brought Maude Lloyd, Walter Gore, Andree Howard, Frank Staff and Hugh Laing, and was presented by Stephen Thomas. The opera was all-British, *Pickwick* by Albert Coates, and starred William Parsons, Henry Wendon and Dennis Noble. It was rehearsed, ready and shortly to open at Covent Garden, and by good luck we got in first. This was presented by Dallas Bower.

In the first week we also televised the American stars Bebe Daniels and Ben Lyon and Henry Hall with the BBC Dance Orchestra.

Soon after the opening came the abdication of the King in December 1936. By coincidence we were showing a display of duplicates of the Tower of London collection of the Crown Jewels, with a historical commentary by Kenneth L. Davy. The Radio Times billing read: " A point of topical interest about this broadcast is that viewers will see a replica of the crown to be worn by King Edward at the

Coronation Ceremony next year. This is King Edward the Confessor's crown."

The news of King Edward VIII's decision to renounce the crown caused much telephoning as to whether it was bad taste to show the item. It was decided to carry on as billed so the topicality was absolute.

Puppets took an early place in programmes, with John Carr's Jacquard Puppets and Scott Gordon's Marionettes. These were based on the human face and puppet's clothes and limbs.

In the second week we got a glimpse of the calibre of Joan Miller. Ronald Adam at the Embassy Theatre supplied us with his entire production of *The Tiger*, about Clemenceau, with William Devlin, Alexander Knox and Joan Miller. Being Canadian, and readily on the spot as the *Picture Page* switchboard girl twice in the day every week, we could do many ambitious American plays effectively, particularly those of Thornton Wilder such as *The Happy Journey to Trenton and Camden* and the Moss Hart-George Kaufman satire on Hollywood, *Once in a Lifetime*. We were thinking big and we had plenty of goodwill.

J. F. Horrabin explained the news with maps, Commander King Hall discussed current events. A.H. Middleton was the first TV gardener, with his own garden in the grounds of Alexandra Park. Mary Adams, who joined the staff in 1937, decided to organise a fire-walking demonstration in the grounds. Red hot stones were heated for hours in a fire and an Indian walked the length of these without damage. An English volunteer who followed got quite badly burned on the soles of his feet.

Under Mary Adams' direction John Piper ran a series *The Eye of the Artist* about current art exhibitions.

Dallas Bower directed a film of TV activities which was called the Demonstration Film and shown every morning for the Trade. It could be seen in the radio shops to

Bebe Daniels and Ben Lyon anchored to the Baird studio floor in *Starlight.* 1936

encourage people to buy television sets. Sherkot, with his comic French goalkeeping act was a hit in this as a juggler, and it ended with the gay tango from *Facade* with Margot Fonteyn and Frederick Ashton.

One day Seth Smith, our first Zoo man, was showing an Australian bush rat which Jasmine Bligh particularly disliked handling. As it became restive he warned her to hold it tight. After a stiff struggle the bush rat got away, leaving its tail in Jasmine's hand.

One night the Crystal Palace, which dominated South London, burned down, and we could see the glow from Alexandra Palace which was on a corresponding height in North London. As a small result, the annual Bird Show came to the Great Hall in Alexandra Palace. We brought some of the birds into our studio. A toucan managed to escape and flew up onto the lighting bridge, making rude noises. As anyone moved towards it, so the toucan moved away. Hours later scene men were still trying to catch it, and at 9.0 pm we had to start the evening programmes, punctuated by these noises which were hard to contend with.

The first outstanding television politician was the Rt. Hon. Leslie Hore Belisha, like me also born in Morocco. *Speaking Personally*, a series produced by Mary Adams, brought Rebecca West and J.B. Priestley. Priestley was always an enthusiast for the medium and was, at one time, by far our most played playwright.

The beautiful Alice Marble not only won Wimbledon tennis, which we televised, but she also came to the studios as a singer. This, with pictures, made all the headlines.

It occurred to me that Yvette Guilbert, the famous French singer, friend of Toulouse Lautrec, could be persuaded over from Paris. She had run a drama school in New York and written the fascinating book *The Song of My Life*. She once said to Grace Moore, "It is not only our errors which ruin us, but our way of conducting ourselves after committing them." I spoke to her by phone and tried to explain that we would give her VIP treatment and look after her as well as we possibly could. "Of course you will," she replied. "Now Mr Madden, never mind the nonsense, "what is the money?" Later came a letter from her. "In regard to rehearsals, the contract reads 'as arranged.' But nothing has been arranged." She liked everything cut and dried.

The staff was strengthened in 1937 by Eric Crozier who handled a 'Comic Strip' series on American humour. Philip Dart took on the Outside Broadcasts, Jan Russell and Moutrie Kelsall to produce plays, and Royston Morley to be my assistant.

Television took a giant step with the televising of the

Coronation Procession of King George VI on May 12, 1937 from a site at Hyde Park Corner. The Derby in 1938 and 1939, the Boat Race, polo at Hurlingham, Trooping the Colour, the Cup Final, Test Matches, the Theatrical Garden Party at Ranelagh, Rugger and Soccer Internationals, all had to have a first time in television. And Bulls Cross Farm, television's own farm, where viewers learned about crops and cattle. The Boon-Danahar fight at Harringay in 1939 was historic since it was agreed to let it be seen in several West End cinemas as well as in the homes.

There were television visits to film studios, to Pinewood, Elstree and Denham. Viewers met Maurice Chevalier, Charles Laughton, Jessie Matthews, Margaret Lockwood, Merle Oberon, Sally Gray, Raymond Massey, Otto Kruger, Valerie Hobson and Sabu on the set as they worked.

Probably the most dramatic outside event was the return from Munich of Prime minister Neville Chamberlain on September 16, 1938, waving his piece of paper signed by Hitler giving us 'Peace in our time'. Indeed it gave us time – one year. THE TIMES on 22nd December, 1933, wrote, "But perhaps the most striking of all was the arrival of the Prime Minister at Heston after his visit to Herr Hitler at Berchtesgarden. No one knew what had happened until, stepping from his aeroplane in front of the television cameras, he told them. This had a quality of history in the making.

One evening about 10:00 pm I was working late in my office, high up in the top of the Tower. The telephone rang and a flat voice spoke, "The Emperor of Abyssinia to see you, Sir." It sounded like a joke. "Just say that again," I said. The Receptionist wearily repeated, "The Emperor of Abyssinia to see you, Sir." Without waiting for the lift, which moved slowly, I rushed down the stairs of the five floors and arrived breathless in the hall, not looking particularly like the senior man on duty. Sure enough, there was Haile

Selassie, the Lion of Judah, with his children and his whole entourage, all in traditional dress. I was a little taken aback but I murmured a welcome in English. This produced no flicker of response so I repeated it in French and Spanish. The Emperor made an impatient gesture like "Cut the cackle and let's get on with it." So I led them into the tiny lift. This took several journeys. Having assembled the whole party on the second floor in the studio corridor, we started along it. Outside the first door of Studio A, under a clearly marked sign "Keep Out," was posted a small boy in uniform, as a guard to prevent entry during transmission and while the red lights were on. Seeing this astonishing party approaching, with me too, instead of exercising his authority as I hoped he would, he lost his nerve and flung open the studio door. Of course everyone stepped in. It happened that there were a series of one-act plays on the bill, one set in a railway carriage. The actors tried to pretend that nothing unusual was going on as this strange procession of bearded Abyssinians was gravely weaving in and out of cameras, sets and props. Luckily everyone behaved as if it was the most natural occurrence in the world. The Royal Party had a good time, made no reference to the fact that they had given no notice of their arrival, and I saw them all off into a fleet of cars. I heaved a sigh of relief. Three days later they did exactly the same thing again!

A delightful intimacy set up between the viewers and the performers. The announcers were looked on as friends. In Christmas week 1938 Gerald Cock, the charming and popular Director of Television, went into the *Witness Box*. He faced a camera and invited viewers to telephone there and then and put questions to him. Viewers were asked to put their phone in the same room as the television set and look directly at the screen. It was so successful the switchboard was jammed.

The first Television Tea Party was held in the Concert Hall of Broadcasting House in June 1939. Some 700 viewers accepted an invitation to meet the television staff, but the total had to be cut down to 150 and after a ballot 75 couples were invited. The staff wore identity badges and met the early viewers. There were questions and frank answers. They told us what they liked and we were glad to know.

Edmundo Ros, originally from Venezuela, came to London with Ciro Rinac's Band. He returned as drummer with pianist Don Marino Bareto's Trio. I was impressed with his personality and advised him to work towards having his own band. He said to me, "How can anyone conduct from the drums?" I said that as far as I knew Gene Krupa did all right, and that my hunch was that he would soon give up drumming altogether. I was right. He was soon a bandleader. In 1940 he had his first band in the Cosmo Club and then he broadcast from the cellar of Martinez's Spanish restaurant, as well as working the Astor and even more night spots, to which the band moved on in taxis, often in dangerous blitz conditions. Edmundo became a great international name, with his Edmundo Ros Club, his broadcasting, his stage work, his television shows and his recordings. He deserves his great success.

In 1955 he made a characteristic gesture when our daughter, Mardie, was having her coming-out dance at the Hyde Park Hotel. He brought his whole band along to play for her party, so with Tommy Kinsman's Band she had the unusual luxury of two bands. In fact he went back to his Club to keep faith with his regulars, and then returned again to Mardie for another session. Mardie studied theatre design at the Central School of Arts and Crafts under the famous Jeanetta Cochraine, who now has a theatre named after her near it.

Mardie went on to be a costume designer in feature

Muriel, Cecil, and daughter Miss Mardie Madden,
a débutante in 1955. Mr Robert Atkins gave a
cocktail party to open the 1955 season of the
Open air Theatre in Regent's Park.

films and the theatre, starting as an assistant designer at Pinewood Studios on *A Night To Remember*, the 'Titanic' film. She married American lawyer Kernan Gorman in 1962, and has three daughters, Jennifer, Caroline, and Annabel. She has lived in Knightsbridge since 1968 and now owns and runs a needlepoint school which she started in 1972.

SHOWS

On Your Toes, Rodgers' and Hart's great musical, was playing in London. Somehow we persuaded the entire company to come to Alexandra Palace as early as May 1937. The stars were Jack Whiting, Olive Blakeney and Vera Zorina, that most lovely creature who made the *Slaughter on Tenth Avenue* ballet a creation all her own. This large company accompanied by Lew Stone's Band was an early high spot and a scoop.

As time went on we tackled the problem of televising musicals from the current theatres. It was done in a big way. After *Under Your Hat* from the Palace Theatre and *Babes in the Wood* from Drury Lane, 1939 shows televised in full were *Magyar Melody* from His Majesty's Theatre; *The Desert Song* from the Garrick Theatre; *Oh Letty*, from the Palace Theatre and Variety; and Continental revue from the Coliseum, among them *Doorlay's Rocket*. We had Lupino Lane in *Me and My Girl* not once but twice. We not only televised the show but the front of the house, the stage door, the dressing rooms, the intervals, the lot. We made a meal of the outings. The real throb of the theatre from open to close.

On televising *Me and My Girl* I quote Gordon Ross in "*TELEVISION JUBILEE*":

In May the King and Queen paid a surprise visit to the Victoria Palace to see the 852nd performance of the show with the Lambeth Walk. Only two hours before the curtain rose the theatre was told of the visit, but as permission would have to be sought beforehand it was not possible to show their Majesties in the Royal Box. The Queen, however, noticed the cameras soon after arriving and pointed them out to the King. Meanwhile Princess Elizabeth and Princess Margaret saw the first act on television in Buckingham Palace.

Somehow everyone was an escapist in the years just before the War. No one really believed it could happen here. As a result a lot of money was being spent in London's night life. The ones who believed war was inevitable were also spending money, to get rid of it quickly. As a result of both kinds of thinking, there was a great deal of talent in the town with big international names and troupes of stunning American dancing girls. Many of the girls married and settled here. I produced, or re-produced (it is usually called 'presenting') many of these programmes. We were lucky to have the co-operation of the MCA (Music Corporation of America) who ran the big cabaret show at Grosvenor House; of Henry Sherek who ran the Dorchester Hotel shows, both with American dancing Girls; and B. Cochran who presented his cabaret at the Trocadero, with English girls. The dance routines and costumes were all first class, and the accompanying bands came too; Sydney Lipton from Grosvenor House and Jack "Dancing in the Dark" Jackson from the Dorchester.

These package deals brought us Chaz Chase, who ate his hat; Gene Shelton, miming threading needles, and the pianists Fats Waller and Art Tatum; Sheila Barrett and John Hoysradt, both impressionists; Tex McLeod, cowboy; Stone and Lee, the highest kicker in the business; Nick Long Junior and Partner. The Partner was Danny Kaye.

Danny looked very different then, with a large mop of

Danny Kaye and Nick Lang Jr. in
Autumn Laughter,
Henry Sherek's Dorchester Hotel Cabaret
presented on September 21, 1938.

dark hair. He told me that Nick Long, who was a tap dancer, worked in the cabarets of the Middle East where it was so hot that after a strenuous routine Danny had to come on, only to find no one understood a word of his American patter. This is how he developed his remarkable act of made-up sounds, getting a response to each one separately and then adding more, getting laughs from the patrons for their own antics. It was brilliant self-help. Years later as the top of the bill at the London Palladium the same Danny was so confident he could lie down on the footlights.

Lovely Hildegarde once, after closing with her familiar song *Darling Je Vous Aime Beaucoup*, spoke a beautiful goodnight with a kiss in close up into the cameras and the curtains closed. As producer I gave the instruction to mix, and at this moment the apparatus jammed in the control room so that nothing could make the fader fade or the mixer mix. The curtains reopened, the studio staff piled the stool on the grand piano, pushed both off, while Hildegarde lifted her very full dress over her head and made for the door. It was an unexpected backstage bonus for viewers.

With so much American talent available I created a series which I also directed, called *100% Broadway*, all-American shows. The star was a young comedian, David Burns. There was also Russell Swann the conjuror; Evelyn Dall, blonde singer; Lee Sims, the pianist; Helen Bennett, a great beauty; Ken Harvey, banjoist; Billy Costello, the original Popeye; and the Girls – and what girls! – Chester Hale's girls, Meriel Abbott's girls, Paul Oscard's girls, Albertina Rasch's girls, Robert Alton's girls. I often think what a story it would make if one could find the names of any one of these troupes, which were mostly about eight girls each, and find out what life has done to each one.

TV cameras can never get down to ground level, which is why so many beautiful girls seem duckfooted with cameras tilting down at them. For variety I used to have cameras off their pedestals, with cameramen full length on the floor holding them upwards. This got unusual effects and had various names, mostly scurrilous, particularly when shooting two lovely blonde German contortionists, Marion and Irma. Years later I tried to trace them, only to find they had a tragic end. They were one of my favourite acts as a director.

I wanted to create something that would be pure television, owing nothing to stage or films, so I devised and directed another series, *Cabaret Cartoons*. Harry Rutherford, the North Country artist, wrote up the name of the performer to the signature tune of Noel Coward's *Tokay*, tore it off and did a progressive drawing of the artist performing on the studio floor – the viewers could see both working in a superimposition and they finished together.

A favourite of mine was a great beauty, Trudi Binar, a former Miss Czechoslovakia, others too, as she made over 100 appearances.

Sometimes a producer would get so excited by a performer's afternoon performance that he would want to book him or her, for a second show perhaps in the evening transmission. The story is told of a keen young producer who rushed up to an attractive Continental singer after the afternoon transmission and said "Can I have you this evening?" The answer he got was, "Yes, but not at my place!"

Two of the greatest illusionists were Gali-Gali with his little chicks and the Mexican, Cantu. I got to know the old juggler Joe Adami's act very well and was always worried about his goldfish in a bowl of water which he guarded so carefully and which he juggled perched on the top of a billiard cue, until one day I found him cutting up a piece of carrot in his dressing room. "Much better than a fish." Not that he ever broke the bowl or spilt a drop of water anyway.

A May 1937 edition of the variety show
Cabaret Cruise was billed as fancy dress night.
The cast included Dixon, saxophonist
and Pal (the seal).

One of our comedians was Cyril Fletcher, then at the height of his 'Odd Odes'. Luckily he lived at Wood Green, so when a variety bill looked a bit thin a favourite story was that my secretary, then Eve Moir, used to wave her handkerchief out of our window at the top of the Tower and up came Cyril to add to or compere a bill of artists in the afternoon. Cyril, was past President of the Concert Artist's Association, denies the story, claiming that the telephone had been invented even then.

A word of advice to producers is never to trust an agent's build-up for an artist and never to book an act unless you have seen this personally. It can be a trap. Wilson, Keppel and Betty were, and seemingly always had been, 2M 1F on the lists, or two males and a female called Betty. Actually the act wore out several Bettys over the years, it was a sand dance. Take Dixon and Pal – Pal was in fact a seal. I knew Dixon's seal well. I was in my office planning schedules and also doing the usual worrying and budgeting when a phone call from the Reception Desk said "Mr Madden, your seal is here. Mr Dixon says he should go into water and he'll be along later for rehearsals." I just said "Put him in the dressing room with a bath." Someone ran the cold bath and in popped the seal. There was only one dressing room with a bath, usually used for chorus girls and ensembles. As it happened the star of the play, Robert Douglas, giving an afternoon performance in Studio B, was in occupation and was at the time in the middle of a long part, the lead in *The Royal Family of Broadway*, a skit on John Barrymore and all the Barrymores, and so he knew nothing of the intrusion. When he had finished, exhausted, he was sitting in his dressing room rubbing his face with grease to take off his make-up, when he saw in the mirror what appeared to be a docile old gentleman with whiskers leering at him out of the bath. I am sorry to say his sense of humour deserted him and there was a splendid row.

On the subject of the Barrymores, there is a story that when they were on tour together in a costume melodrama John and his brother Lionel had to fight a duel, ending with John being run through the heart. One night John battled so well that Lionel's sword was twinkled out of his hand and flew in an arc into the orchestra pit. John raised his head and said "And what am I supposed to do now? Starve to death?"

In my capacity in charge of programmes I wanted to engage Madame Koringa, the great attraction of the then Olympia Circus. She was unique and in her act she put daggers through her arms and legs without drawing blood and lay on a ladder of sharp swords - cigarette papers were cut on them to show how sharp they were. She also wrestled with crocodiles and in the Circus (although we didn't try it), was buried in sand for minutes. In fact she told me she could do it for much longer.

I went to see her to discuss her dates. She only spoke French and never disclosed her origins. She was agreeable and had two spare days after the Circus was to close on a Saturday some weeks later before going to Hamburg. But she made the condition that as she had to vacate Olympia and we were delaying her departure, we must accommodate her whole menagerie at our place for a few days. There were eight crocodiles, several eagles, a number of enormous snakes and native attendants, male and female. I agreed at once and being very overtired, working almost day and night, it completely slipped my mind.

About 3:00 am on a Sunday morning I was woken in my flat in London's Dolphin Square by an infuriated House Manager who was in such a rage he could hardly speak. He told me to dress at once, get a taxi and go straight to Alexandra Palace to help him cope. It seems that wild animals in vans with keepers were outside and demanding admittance. All available staff converged, the Scene Dock

Madame Koringa,
the Female Fakir, January 28, 1938.

was opened and the beasts let in. The crocodiles in particular were put in a tank on top of one another, warmed and in water. They were only strapped down. Apparently they were used to this.

Gradually all was explained. Koringa, 'The Only Female Fakir in the World', was of course in a hotel in town and oblivious of the commotion, and the natives and the animals were all dossed down by the BBC, more or less together. The eagles were a lot more menacing than the pythons or the crocodiles. They obviously hated everyone in show business.

In the early hours the top, and largest, crocodile managed to get free, slid off the tank and started slowly exploring the whole ground floor of Alexandra Palace. The crocodile pushed his way through three swing doors, past the transmitter halls and canteen, and ended up in the front hall of the building. Imagine the surprise of the first cleaner letting herself in with a key to find herself confronted with an eight-foot crocodile facing her at the front door. The screams could be heard almost at Broadcasting House!

Madame Koringa came again after the war with different crocodiles and new snakes. There was an incident when one or these huge snakes managed to wrap itself round the camera so that the wheels of the dolly truck could move neither forward nor backward and the cameraman was then standing on his seat as the ugly face got nearer. The producer, looking into little monitors, could not understand why his orders were disregarded and got more and more angry. Koringa in her act used to build up a ladder of swords, all razor sharp and then climb up and lie suspended on them. She also allowed all the studio men to smash up a number of beer or lemonade bottles and any other glass or porcelain handy, and then not only did she lie on them but allowed a gigantic stone to be put on her chest and hammered on by all and sundry. She is unique among the great stars, no one has taken her place.

Of the great performing innovators she would join a select list of mine with Al Trahan (with Lady Yukona Cameron), who said, "I play with the accent on the rough, I do an act which I call comedy with violence – in five years I have torn up sixteen thousand, four hundred and fifty shirts and worn out over one thousand, two hundred and fifty six suits, I break over nine hundred stools a year and an equal number of grand pianos. In this list I put Olsen and Johnson who created *Hellzapoppin'*, Schnozzle Durante of Clayton, Jackson and Durante, Owen McGiveney's quick change act, Joe Jackson and his bicycle, and, of course, Charlie Chaplin. These artists can never be repeated, nor their material.

I was particularly interested in fast camera work and what I could do to show off to best advantage a certain knife-throwing act. A throw across a small studio under powerful lights was not the same thing as in a circus tent. On the day I was summarily sent for to the Boss's office. "Cecil, I see you've booked these knife throwers again." "Yes," I said, "And why not? They're very good." "It's too dangerous," he said, "You're to cancel them at once." This I said I could not do. It was now a professional matter with signed contracts which could not be broken. Besides the press had been invited to a reception in London to judge the whole show, so it would have caused an unhappy story everyone would wish to avoid. "Well, it's your own responsibility, take no risks." Thoroughly alarmed I checked the studio set up, distances and so on, and then went down to meet the coach bringing up the artists. Imagine my dismay when I heard a blazing row in progress between Mr X and Mrs X, accompanied by blows in which she gave as good as she got. She was a blonde and pretty tough with all her attractiveness, which was considerable. Moreover Mrs X. had a very nasty bandage disfiguring one of her legs at

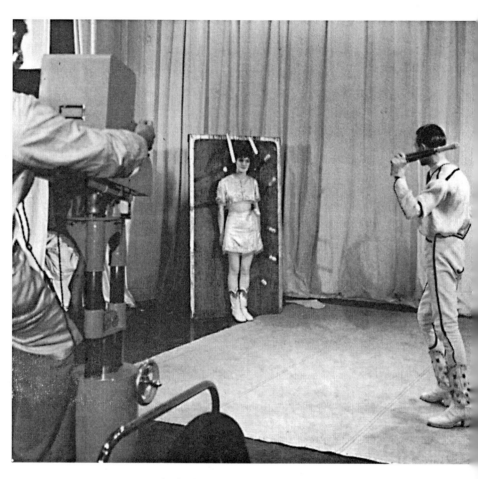

The knife-throwing Denvers in *Variety*,
producer Cecil Madden, October 24, 1936.
Curtains provide a very basic backdrop.

the ankle, which looked as though a knife or a hatchet had recently missed the board. They fought in the lift and in the dressing room. By then I was getting the jitters as he was truculently laying down the knives and clashing them together with maximum noise, as knife-throwers do, holding them up in a kind of steel fan with the blades in his fist.

He would first throw twelve knives, then cover his wife with newspaper, blindfold himself, then throw flaming hatchets round her head. She told me he threw so close they would pin her hair to the board.

Having laid out the positions, he sent for his sullen, cursing wife, and pushed her against the board accompanied by various tasteless remarks for the benefit of the studio staff like, "I've got you where I want you." By then I was losing my nerve fast so I said to Mr X, "Look, X, I know your act perfectly so there is no need to go through the whole routine of throwing the knives and hatchets for the rehearsal." To which he replied, "That's all right old boy, we've been sleeping rough lately. We haven't worked for some time so I'll have to bash through it a few times to get my eye in, as I'm a bit rusty." Fortunately he was a brilliant artist and all went well.

Having only two studios, mostly used as four by dividing them in half, the sides got cluttered with props. One variety bill called for a scene in a taxi so an old one was bought for £5 and sawn in half. In their enthusiasm the studio staff rushed this off to the side where it struck the telephone switchboard standing ready for *Picture Page*, which started off its buzzer. This was a piercing noise and nothing would stop it until a stage hand gave it a sharp knock which silenced it so effectively that when the time came for *Picture Page* it would not work at all.

I had some reputation for doing girl shows, so to fool everyone I engaged every male dancing troupe I could find, the Lancashire Lads, the J.W. Jackson Boys and so on. The place was teeming with troupes of youths in white flannel outfits, which were then traditional for dancing boys. Nelson Keys, the brilliant little comedian, compèred sitting in a hot bath in a dressing room. We switched commentaries on films of Hawaii and the Industrial North.

We booked every pantomime animal we could find, such as Fred Conquest's Goose and many others. The passages and studios became clogged with pantomime Cats, Monkeys and the rest. Another time we engaged as many carnival Grotesques as we could find. It became a tradition in early television that I should produce a 'crazy show' of eccentric performers every April 1, two in fact, one in the afternoon called *Nice Work*, and in the evening *If You Can Get It*.

There came a demand for a visual tour of the studios. To sugar the pill we asked 'The Prime Minister of Mirth', George Robey, to conduct this. He was game for anything new.

It was the time of the Show Dance Band; Jack Hylton's, Jack Payne's, Geraldo's, Ambrose's, Henry Hall's. We televised no less than 35 different dance bands, including Ray Ventura over from Paris, and the Lecuona Cuban Boys, genuinely from Cuba. We put on 150 cabaret shows and revues, 98 star musicians, 25 cartoonists, 80 ballets, 50 operettas, 42 personalities *Speaking Personally*, 57 *Starlight* stars, 56 public events, 165 documentary and light features and 17 puppeteers, not forgetting Percy Press and his irrepressible Punch and Judy.

As a programme planner with little money to spend I was always tearing my hair for cheap but compelling items.

PICTURE PAGE

Picture Page, the first television magazine, ran for seven years. In its day only relays from theatre and newsreels got a higher vote. Here is not what I say but *The Times* of 10/7/39:

> *Picture Page* was specially invented for the new service by Cecil Madden, the programme organiser, and has been a twice-weekly feature from the beginning. It provides a unique contact between viewers and personalities of the day. It has an office and staff of its own, the outside staff whose duty it is to capture people in the news and lure them up to Alexandra Palace, and the inside staff who introduce and interview them before the cameras.
>
> The array of celebrities who have appeared in *Picture Page* is formidable and the topical quality of the programme is remarkable. If the flying boat Yankee Clipper has arrived in the morning from America, Senator Lundeen is there to tell us about his trip. If an exhibition of Soviet Art is to open, Mme Maisky is there to show us some of the exhibits, and while Mr Gielgud's "Hamlet" production is speeding to Elsinore, Miss Sophie Harris of "Motley" describes how the show was designed. Less recently the cast of "The Women" appeared on the screen before they appeared on the stage, and Mme Paxinou, the Greek tragedienne, who was to be famous a week later as "Electra." Last week, the Varsity match being imminent, both captains were in the studio which also held an Indian Yogi and a Red Indian Chief awaiting their turn. The smile on the face of the game warden from Tanganyika gave viewers quite a new sidelight on lions.

Picture Page's signature music was *I've Had My Moments* (Billy Cotton's Band and Leo Reisman's), linked by "Song of Surrender" (Wayne King's Orchestra) and closed with "Red White and Blue" (Jack Hylton's Band.) It opened with a boy bugler from HMS *Warspite*.

Here is Grace Wyndham Goldie, critic of the Listener, on July 13, 1939:

> *Picture Page* is one long triumph. There is something of everything and nothing for long. It is, in fact, a kind of high speed television circus. It exploits just these things of which television is master. Television still does the individual turn and the individual interview better than anything else: it is still at its best when it is intimate, and *Picture Page* is full of individual interviews and can be as intimate as you like. Moreover television can create a valuable friendliness by letting us see the same personalities every week. And in *Picture Page* the novelty and variety are always presented by the same pair, Leslie Mitchell and Joan Miller. All this, plus the drive of Cecil Madden, the editor and inventor of *Picture Page* and the hard work of Joan Gilbert, his assistant, make it the great success that it is. One of their great problems is to make it run smoothly without losing spontaneity. This can only be done by the most skilful handling of a collection of frightened and embarrassed people. And I know how well they do it because last week I was one of them.

Joan Miller at the *Picture Page* switchboard was the first person to be seen by television in America from Europe. One night early in November 1938 radio engineers were sitting in front of a British television set in Riverside Receiving Station, New York, testing an aerial, when they were amazed to see a woman's face swim rather indistinctly onto the screen on the London wavelength. It was a freak then, a freak of transmission and reception, but still it was historical.

Joan Gilbert, presenter of *Picture Page.*

At first we cued Joan Miller through headphones, but later we devised an electrical ankle signal, giving her a mild shock.

Out of 1,855 items pre-war alone, American guests included Sir Hubert Wilkins, the explorer; film star Ray Milland; Erskine Caldwell, author of *Tobacco Road*; James Thurber, the shy humorist in the unlikely guise of tennis correspondent for the *NEW YORKER*. Adolf Zukor, pioneer of the cinema in Hollywood, afterwards sent us his book *The Public Is Never Wrong* inscribed 'You made me a TV star!' Rouben Mamoulian came to Alexandra Palace long before he staged *Oklahoma*. We also hosted Richard Rodgers the composer; James Fitzpatrick of the *As the sun sinks in the West* film travelogues and Bela Lugosi, star of *Dracula*. Asta, the famous performing dog of the *Thin Man* films, insured for thousands of dollars, looked charming but flatly refused to perform in any way, to the fury of its trainer. We found out afterwards that a snake had been in the studio and somehow the dog knew this. Distinguished visitors from overseas included Mme. Maisky the Russian ambassadress, Count Tolstoi, Mme. Nijinksa, French writer Andre Maurois, Oscar Kokoschka painter, Stefan Zweig the writer who committed suicide, the Grand Vizier of Morocco and Boris Smirnoff the Russian born French Artist, who became a good friend and I had quite a few of his paintings.

Leslie Mitchell one day arrived so tired he opened the station by making the closing announcement. Leslie once failed to brake his car properly as he rushed inside the building. Looking out from our window in the Tower, six floors higher, we were horrified to see the car drive off silently, dive over the embankment, cross the drive at gathering speed and shatter itself on a tree down by the Alexandra Palace golf course.

Marion and Irma, the two German girl contortionists, insisted on a small white carpet to stand on for their acrobatic act. So we all went to the scene dock and selected a small white carpet rolled up and propped against a wall. We shook it open and five mice ran out. How the girls screamed!

The weather at Alexandra Palace was always tricky in winter, and once I got lost in the grounds in a taxi in thick fog and snow that had turned to ice, immovable for four hours with six clerics, all of different denominations, one a bishop and one a chaplain from Tristan de Cunha who had seen no-one new for five years. The milk of human kindness was not apparent that night.

Once we played *Picture Page* in public before an audience at a Radiolympia Radio Show and had hired a revolve, allowing for acts to come round with their own little sets complete. A young elephant from Chessington Zoo enjoyed the revolve and was evidently in a playful mood. He spotted a bucketful of red paint backstage, filled up his trunk with this like a fountain pen, waited till he was squarely revolved in the centre of the stage and then blew it out over everything.

Robert Sherwood, the playwright of *Abe Lincoln in Illinois, Idiot's Delight* and *The Petrified Forest*, refused thus: "I am greatly flattered by your kind invitation to appear on your remarkable programme but I think it would be a mistake for you even more than for me. I am a rotten speaker equipped with one of the worst accents you ever heard, I could easily set back the progress of television for years."

Lilian Baylis, great woman of the theatre, came with her three leading ladies, Pearl Argyle, Marie Ney and Joan Cross, representing ballet, plays and opera, on the opening of the Old Vic season.

One of the most attractive visitors was Corinne Luchaire, French film starlet, a beautiful girl (in white shorts), then filming in England and later sadly to be tried for her wartime association with Otto Abetz, occupying Governor of Paris. She was by then a shadow of her former self.

On the last night of television, when war was obviously imminent, it happened to be *Picture Page* night (262nd edition) edited by me as usual, and this day produced by Denis Johnston. It contained blooms from the Dahlia Show; Colonel Bennett with banking relics; Dr. Tangred Borenius on Clarendon Palace excavations; Marjorie Cottle on motor cycle trials; Leslie Charteris who wrote *The Saint*; José Terina who tore up telephone books; and Basil Radford and Naunton Wayne, the film comedians.

After the war I never went back to *Picture Page* myself, though as Planner I revived it for four more years. Joan Gilbert took over the editorship and later the interviewing too, giving it a lot of her own charming personality.

It was an early forerunner of television's *Tonight* and, if it did nothing else, twice a week for seven years it was a peacemaker and a tastemaker. It had no edge, it played straight. In its early years it had a small secret. Every programme contained a professional speciality act. I have always admired people who do one thing perfectly.

THE PLAY'S THE THING

'A play a day' was the target we set ourselves at the outset, and so it turned out. The process nearly killed everyone. But this was something I was particularly proud of. Yes, Shakespeare was absolutely right, the play's the thing and if he had been living today he would have embraced television.

"What is Drama? It's what literature does at night." (George Jean Nathan).

And Acting? "Anybody can act. Most people in England do nothing else." (Oscar Wilde).

At the outset the London theatre was ready to play, a debt that has scarcely been repaid to the theatre, though it may have been to drama. We were offered help by such men as F. R. Pryor, who owned the old Kingsway Theatre and who wrote most of *Marigold*, a hit in his own theatre; Anmer Hall, really A. B. Horne the insurance financier, who owned the Westminster Theatre and occasionally acted there; and Henry Sherek, both an agent and an impresario. And most of all Lilian Baylis, that blithe spirit from the Waterloo Road, was always ready to play, but always insisted on the words 'By permission of Lilian Baylis' in the billing. Firstly she offered her ballet, the redoubtable Vic Wells, and more so she offered her production of *Macbeth* at the Old Vic, starring Laurence Olivier and Judith Anderson with Andrew Cruikshank and the entire company, together with all costumes 'and certain props' for £75. The stage production was by Michel Saint Denis. She consulted no one but herself and assumed that everyone would jump at her bidding, which they always had. The BBC normally provided a small shooting brake from Broadcasting House in Portland Place where artists usually assembled for the ghastly journey north to Alexandra Palace. A tremendous correspondence then began between Miss Anderson (later made a Dame of the British Empire) and the booking manager, Bill Streeton. She said she could not see why Lady Macbeth should travel in a shooting brake and furthermore she had no intention of doing so. She added that it might be difficult for us to televise the play without Lady Macbeth. "I shall take a taxi from where I live," she wrote, "and I shall expect you to pay for it at the door." He did. Laurence Olivier reacted differently, understandably. He refused to go at all, since it was not part of his Old Vic contract. Lilian Baylis, then ill, was not to be brooked and she said that she had given her word. To make matters worse she actually died on November 25, 1937, so the date was changed to a week later. No-one let her memory or her word down and *Macbeth* took place at Alexandra Palace.

The Habima Theatre from Tel Aviv paid a rare visit to London with their entire company and their own great star, Hanna Rovina. They came to television and gave two performances of *The Dybbuk* and *Uriel Acosta*. They were long, and in ancient Hebrew, but enthralling in their way. The production derived from Vakhtangov's when the Habima was a studio of the Moscow Art Theatre.

I myself much preferred taking units to theatres, and in these days there was no threat to the Managements so we were allowed to televise a whole play. The first ever was J.B. Priestley's *When We Are Married* from the St. Martin's Theatre in 1938, with Frank Pettingell as the photographer who got drunk at a wedding reception. It was the audience and their laughter which showed the way television comedy would go ultimately.

Another notable theatre visit was for Michael Redgrave, Peggy Ashcroft and George Devine in *Twelfth Night*, televised in its entirety from the Phoenix Theatre. It was both presented and directed by Michel Saint Denis. This charming man and great producer has rendered much service to the British theatre but his finest hour was yet to come. During the war, as 'Jacques Duchesne', he nightly called the French from London and prefaced General de Gaulle's rallying words to the Free French that liberation would come.

The Bard was always ideal television, short scenes, opportunities for close-up, great characters, colourful settings. Margaretta Scott starred in the first television Shakespeare, *As You Like it*, in 1937.

Malcolm Keen was Long John Silver in *Treasure Island*; Eric Portman played Trino in *A Hundred Years Old*. Leslie Banks played *Cyrano de Bergerac* with Constance

Cummings as Roxanne; Ralph Richardson and James Mason played Priestley's *Bees on the Boatdeck*; Sara Allgood, Marie O'Neill and many of the great Irish players from the old Abbey Theatre recreated the O'Casey plays; Sybil Thorndike was Widow Cagle in *Sun Up* with Finlay Currie, one of the finest old woman parts ever written. I persuaded her to try it – she had to smoke a pipe throughout. It is about mountain folk so primitive that when Widow Cogle's son is called up to fight the Germans she thinks it is a war against the Yankees. Ernest Milton was magnificient in Pirandello's *Henry IV*; Greer Garson as Yasmin in Flecker's *Hassan*. In a famous little one-acter Wilfred Shine played *Waterloo* with Mary Kerridge as a child.

There were other memorable moments: Richard Murdoch in Noel Coward's *Red Peppers*; Esmond Knight in *Night Must Fall*; Anthony Quayle in *Trelawny of the Wells*; Reginald Tate in *Journey's End*; and May Whitty in *The Royal Family of Broadway*.

Wendy Hiller starred in a new play by Yvette Pienne, *The Fame of Grace Darling*, the first example of a girl ruined by modern methods of publicity. Somehow everyone imagined Grace Darling as a girl who rowed out alone to a wrecked ship and managed to rescue everyone. In the light of later knowledge it seems that she did actually accompany her father to put out to sea in a 16-foot coble in a storm to save the lives of the nine survivors of the wreck. She attracted the reporters by being a young girl with a lot of hair who was on the spot, or there may have been darker reasons, to divert attention. Postcards came out showing her with her blonde tresses in a boat. She died at 26.

My planning was based on a Sunday night play. These started in 1938 and were a controversial idea at the time. Broadcasting House wanted us to follow their own Sunday pattern, bits and pieces. I was sure a solid wedge of dramatic material was needed, and with Cock's support we started this policy. It caught on at once and has lasted durably. The first weekly television series was *Ann and Harold*. It starred Ann Todd. Charles Heels starred in a series, *The Adventures of Percy Ponsonby*. As he needed a stooge, a delightful old character actor, Harry Atkinson, from the Savage Club, was engaged to support him. He never spoke a word but he was always there, whether watching cricket at Lords or in the next chair at the barber's.

But the hero of this dramatic scene, if this is the right word, was Cyril Phillips, then managing the Birmingham Repertory Theatre. I approached him with an idea. This repertory company, one of the best in the country at the time, had a policy of a play a month, and every play ran for four weeks. This was a neat pattern. Our suggestion was that on the third Sunday in every month they should bring their productions (which were all directed by Herbert Prentice) to the Alexandra Palace studios. It was not an impossible distance as the Palace was well in the north of London anyway. Our television producer studied the play in the theatre, went to Birmingham for some time in advance, rehearsing his new moves for the cameras with the artists on their own stage, then on the Sunday at crack of dawn a coach started for London from Birmingham's Station Street. The scenery had been reconstructed in advance in our workshops. The actors rehearsed all day in the studio, performed the play about 9.30 pm and then, late at night, the coach rolled back to Birmingham. Birmingham was not even in the television area then, but this gesture suited everyone, it brought the plays and players to a London audience and it gave television a production to some extent ready made.

One day we were televising Bernard Shaw's one-act play *How He Lied To Her Husband*. Someone suggested Shaw might like to be asked to come to the studio so I

An afternoon performance of the one-act play
How He Lied to Her Husband in July 1937 was
honoured by a visit from its author,
George Bernard Shaw.
At the end of the production he was invited to
make 'on air' comments. With Shaw (centre) were
(l to r) Greer Garson, Derek Williams,
George More O'Ferrall (producer on floor)
and D. A. Clark-Smith.

waited until lunchtime when Miss Patch his secretary, might be out and caught him on the telephone myself at his flat in Whitehall Court. I told him about our production. "It's a very bad play, you know," he said. However, I invited him to join us. He thought for a moment. "I think I will," he replied. Sure enough an hour or two later an ancient car drove up to Alexandra Palace and out came the great man in splendid form, wearing a kind of tweed knickerbocker suit. He was looked after by the performers of the play: Greer Garson glorious in the period dress, D.A. Clarke-Smith and David Hoffman. He was given tea and enjoyed himself hugely. He popped in and out of a property door and posed for a photograph with the producer and the cast. THE OBSERVER wrote, "*How He Lied to Her Husband* is thirty years old, but it might have been written for television... After the afternoon show 'G.B.S.' himself appeared before the camera and was amusingly rude to the child of his less mature genius." I am sure that, as a result of this personal contact with the new medium, he not only allowed us to televise the third act of his new play "Geneva" but wrote a special introduction to cover the first two acts, which was printed in THE TIMES.

Later, when we televised the West End production of Shaw's *Buoyant Billions*, I had the sound recorded onto a number of discs, some three hours of playing time and therefore a large number of records. In the interests of posterity I then asked Roy Limbert of the Malvern Festival if he would like to keep these somewhere, such as under his bed, as a valuable Shaw Archive for a possible Shaw Museum one day. Frances Day played 'She' in this production, looking piquant and beautiful.

The next I heard was this postcard from the great man:

from BERNARD SHAW, Ayot St. Lawrence, Welwyn.
23.12.1949.
Cecil Madden Esq.

"A letter with the reference from you to Roy Limbert
mentions 34 discs recording a blasted failure of my play
"Buoyant Billions" to draw more than £500 a week at its
first production in London. I authorised its television
but not its recording. Be good enough to see that these
damned discs are utterly destroyed, as they will be if
ever they come into my hands.

G. Bernard Shaw.

Whilst on the subject of Bernard Shaw, and since
Pygmalion was televised several times, here is a splendid
example of Shaviana:

To David Manderson:
4 Whitehall Court,
London, S.W.1.
2nd December 1938.

My licence for the performance of my play *Pygmalion*
by the Derek Salberg Company in Wolverhampton did
not include an authorisation to advertise it as 'the
brilliant comedy by Oscar Wilde.

"Is Oscar's name a bigger draw than mine? And if so,
what royalty do his representatives receive for the use?

G. Bernard Shaw.

The reply to Shaw was as follows:

Dear Sir,

I regret that some confusion in the mind of the resident manager of this theatre caused him last week to attribute to the late Mr Wilde a play which, I understand, has been written by you.

Mr Purdey (the Gentleman in question) is disinclined to offer an apology as he contends that this substitution accounts for the show having played to three times as much money as it did when it was billed as having been written by you. He also contends that this will result in your receiving larger royalties than he believes would otherwise have been the case, and he is therefore unable to see what you are grumbling about.

                    Yours faithfully, David Manderson.

His reply, on a postcard, was:

Please give my compliments to Mr Purdey and beg him to continue the attribution, which was a most happy thought. I am not grumbling. I am rejoicing.

                              G. Bernard Shaw.

There is a story that when Bernard Shaw had a very bad notice of one of his early plays someone asked him what he thought of this. He replied, "They should send a better class of critic."

In three formative television years viewers saw nearly 400 plays, almost all given two performances, fifteen being new writing, plus ten relays from West End theatres. Thus our early target of 'A play a day' as the solid drama foundation of the service was carried out.

And drama was not the only thing on television. Ballet at once seemed ideally suited to the medium. The close-up could humanise the whole conception. To me the high spot was when Colonel de Basil in person brought his Ballets Russes, not only to dance *Les Sylphides* and *Aurora's Wedding* but also for a rehearsal programme, mostly of Gluck's *Orphée* with Lichine, Baronova, Serova, Riabouchinska and Paul Petroff. The Ballet Russe de Monte Carlo presented *Le Spectre de la Rose*.

Lilian Baylis immediately offered television the Vic Wells Ballet who came to dance *Job, Carnival, Swan Lake*, and *The Rake's Progress*, among others. Several performances featured a brilliant young group, Margot Fonteyn, Robert Helpmann, William Chappell, Joy Newton, and Harold Turner. D. H. Munro was at his most imaginative as creator of the chess board ballet, Ninette de Valois' *Checkmate* to Arthur Bliss's music.

Agnes de Mille's Ballets Joos performed for us. Argentinita, the great Spanish dancer, came to perform,

Les Patineurs with Margot Fonteyn, Robert Helpmann and the corps of the Vic-Wells Ballet. Producer D.H. Munro, May 3, 1937.

accompanied by the old guitarist Ricardo Montoya. The lights failed and he was found miserably wandering in the wrong studio, striking matches. These were magic nights of Danilova, Markova, Dolin and Tamara Tourmanova, with fascinating introductions by Michael Folkine.

And the great music stars were ready to come too: Piatigorsky, Moseievitch, Hambourg, Elizabeth Schumann, Rose Bampton, Peter Dawson and Paul Robeson. Ivor Novello brought his entire Drury Lane Company and even played the piano in the orchestra.

Television's own original orchestra of 25 was constituted more for the wish than its need. Many French horns restricted their repertoire. An accompanying orchestra of 17 would have been more practical. Still it was great while it lasted. Hyam Greenbaum had been with Charles B. Cochran conducting his famous musicals, but was a classicist at heart. He envisaged television as simply playing good music which the cameras would watch. True, this could be done, but unfortunately not for long.

The second violin then was Eric Robinson. Eric and I worked together, in one capacity or another in television from the start at Alexandra Palace, to the outbreak of war, then in the Allied Expeditionary Forces Programmes during the war, and in television again after the war – some thirty years. He wrote an admirable book himself, *Conducted Personally*. Eric's versatility is great. When he announces as well as conducts, if he is breathless or fluffs a difficult name like Margherita Carioso, he may upset the musicians but the ordinary viewer identifies with him. In early days small groups were made up from the full orchestra. One of these was the jazz ensemble, Eric Wild and his Teatimers. They sat all over a vast cut-out teapot, and perched near the handle with his wide grin was the guitarist. I need hardly say that this was Eric Robinson again.

Many people are now familiar with the wartime

The scenery workshop – suits and overalls. The giant teapot was used as a setting for Eric Wilde and his Teatimers. 1937

For this performance, 'Pastiche' the Teatimers backed the American actress, Claire Luce.

This typical room setting at the 1939 Radiolympia show was used
to show off the latest model of a Philips television set. Prices by now
had come down and this one was on sale at 35 guineas. Total sales
had risen rapidly to about 20,000 but within a fortnight
television had closed down for the war.

adventures of the Trapp family escaping from the Nazis, through the dramatisation of their own books told in music by Rodgers and Hammerstein in the *The Sound of Music*. Few realise that in the early days of television the whole Trapp family came over to be televised at Alexandra Palace, and very delightful they were with wonderful manners and discipline.

AU REVOIR TELEVISION

When television closed there were perhaps 30,000 sets in viewers' homes. At the time it seemed like Adieu. In the event it was Au Revoir.

The annual radio show at Olympia was still on and as late as noon on September 1, 1939 the television announcer was giving out a list of things to come. Five full-length plays were in rehearsal for the following week, two new editions of *Picture Page* magazine, two top ranking stars, much more besides.

But up at Alexandra Palace in the Central Television Control Room there was an air of foreboding. A telephone message which had been dreaded for days had still not come. It could happen any minute now.

So the station kept on the air. The announcer smiled and this merged into a Walt Disney cartoon film, *Mickey's Gala Premiere* which ran for a few minutes and was suddenly stopped, just as a cartoon Garbo said "Ay tank ay go home." These were the last words viewers heard from their screens. The order to close down came at 12:10. Without fuss, without even a closing announcement, the first high definition television service in the world was arbitrarily cut off. It promised to be a most successful television winter. It was so on paper. But it was not to be.

The staff dispersed, many to the services, others to keep the radio services going. It was a miserable business seeing the great Olympia Radio Exhibition dismantle its stands including our own stage.

We dragged ourselves to Alexandra Palace to take down all notices from office walls. Everyone was despondent. All our hopes had gone, our efforts wasted. It was obviously going to be a long war. It was.

But television did come back, in 1946. We shall come to this in good time.

Valerie Hobson and Richard Coleman
in *Cabaret*, July 5, 1937.
A painted backdrop gives increased
movement and sophistication.

4

WAR

CENSOR

At first the BBC did not know what to do with its senior staff. The American Liaison Unit was formed to self-censor the endless broadcasts by American commentators in London, mostly in the middle of the night London time. This unit contained Roger Eckersley, R.A. Rendall, S.J. de Lotbiniere, Denis Johnston, Cecilia Reeves and myself. The main broadcasters were H.V. Kaltenborn, Fielding Eliot, John Gunther and Ed Murrow.

September 5, 1939 was the day Germany invaded Poland. H.V. Kaltenborn who earlier had said, "I predict there will be no war," made another shattering pronouncement, which proved too much for the American engineer on duty in New York who took it off with, "And another Indian bit the dust."

Censoring is a dull business, the very opposite of creative. The only interest to me was to put on headphones and listen to Bill Shirer in enemy Berlin talking to New York, knowing the Nazi censors were breathing over his shoulder. The American engineers left it all on the line for us to hear in London. On our headphones we heard the first air raid siren sounding in Paris. At that time Paris and London were linked together to New York. Berlin was linked direct to New York, so through the New York control room one could hear everything that was said in Berlin in the broadcasting studio used by the neutral Americans.

One night Fred Bate of NBC was giving a little talk, mostly to fill his scheduled time, which was usually five minutes from London, five minutes from Paris and then five minutes from Berlin. Fred Bate was talking about London in the blackout, how people carried gas masks and tripped over sandbags and so on, just filling time. So I left him to it and walked down a passage in the basement of Broadcasting House to the nearest ticker tape machine. Suddenly up came the story of the sinking of the *Athenia* by German action. This liner was bound for America from Scotland, full of the wives and children of American diplomatic and consular officials. This was real news. I tore off the sheet from the ticking machine, rushed down the corridor, put it in front of Fred Bate's face and he simply read it. It caused an instant sensation in New York, special editions of newspapers were rushed out with enormous headlines, all having to acknowledge NBC for the scoop.

What I had failed to realise was that just after I had left there ticked up a *Stop* notice, putting an official stop on the information until a fixed time several hours later when all sources, including the press, were authorised to use it at the same time. NBC really had a splendid scoop, and I left the department! There was no place for censors to do the work of broadcasters – neutral ones at that.

Entertainment was being organised for ENSA by Basil Dean and Seymour Hicks. F.W. Ogilvie was Director General of the BBC then, and on September 5 he decided to broadcast on all the American networks, an event that I produced.

George Barnes was running the Talks Department, and in an effort to liven broadcast talks he asked for my help to produce a series which he wished to call 'Close-Up.' I thought shock tactics were called for and some showmanship. With Leslie Mitchell as interviewer I paired show business personalities who might normally never meet, such as Rex Harrison with Evelyn Dall, the blonde American singer; Bobby Howes with Wendy Hiller, the actress; Leslie Howard with Barbara Mullen; Robert Montgomery, the American film star, with Valerie Hobson. Others were Binnie Hale; Cyril Ritchard; Jessie Matthews and Sonnie Hale; Florence Desmond with Tod Slaughter, the melodrama barnstormer; Stanley Lupino; Stanley Holloway; Richard Hearne and others. Leslie Henson forgot to come and Judy Kelly had to carry on alone. So we got Leslie along next time with Clifford Mollison and Pat Burke. He was very contrite.

On May 5, 1940 Germany invaded Holland, Belgium and Luxembourg. On the next day Admiral of the Fleet Sir Roger Keyes gave a talk on Zeebrugge, the famous raid he had led. He was then an MP and the next day he made a famous outburst in the House of Commons. At 68 he was put on the Active List again.

On May 15 Queen Wilhelmina of the Netherlands spoke from Buckingham Palace to the British people. I suggested she should repeat this to America, and at 2:00 am she did.

On June 1 1940 *THE TIMES* published the list of the new Government. Prime Minister and Minister of Defence, Mr Winston Churchill; Lord President of the Council, Mr Neville Chamberlain; Lord Privy Seal, Mr C.R. Attlee.

On June 4 the five days of evacuation from Dunkirk was completed. At the time of Dunkirk it seemed likely that Hitler would invade Britain and the BBC organised its own

Home Guard. I have looked up a 1797 poster:

Fellow Citizens, Bonaparte threatens to invade us. He promises to enrich his soldiers with our property, to glut their lust with our wives and daughters, to incite his hellhounds to execute his vengeance he has sworn to permit everything. Shall we merit, by our cowardice, the titles of sordid shop-keepers, cowardly scum and dastardly wretches which in every proclamation he gives us. No, we will loudly give him the lie. Let us make ourselves ready to shut our shops and to march to give him the reception his malicious calumnies deserve. Let every brave young fellow instantly join the Army or Navy, and these among us who, from being married or so occupied in business, cannot, let us join some Volunteer corps where we may learn the use of arms and yet attend our business.

On June 11, 1940 Italy declared war on France and Britain. Mussolini said: "The hour of destiny has arrived." Duff Cooper said: "Mussolini will increase the number of ruins for which Italy has so long been famous." President Roosevelt said: "We will extend to the opponents of force the material resources of this nation." On June 17 Paul Reynaud resigned as Premier of France: Marshal Petain succeeded him. On June 18 Hitler and Mussolini met, and on June 21 in Foch's railway carriage at Compiegne Hitler told France his terms. George Slocombe, last British journalist to leave France, wrote in the Sunday Express on June 30 1940, "I have seen the fall of France. Great armies did not do it. Only 200,000 mechanised troops, plus corruption, treachery, sloth, vanity. Remember it can happen here."

My youngest brother Colin received the D.S.C for 'Good services in successful operations which prevented much war material from falling into the hands of the enemy.' In fact with a party of Marines he sank a large liner in the entrance to the port of Ymuiden, so blocking the port of Amsterdam for the entire war, and managing to get his men away. The King held the investiture at Buckingham Palace on September 3, 1940, in Air Force uniform.

The London theatre list at the time was small but escapist: *Swing the Gate* (Ambassadors), *White Horse Inn* (Coliseum), *New Faces* (Comedy), *Come Out of Your Shell* (Criterion), *Black Velvet* (Hippodrome), *Haw Haw* (Holborn), *The Tempest* (Old Vic), Chu Chin Chow (Palace), *Garrison Theatre* (Palladium), *Present Arms* (Prince of Wales), *Shephard's Pie* (Prince's), *Rebecca* (Queens) and *Up and Doing* (Saville).

BLITZ ROUNDUPS

On August 8, 1940 "Massed German raids on London began" THE TIMES. On August 24, "First bombs on Central London" THE TIMES. The Blitz on London had begun in earnest. America was still neutral.

I had one of my best ideas then, to mount an Outside Broadcast round-up programme, with nine points in half an hour, to be heard at home and overseas. I proposed to the American networks that they should come in too. NBC were reluctant to join with CBS and CBS had already accepted.

I called it (there were just two such in all) *London After Dark*. It was London on Saturday night August 24, and as luck and planning would have it I produced it myself and it was meticulously planned with 20 microphones at varied locations: St. George's Hall, for the organ there; Trafalgar Square, on the steps of St. Martin's Church; The Savoy Hotel, for the dance band; the Savoy Kitchen; Primrose Hill for the anti-aircraft gun-site; Dolphin Square flats for an Air Raid

Precautions unit; the Palais de Danse, Hammersmith, for Londoners dancing; the Piccadilly Hotel, on a balcony with a view up Regent Street; and Euston Station for the Services Canteen and the platforms. The technical side was in the hands of R.H. Wood.

This was my own directive to all staff and commentators taking part:

> If there is an Air Raid Alarm between 11.30 pm and midnight, the Home Service will fade, Overseas and USA will continue. In the unlikely event of bombs falling within range would Commentators (assuming that they are still in one piece) observe the following points:
>
> 1) Be truthful but discreet and remember that impromptu remarks made in the excitement of the moment are liable to exaggerate rather than minimise distress.
>
> 2) Avoid horrors – in fact unless there is reason to do so do not mention casualties.
>
> 3) Use utmost discretion in assessing damage, if any.
>
> The general rule must obviously be to avoid saying anything which is going to give information of an encouraging nature to the enemy or of an unduly distressing nature to our friends. The Censorship regulations have been considerably relaxed on this occasion and we should none of us do anything to prejudice the future.

This turned out to be an historic programme even though, because of a Raid, it was never heard in Britain. For Gerry Wilmot made his opening announcement in Broadcasting House at 11.30 pm on August 24 1940, Sandy Macpherson played a few chords live on the organ and at 11.32 the air raid sirens started, and so the Home Service faded out. Overseas carried on as arranged and we went over to Ed Murrow of CBS in Trafalgar Square. And of course he was heard live over the whole CBS Network and CBC in Canada. Bombs were heard falling on the docks. Here I quote Abel Green, Editor of VARIETY, on August 28, 1940:

One of these fortuitous 'breaks' fell to Ed Murrow's lot in his London war-time pick-up. After the announcement had laid the plan, the mike switched to Trafalgar Square with Murrow presiding. Just as he got on the metropolis was being subjected to an air raid alarm and bombing, and excitedly he relayed the coincidental fact. The fearful sounds of the air raid sirens and the attendant excitement were picked up. Considering how terrorising are the sounds of these sirens, the slightest imagination can conjure up how terrifying must be the war of nerves on the scene of action.

Larry LeSueur, Vincent Sheean, Eric Sevareid (for CBS), Bob Bowman for CBC and Raymond Glendenning, Wynford Vaughan Thomas and Michael Standing for the BBC all spoke at their various allotted spots. Here is Abel Green again: "Sevareid mentioned that soldiers on leave in the Dance Hall took off their boots at the door and donned dancing pumps loaned to them by the Hammersmith Palais. The evening wound up with J.B. Priestley in Whitehall. America's TIME magazine of September 2, 1940 wrote a long review starting with "Unexpected was the co-operation of Herr Hitler..." ended by quoting some of Priestley's words:

I'm standing at an open window in Whitehall. Just opposite me is the tall, pale, rather ghostly shape of the Cenotaph commemorating a million dead, many of them friends of mine, boys that I played with as a boy, men that might have been leaders now. Behind the great Government offices, the Home Office, the Colonial Office, the Treasury, is the heart of our great capital city. It is also historic ground. Henry VIII married Anne Boleyn near here. Elizabeth saw Shakespeare's plays and the masques of Ben Jonson here. Charles I was executed a few yards from where I am standing. It's historic ground and I think today it's probably more deeply sunk in our world's history than ever because it's the very centre of the hopes of free men everywhere. It's the heart of this great rock that's defying the dark tide of invasion that has destroyed freedom all over Western Europe.

Not until April 1941 would the Censors release the bombing of St. George's Hill and the destruction of the famous broadcasting organ.

Night after night the artists came to Broadcasting House to sing. Patricia Burke, Evelyn Dall, Stanley Holloway and Frances Day were regulars of the nightly *Starlight*. Space was so scarce in Broadcasting House the artists had to perform while staff slept at their feet on mattresses. At that time Jill Allgood was my assistant and Robert Beatty the Canadian actor and Gerry Wilmot were the regular announcers.

On July 24 I find I wrote a memo within the BBC saying, "Things have come to a pretty pass if we cannot get copies of *VARIETY*." Soon after *VARIETY* put a photograph on their front page of Patricia Burke and myself, taken one midnight, reading *VARIETY*. This picture was reproduced the world over.

From: Director of Office Administration.
To: Each room.
August 28, 1940.
It has been noticed that the number of private calls
made during evenings has increased very considerably.
No private calls whatsoever can be accepted by PBX
during, and immediately after, an air raid warning.

L. Harvey.

One of the most savage raids was on September 7, 1940.
To quote a daily newspaper: "Five hundred Nazi raiders.
Hitler launched his biggest and fiercest raid of the war on
London. Hordes of bombers, at least 500 in waves of 100
strong, dropped hundreds of high explosive and fire bombs
at points in the London area. There were hits on a
children's home, a convent and a variety theatre. For 98
hectic minutes anti-aircraft guns turned on their most
terrific barrage. British fighters darted in and out of the
raiders. Early this morning waves of raiders were still
dropping bombs."

Following the first *Blitz Round-Up* programme I was
pressed to produce another. This took place on Saturday
September 21 and achieved the impossible, with NBC, CBS,
CBC, and BBC all co-operating. NBC men were heard over
CBS and vice-versa, something only a war could bring
about. I suggested that Fred Bate of NBC should choose his
own spot. He chose Buckingham Palace. The Palace had
already been hit once and by coincidence it was hit again,
this time in the stables, on the very evening of the
broadcast. Not, however, during the broadcast. Ed Murrow
was on a high spot and Rooney Pelletier in the crypt of St.
Martin's Church. Howard Marshall was the commentator.

London's theatre list on September 9 still had 19 shows:
Once a Crook (Aldwych), *Swinging the Gate*
(Ambassadors), *The Infernal Machine* (Arts), *White Horse
Inn* (Coliseum), *New Faces* (Comedy), *In Town Again*

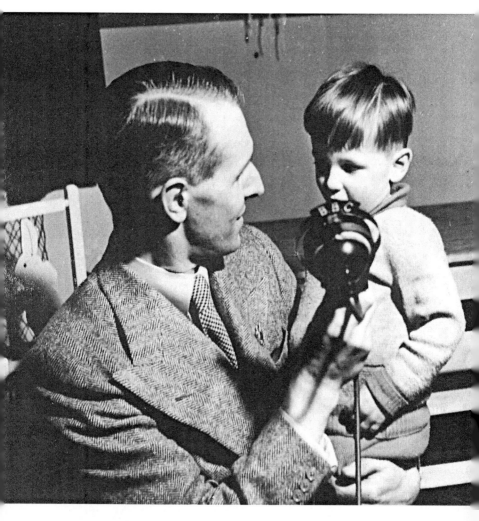

Cecil Madden
interviewing children from a Nursery Training College which was a
temporary home to destitute war orphans aged from infancy to four years.

Cecil Madden
broadcasts from a Nursery Training College.

(Criterion), High Temperature (Duke of York's), *The Millionairess* (Globe), *Thunder Rock* (Haymarket), *Black Velvet* (Hippodrome), *Applesauce* (Holborn), *Chu Chin Chow* (Palace), *Top of the World* (Palladium), *The Devil's Disciple* (Piccadilly) Shephard's Pie (Princes), *Up and Doing* (Saville), *Women Aren't Angels* (Strand), *Cottage to Let* (Wyndhams), *Revuedeville* (Windmill).

On September 10 it was down to nine, on the 11 down to five, on the 13 down to two, And on September 14 only one, the Windmill.

On September 27 there were tremendous day raids on London and the next day too. *THE TIMES* reported "130 daylight raiders destroyed, while the RAF lost 35 fighters."

I was asked to produce a programme for the Ministry of Information: *The Battle for Britain*. It features Negley Farson, T. H. Alderson, first man to win the new George Cross, and Jack Buchanan, musical comedy star. Leslie Howard, the film star, spoke in it, of pilots who had been shot down and endured long exposure in a dinghy, and of the sinking of the *City of Benares* carrying children to Canada.

I lived then at a block of flats called Dolphin Square in Pimlico. The night of September 22 was one to remember. Here is the *EVENING STANDARD* "Aerial Torpedo hits London flats. Seven killed, many injured." The missile plunged into the lawn and buried itself in a deep shelter in a corner of one section of the flats. None of the casualties was a tenant of the flats, they were people who only an hour before had been evacuated from a nearby street because of the danger of an unexploded bomb. The shelter under the flats was full of men, women and children. Few escaped injury. I was at the foot of the lifts when the explosion came. My wife and baby daughter were out of London, renting a house in the country with her mother. A little while later I went outside to see our burning sofa being thrown to the ground.

Stéphane Grappelly,
the famous French swing violinist (right) taking part in the BBC
programme Starlight in 1942. Centre is Cecil Madden, then Head
of the BBC Overseas Entertainment Unit and left RAF Flight
Sergeant Steve Challen D.F.M. From Hamilton, Ontario.

MESSAGES

The first person to send me a message programme, accidentally, was Frances Day. She used to do a nightly 2:15 am programme called *Starlight*, which I produced, from the eighth floor studio under the roof of Broadcasting House. I have a photo of us both, with Harry Jacobsen, who accompanied her and played solos, taken on August 8, 1940, the night the massed bombing began. Soon after this Broadcasting House was blitzed and from then on we had to work in the basement. One night she arrived in her usual gay fashion, in a diaphanous evening dress with some Canadian airmen she had met. I had not the heart to stop them saying hello to their folks in Canada. She later did a series to Canada and many programmes for Forces from the Hammersmith Palais too.

Programmes interspersed with messages and entertainment were the new idea. The entertainment was popular dance bands. I proposed a Dance Band Scheme to the BBC to put a number of named bands under long contract and a tie-up with ENSA too to ensure their availability. The first two bands were Geraldo's and Jack Payne's. Others were Joe Loss, Debroy Somers, Billy Cotton and Edmundo Ros. They competed with each other, orchestrations were very individual and all this kept up the high standards. ENSA demanded a quid pro quo and Geraldo and others later set off on a tour to play for the troops in person.

The Message office was the cloakroom of the Criterion Theatre. It had white tiled walls and the names and addresses could be written programme by programme all round the room in ink, and washed off at will. A natural unfiling system.

Ronald Shiner called the British Forces in Malta. He was

in the police, then he became an actor. Franklin Englemann took over the messages to India, Alick Hayes to the Far East and Palestine. Ned Williams (also known as Robert Harbin, the illusionist) compèred *Songtime in the Laager* to South and East Africa and Rhodesia. Freddie Grisewood ran *Your Cup of Tea* to Forces from their families. There were two ANZAC programmes; Joseph Sultana ran a Maltese programme; Michael Cacoyannis broadcast to Cyprus. He was very young then, but keen, and became a noted film director. Joan Gilbert did a regular programme, both at the Union Jack Club and at the Overseas League.

We had sackfuls of grateful letters, such as this one from India: "It is impossible for me adequately to express our sincere appreciation in enabling our daughter to speak to us. She enlisted in the WAAF immediately war was declared. The fact that she has been allowed to speak to us in her 21st year has added sentimental value to the message deeply appreciated by my entire family."

I particularly remember the New Zealand VC Sergeant Pilot James A. Ward who climbed out on the wing of a Wellington bomber which caught fire and put out the flames. He broadcast a message home in the Criterion Theatre. Soon after he was reported missing.

I always asked every serviceman from Canada, South Africa, Australia, and New Zealand to sign big cards. As many of these became casualties I sent the huge cards to national museums in Canada, South Africa, Australia and New Zealand, through the Foreign office, so they could all be displayed in their home lands.

HUB OF THE UNIVERSE

How could anyone believe one would spend almost the whole of a great war in a London theatre, and underground at that? Yet I did work for four years broadcasting in the beautiful little Criterion Theatre underneath Piccadilly Circus.

This theatre was built by Spiers and Pond in 1873 as part of a large restaurant block on the site of what was once a famous old posting inn, the White Bear, which had flourished there since 1635 or earlier. The Criterion Theatre opened in 1874 with a comedy *An American Lady*. Underground theatres are now prohibited by LCC Regulations though they thrive in Italy, with shops and blocks of flats towering above, as the most economical way to use ground space.

Piccadilly Circus used to be called 'The Hub of the Universe' which was written on the London Pavilion Theatre, opposite the Criterion, as the centre of London. But a very strange atmosphere it was then, with Eros removed for the war and its pedestal covered in and adorned with Government posters as follows: "USSR, USA, U."

The theatre itself had 18 exit doors and was surrounded by licensed bars. As you go in to the stage door which is in Jermyn Street, down iron steps and still on down, you come to a long iron-floored passage, which runs alongside the main drains of London. I was Air Raid Warden for the theatre then. I was always so glad the theatre was never hit, for many reasons. How awful to lose a theatre or to be drowned in a drain!

The BBC staff was evacuated to Evesham and other places, my office in the annexe of Broadcasting House had suddenly disappeared (by a bomb) overnight, and hearing the BBC had used emergency powers to requisition the Criterion Theatre, I decided to be the occupant. On November 11, 1940 I moved whatever was left of our sodden office possessions (including a shark's tooth I had been trying to lose for years) and with Jill Allgood to assist me and Jean Metcalfe as secretary we took possession of Dressing Room No. 10, once famous as used by Marie

Tempests, and many earlier great ladies of the theatre.

We arrived without stationary but we found a stock of slips, "With the compliments of the Management" Criterion Theatre, Piccadilly Circus, W.I. I had always wanted to run a theatre and for the next years we were indeed the Management and the beautiful theatre was a real home from home.

On November 22, 1940 Air Marshal O.T. Boyd was shot down and taken prisoner by the Italians on his way to take up his post as Deputy Air Officer C-in-C Middle East Command. I had visited him at the beginning of the war at Balloon Barrage Command HQ in North London with Monsieur Antoine of the French State Broadcasting. Later the same evening I had to impersonate him by proxy in French and answer simple questions on balloons on Antoine's tour of London. Antoine returned to Paris, which was soon to be occupied by the Nazis.

George S. Kaufman, the American playwright and brilliant director wrote me on January 3, 1941: "Every word I hear from London thrills me. I only wish this country were behaving half as well. Mr Roosevelt, to my certain knowledge, is ready to go the limit but there remains a large fraction of the public who must be brought up to 'the fighting point."

London prices were still reasonable. Supreme de Volaille Marechale at the Dorchester on November 27, 1940 was 5/6d, or Delice de Sole 3/6d. Or at the Écu de France Le Merlon Frit 3/-, Poulet en Cocotte 5/9d. The Menu (Non-Rationne) had 'Ministry of Food Order. One dish only of either eggs, fish, meat, poultry, game or cheese may be served at a meal.'

Sam Behrman's play *No Time for Comedy* was opening at the Haymarket and he was giving his royalties to the Red Cross. Rex Harrison, Diana Wynyard, Elizabeth Welch and Lili Palmer with Carol Reed came over to the Criterion after the first night and broadcast a scene to the author in California. He cabled "Broadcast thrilled and moved me beyond words."

So this is the story of West End theatre, occupied by the BBC as a studio, and in the shape of myself as its wartime Management. The first thing we did was to move in two grand pianos. This was most difficult as everything had to come in through exit doors, along curving passages into the stalls and then lifted over the orchestra pit and over the footlights onto the stage. When the pianos, like vast waterlogged elephants, were put onto their legs, they slowly sank right through the stage, nearly crushing Mr Brooks, the old electrician, who slept immediately below and always wore his bowler hat. The hat probably helped to save him. It took time to get the pianos up and out again and lay an entire new stage, a great feat in wartime.

The theatre staff consisted of Mr Brooks, Bert his assistant electrician and Mrs Fenton who had even then been chief cleaner of the theatre for 45 years. Small and thin, always dressed in deep black, she was very concerned about my health and ordered immense quantities of milk for me. Earlier, having had a flat in Dolphin Square which I rarely visited at all, I had forgotten to stop our family's three pints of milk a day. The doors had a system whereby the milk could be pushed into the flat by the milkman via a trap and thus went into the flat round a corner. So the milkman had no idea whether the flat was actually occupied or not. I once let myself in after 21 days to find 63 full bottles in the passage. With an ulcer to kill and in a fit of economy, I gradually drank them all.

The theatre's own staff, Mr Brooks, Bert, Mrs Fenton and the Fireman, were remarkably philosophical about the disappearance of plays and the public and their places being taken by broadcasters and microphones. It was all the same to them. No one could call them stage-struck, like me.

Mr Brooks,
electrician for the Criterion Theatre, arranges lighting for
Cecil Madden who stands at a corner of the stage, 1940.

The Fireman was another phlegmatic character. He was pathologically opposed to anyone smoking and was very unpopular with the bandsmen who had no illusions about fire risks or the traditions of the Theatre (with a capital T!). I have often said: "All men are created equal - except musicians." However our friend the fireman was yet to have his moment of glory.

On the night of December 8 /9 I am convinced that the Fireman of the Criterion Theatre and I saved this lovely little theatre from being burned down. When theatres catch fire they quickly create a vacuum in the auditorium which blasts into and destroys the walls. Here is the newspaper headline about that night. "Nazis try a Coventry on London. For hours wave after wave of bombers flew over, preceding their high explosive with showers of fire bombs." An incendiary bomb had fallen into the building in Jermyn Street immediately opposite the stage door, and got it well and truly alight. We kept a hose on it for hours on end until the Fire Brigade could take over.

As we had to spend all our days and nights in an overheated atmosphere I persuaded the BBC to install a bath. This they did in the only place for it, a dressing room, reached on a much higher level than the stage door, which was down and then up some side steps. The bath improved everyone's morale when we were sleeping in stage boxes or in passages, and I fondly imagined recently that it might still be there. Donald Albery, whose family owns the theatre, told me regretfully that he had had to remove it to allow actors to sit down as soon as a play came in post war with a large cast. Alas, the Criterion dressing room accommodation is very limited.

Jean Metcalfe, a most amusing girl and not the ideal typist, one day turned from her typewriter and told me she had ambitions to be an announcer. Knowing BBC female hierarchical grades I felt her chances were slim and she might well suddenly be sent to an outpost, such as the BBC had at Bangor where the Variety Department was merrily ensconced at the seaside, far from all noise and tumult. What was known as 'being sent to the salt mines' was then far from a true analogy. "It's no good trying to put me off, Mr Madden," she smiled from behind her typewriter. "My mind is made up." Sure enough, less than two weeks later her voice was gaily announcing the news from 200 Oxford Street, the BBC Overseas Headquarters in the old Peter Robinson shop building. She has done very well ever since. One of the Corporation's charming and unlikely staff just then was someone I used to meet for lunch in the canteen, George Orwell, the writer.

Replacing Jean Metcalfe on my staff came Mrs Omelist, who kept our schedules in order on a series of expandable rollers, allowing for easy snipping off and pasted insertions, like vast toilet rolls as more and more programmes by day and night were demanded of the Unit. Also came Joy Russell Smith, who arrived a highbrow music lover but who learned to see that anything can be of high standard, in whatever field. Much later she took over auditions and, to her eternal credit, discovered Frankie Howerd for the nation, before she left for America.

Dame Marie Tempest came to visit us in her old dressing room. She recalled others who had used it, Mary Moore, Lilian Braithwaite, Alice Delysia, Kay Hammond.

This is what THE PERFORMER said on January 16, 1941:

One of London's famous old theatres has been taken over lock, stock and barrel. The theatre lights are dimmed. Only the stage where BBC microphones now stand is still brightly lit. Gramophone turntables occupy most of the space in the ante-room of the Royal Box, and the Royal Box itself is filled with broadcasting apparatus. Office desks have replaced the ornate furniture of the star dressing room, but the room with its large mirrors and elaborate frieze of Hyde Park in the time of Queen Victoria still retains an atmosphere of past glories, although a steel helmet is seen hanging from the old fashioned gas bracket on the wall. The theatre now never sleeps. Radio programmes go out from it at all hours of the day and night under the general production of Cecil Madden who handles all special events and vaudeville programmes. Mattresses, sleeping bags and rugs are provided for the radio stars and BBC staff who, in brief off duty periods, snatch sleep in stage boxes, dress circle, stalls and orchestra pit, a sight which would have astonished the theatregoers who, in another war 25 years ago, thronged into the theatre to see its longest run.

One of the star dressing rooms in the theatre, lined with mirrors, was my office. It was full of light-brackets and a blaze of light. When Sir Charles Wyndham took over the theatre he had a hole bored through from his dressing room through which he could watch the stage. One of Sir Charles Wyndham's successes at the theatre was his production in 1890 of Oliver Goldsmith's *She Stoops to Conquer*. Always elegant, the Criterion had a tradition of luxury and was noted for long runs. One farce, *A Little Bit of Fluff* with Ernest Thesiger, was playing almost throughout the First World War, 1,241 performances. In an empty drawer in the Manager's old office I found, tucked at the back, an intact copy of the celebrated poster for this play, so well known to officers on leave in the First World War. It is a painting of a redheaded girl by Barribal, with the 'kisscurl' then in vogue.

Our work was intense, and it was desperately hot with no air conditioning. When I undressed down to my underpants to lie down in my upper circle box I was so overtired I would have a recurring nightmare that when I woke up the war would be over, the theatre would be itself again, a First Night would be in progress with a fashionably dressed audience in the stalls.

Calling All Stars was an idea I carried out at Christmas 1940 with all the stars sending messages to their counterparts in America. The list of names was impressive, Marie Tempest, Robert Donat, Myra Hess, Sam Eckman, Emlyn Williams, Hartley Power, George Arliss, Clive Brook and thirty others.

Our Unit, familiarly known as The Madden Unit and officially as the Overseas Entertainments Unit, grew fast.

Above the Criterion Theatre was the Criterion Restaurant. Above the auditorium was the kitchen, above the stage was the cellar. I had visions that if a bomb fell on the restaurant we should either be smothered in spaghetti or asphyxiated in alcohol. The BBC, alarmed at the underground conditions which might affect our health, in their infinite wisdom gave me a daytime office in the Winston Hotel next door. It was much frequented by servicemen for single nights, and was very lively. Unfortunately I never had much time to go up to my room but Stanley Maxted, the Canadian commentator, actor and producer, enjoyed the use of it.

In the permanent artificial light it was easy to lose all sense of whether it was day or night. With work and broadcasts and bands and artists and programmes and servicemen all round the clock, even the day got forgotten. The endless summons to meetings brought me to earth.

We closed the Box Office entrance in Piccadilly, the Royal Box became the Radio Control, boxed in with glass and looking down on the microphones on the stage. The Royal Ante, where Kings had retired between the acts, was fitted up with turntables to play gramophone records. The bar became a canteen. We asked for a refrigerator and one came, a huge monstrous white elephant of a thing which blocked the way up the stairs for some years; and which never worked as the current was wrong. All efforts to get it taken away failed too. It lay, lumbering, wonderful and unwanted. Once some music was put down and lost, and a broadcast nearly ruined. The music turned up three years later - inside this refrigerator, together with a vintage brown derby hat.

During the Blitz the wailing sirens invariably started at about 6:00 pm, the alert lights turned red and the raids were on. Dull thuds and explosions from all sides, firebells ringing, the theatre became one vast air raid shelter. One wondered who everyone was. The stalls, pit, dress circle and boxes became a sprawling mass of bedding, bald heads, blonde hair and pillows, an amiable camp with snoring in all keys. Vera Lynn had her own pitch in the old orchestra pit. She never missed a night. My own upper circle box was next to Joan Gilbert's. It was a strange feeling to undress in a theatre box with one side open and someone doing much the same opposite, the yawning cavern of the old theatre below with its pink plush seats and beautiful lines. It is a theatre of elegance and it was a delight to work and sleep in such artistic surroundings, peopled by so many charming ghosts.

Sometimes the ghosts took the form of mice who would run over my face, presumably on their way to listen to the next programme taking place on the stage. Programmes were continuous, night and day. Frances Day, very intimate and glamorous, would give place to Jack Payne's Orchestra or Geraldo, to be followed by Edmundo Ros and his Band, then Robin Richmond, and so on into the daytime broadcasting.

As the whole theatre used to shake whenever a bomb fell near, and too many fell much too close, I installed a rope from my box to the stalls in the case of a crash. Though I never had to shin down it personally, it caused endless amusement to audiences and visitors. The only person who actually went down it, to my knowledge, was Vic Oliver.

It was the middle of 1940 and our call sign, 'This is London calling – Hello Forces Overseas!' become known to every British serviceman outside Britain, from Durban to Darwin.

At the time I made a list of young artists of promise: Lesley Osmond, Carol Raye, Sylvia Marriott, Sylvia Saetre, Hilary Allen, Anne Shelton, Carole Lynne, Pat Kirkwood, Irene Fieldhouse and Jacqueline Wauters. Jacqueline I found in the French Club and she should have stayed on and become a star. She married and went to Belgium.

One Blitz night we put on a quiz with strong teams: Bea Lillie, Harriet Cohen, Virginia Cherrill (then Countess of Jersey), Negley Farson, Edward Sieff, Manning Sherwin, Carroll Gibbons, Joyce Grenfell, and Gerry Wilmot.

Our story of a staff living and working in an underground London theatre penetrated to America. In March 1941 Mary Welch of *TIME-LIFE* decided to feature us as a 'Theatre at War'- which indeed we were.

Here is what I myself broadcast to America in the North American Service, from a platform of the Piccadilly Tube below our feet in the Criterion Theatre:

There are 279,000 children still in London, and whilst they're not all here quite a number are, here on the platform of the Piccadilly Tube in the heart of London's West End. It's one of the saddest results of the war, that women, children and men – in that order, men are in the minority here – have to be here at all. Many are bombed out of their homes – all look tired but they feel safe here about a hundred feet below ground – and their spirit and fortitude are great. The Underground authorities are simply marvellous to them – they're doing their very best for these visitors of theirs in these difficult times and impossible conditions. As I was coming down to the platforms the sirens sounded the nightly alert and almost simultaneously there were bombs and gunfire - the anti-aircraft barrage. They're very crowded and it's very hot and nothing is private - but at any rate they can't hear the noise which we now call the Blitz.

The English people have always been friendly but now with their bundles and mattresses they are even more matey than ever. Don't run away with the idea that this is just the poor - it's everybody! Just a few feet away from me is an old lady huddled in a fur coat - and on the other side a very weary mother with four little kids climbing all over her, she's given up the unequal struggle of trying to get them to sleep and has fallen asleep herself. And to give you an example of the humour of these people - many of them have been here for seven weeks - someone, seeing me with a mike, asked me if I was going to sing! I said I'd spare them that!

Well, what with going down mines, I never thought I'd be going below ground to broadcast a dormitory, and a Cockney one at that! It's lights out here at 12.30, so goodnight and good luck from under London in a subway Tube platform shelter.

Captain Knight's famous golden eagle, 'Mr Ramshaw' was brought along to the Criterion Theatre soon after his own return from America. Both Captain Knight and the eagle had been on their way to America in the SS *Volendam* which was torpedoed off Liverpool and abandoned. The eagle had to be abandoned too in the ship, but was found days later by Captain Knight off the coast of Scotland, quietly sitting in the same waterlogged cabin in which he had been left. Some time later both started out to America again, and this time arrived safely. Nothing daunted Mr Ramshaw, the all-British eagle, broadcasting, films, television. At the Criterion Theatre awaiting his performance, which consisted of flying round the audience, wings outstretched, it became a problem where to put him after rehearsal, so he was dumped in the small gramophone room in the dark without his hood. Imagine the terror of a secretary hurrying through this underground room in the middle of the night on finding a large eagle sitting on a gramophone turntable tearing up a raw rabbit, the room full of blood and feathers. This same eagle flew round General Eisenhower too at Rainbow Corner a little later. Neither thought this sort of visual broadcasting of mine in the least surprising. I have a photo of the General with the eagle behind him to prove it.

Jill Allgood ran her own Blitz series, *Something Going On In Britain Now*. One November night in the Blitz we had arranged to broadcast from the Euston Station Services Canteen, myself doing the interviewing. The Foreign Broadcasters were to come too. But at 6:30 Broadcasting House heard that Euston Station was the bombers' target and our foreign friends were all cancelled. Wynford Vaughan Thomas and I, and the OB Engineers, duly met at Euston and we did the programme, only to find that the Recording Department at Maida Vale had gone below and had recorded nothing. So we waited until they came up, did the broadcast again, and then later we recovered the effects microphone, on a railway bridge, with the aid of a petrol lighter. Clambering over the parcels and mails abandoned in the dark, we dubbed it "The Dunkirk of Broadcasting", as we were the sole survivors. It was indeed a terrible night in London with terrific damage, and we went back to sleep at the Criterion Theatre which shook with the noise.

Quentin Reynolds had just returned from a memorial

service in St. Paul's Cathedral for Billy Fiske, the first American flier to be killed over here. He said, "It was pretty exciting hearing *The Star Spangled Banner* in St. Paul's."

The ARP On Duty gave insight into a station in action, and off duty too. The American Red Cross girls in Britain gave the USA stories of the work of their ambulance units here in air raids. Ensign Scott recalled her escape from France, field Ensign Betsy Dumbell told how she had fallen into a bomb crater and found herself on an unexploded bomb. There were visits to munitions works and the docks, all dangerous areas at the time.

Blitz Sketch Book gave stories of ordinary people and service men. *Marching to Victory* had marching songs, Newfoundland artillerymen and Indian Troops who were at Dunkirk, Free French training and Maoris in the English countryside.

Even the old soldiers of past wars, the Chelsea Pensioners, were attacked. We had just finished broadcasting from the Royal Hospital, Chelsea, when bombs fell on the Infirmary and destroyed with it Private Rattray, then the oldest living soldier at 101. Luckily he was asleep at the time, with a handkerchief over his face.

The National Gallery ran lunchtime concerts by Dame Myra Hess. All the great national paintings had been removed to caves in the Welsh mountains, and the walls covered with paintings by the late Charles Conder. How annoyed he would have been to be considered expendable.

We met Mrs Fortune. Mrs Fortune did munitions work in the First World War and abandoned her housework at home to become a railway porter at a London terminus. Doing this job she was injured and lay in hospital in a plaster jacket. Aged 48, mother of eleven children and grandmother of six more, she sent messages to her sons serving in India and Egypt.

And we arranged a series of midnight shows direct from the basement of the Players Theatre, which had moved from its traditional home under the Charing Cross Station arches to Albemarle Street.

Jill Allgood herself had a narrow escape at Broadcasting House on the night of the famous bomb that exploded during the Nine o'clock news. She had arranged a studio on the fourth floor for Una Marson, the West Indian girl broadcaster, to interview Ken Johnson, the West Indian bandleader, late at night, this being early evening in the Caribbean. About 8:50 she decided to go up to the Fourth Floor to check that everything was arranged, and walked through the central studio passage of the Tower. Soon after nine o'clock she came back round the outer corridor and had just started down the stairs when a delayed action bomb exploded between the third and fourth floors, killing several of the staff. As a matter of interest, despite everything Ken Johnson appeared at the fixed time, nonchalantly picking his way through the masonry in the streets outside, and gave his talk from an improvised studio in the basement; the records of it still exist. He died soon afterwards in a bomb explosion in the fashionable Café de Paris in Coventry Street.

On the night in May 1941, when the House of Commons was blitzed, Westminster Abbey was also damaged. The night over, our Unit immediately decided to get hold of a recording van and do a commentary from both. It became impossible to obtain a BBC van so we telephoned ENSA who were very ready to oblige with one of theirs. I assumed it would be a plain van like our own, and we arranged to meet it outside Westminster Abbey. ENSA were, at that time, very proud of a set of records sent to them from New York by their American Committee and were advertising them everywhere. As it happened the van got there before us and the driver, being of an adventurous turn of mind, had driven right inside the Abbey and was installed in the middle of a pile of rubble and actually alongside the altar. When we arrived we were met by an infuriated Dean, still wearing pyjamas under his cassock as he had just been bombed out of his own house. Without a word he marched us straight to the van and we were horrified to see, emblazoned in enormous coloured letters all over its sides, 'Gertrude Lawrence Calling.'

Noel Gay, despite his enormous song successes like *Run Rabbit Run*, *Something About a Soldier* and *The Lambeth Walk* had a most modest personality and was always ready to co-operate. When Jill Allgood started a programme for men in hospitals called *Here's Wishing You Well Again*, Noel at once wrote the perfect signature tune. Our signature tune for the *Merry-Go-Round* programme, called *The Army, the Navy and the Air Force* was also by Noel.

Joan Gilbert recorded a Service pantomime, *Off White and the Seven Oafs*, a joint RAF-WAAF effort, and presented to Radio News Reel.

Vivian Van Damm used to take his full Windmill company, comics, show girls, dancing girls and all, to the RAF stations on Sundays. On March 29, 1942 it was the turn of RAF Fighter Command. Along went Johnny McGregor the comedian, Charmian Innes comedienne, Margaret McGrath, Sonia Stacpoole, showgirls and others, also Joan Rock whose Fan Dance and Dance of the Seven Veils were sensational at any time. I was invited to bring along BBC microphones.

The RAF's great gag was to liven things up by suddenly turning on an immense concealed searchlight. When veils were off, fans were down and blackouts were due. Van Damm used to get into a rage and swear never to bring the Windmill again, but the girls laughed and took it in very good part. For the boys, home was never like this!

Here's Wishing You Well Again.
A special gala edition broadcast December 31, 1943. From Centre: East
End Policeman; Countess of Limerick, Deputy Chairman of the Red Cross
& St John's War Organisation; Mrs Florence Fortune, housewife and war
worker, mother of eleven, grandmother to seven, with five serving
overseas; Dr Debreu, sold newspapers in Piccadilly for 22 years; Lupino
Lane, musical comedy star; Godfrey Keaton, BBC narrator for the
programme; Jill Allgood, producer of the programme; Cecil Madden,
Head of BBC Overseas Entertainment Unit; Bebe Daniels, American star;
Anne Shelton, singer; Cyril Fletcher, comedian; Patricia Hicks, compère
of the programme; Paula Green and Olive Groves, who sang with
Mantovani's Orchestra. Mantovani is on the left.

NIGHT OF THE CAFÉ DE PARIS

Opposite us, on the other side of Piccadilly Circus in Coventry Street, was the famous Café de Paris, celebrated for stars, glamour and luxury. Being well below ground, seemingly safe and always elegant, it still drew a smart crowd in wartime, as it always had in peacetime. Two bands were in residence, Ken 'Snakehips' Johnson's and Nat Allen's.

The night of Saturday March 8, 1941 was a night never to be forgotten. While actually leading the orchestra on the stand in the circular ballroom Johnson was killed. The raid was a terrible one. Here is the *EVENING STANDARD'S* description:

The first bomb fell on the piano. It scattered the band, killing Ken Johnson and several of his Orchestra. Before the dancers could get off the floor the second bomb crashed through the glass dome, right in the middle of the ballroom. Couples were torn from each other's arms. The whole Café was plunged into darkness. For a few minutes there was pandemonium. A young attendant in the balcony shouted, "Pull yourselves together." Then those uninjured started to pull young women and their men friends from the debris.

Martinus Poulsen, the Restaurateur, and Mr Charles, the Manager, were killed.

Joe Denise, guitarist, who was playing on the stand when the bomb came down, told me his story:

Well, the band was playing as usual when suddenly there was a terrible crash and I found myself lying on the floor. The first thing that flashed through my mind was that it was silly to think that the place had been

151

damaged, as it was considered so safe. I made two attempts to stand up, but found I couldn't. I felt no pain and couldn't imagine that I had been injured. But then I looked down and saw that my leg had been shattered. There was a general scramble to get off the stand as debris was falling all around. The drummer dragged me out backwards through a little door at the back of the stage into the kitchen, which had not been damaged. Everything was very hazy for a few minutes but I do remember feeling great pain in my leg. A Canadian soldier applied a tourniquet but this only made the pain worse, although of course it saved my life by stopping the flow of blood.

I lay there for about five or ten minutes and then the drummer, who was uninjured, came in and told me that our band leader, Ken Johnson, and the tenor sax player had both been killed. Naturally this upset me very much as they had both been my friends for many years. It seemed an age before anybody else come to see me but at last some ARP men appeared on the scene and improvised a stretcher for me out of a large piece of plaster from the ceiling. No sooner had they laid me on this than it crumbled to pieces from my weight, so off they went to look for something else to carry me out. Well, at last they found a ladder somewhere on which they carried me out of what remained of the Café into the foyer of the cinema next door. I lay there for, I suppose, half an hour, completely in the dark and with the air raid still going on overhead as fiercely as ever. After a while a priest came along and asked if there was anything he could do for me, and I'm afraid I was very rude to him. He was an understanding man and he went off to see what he could do for the other casualties who were lying all around me. At long last the rescue party got me onto a stretcher and left me in the street to wait for an ambulance. The raid was so serious that every available ambulance was in constant use that night, so it was some little while before I was transported to Charing Cross Hospital. From then on, everything was hazy, and I was operated on."

Tom Bromley gave me his account:

I was playing with the band as usual. We had just relieved Nat Allen's Band and were in the middle of our first number when suddenly there was an explosion. I felt my bass being torn out of my hands and saw it flung across the room. Somehow or other I wasn't knocked down by the blast but I saw someone lying very near me who was obviously seriously injured and I tried to move over to see if I could help. Then I realised that one of my legs was completely useless. It folded up underneath me the moment I tried to put any weight on it. There were only a few emergency lamps which had not been put out by the explosion. I lowered myself to the floor as best I could and looked at my leg. There was no doubt about it because several pieces of bone were actually sticking out through a hole in my flesh. I waited for what seemed an age and I was dimly conscious of others who were not injured trying to assist those who were even more seriously hurt than I was. At last I felt I could not stand that terrible scene much longer so I dragged myself on my two arms and my one good leg across the floor of the stage to the back exit, as so far as I could see the front entrance was completely demolished and blocked by a heap of debris. I crawled up the stairs and finally into the street where I lay on the pavement. Presently someone brought me a cup of tea and told me that doctors and first aid people were up to their eyes working on casualties further down the street and in neighbouring buildings, but they would attend to me as soon as was possible. I lay on the pavement for about an hour and a half. I remember putting a tourniquet on my leg with a handkerchief and a pencil and at long last the ambulance squad took me in hand. I was transported to a nearby First Aid depot where a doctor examined me and found that I had a serious compound fracture and that part of the bone of my leg had been blown away altogether. I was at the First Aid depot for about half on hour and then was taken to the Middlesex Hospital, and I was there for some months while the surgeons patched me up and grafted bone from another part of my leg into the hole which the bomb had made.

Nat Allen, who ran the second band at the Café de Paris, had a miraculous escape. Ken Johnson's Band had just relieved him and he had been asked to join a 21st birthday party on the floor, but having a headache Nat begged off and asked his band if they would like a cup of tea in the Corner House next door. They said they would, so Nat had just led them up the front stairs into Coventry Street when the bomb went off inside below ground. Nat Allen lost all his instruments and later that night came over to the Criterion Theatre where we promised him enough future work to get himself and his boys on their feet again.

SWEETHEARTS OF THE FORCES

I had the idea of creating Radio Girl Friends for the Forces, and this turned out to be very successful. These girls were all in charge of their own programmes, with messages and music. Joan Gilbert was the first, broadcasting to the Gibraltar Garrison. She became Sweetheart of the Rock for years, and later was able to visit her supporters at the

Governor's invitation. Jane Carr did the same for isolated spots, such as Reunion and the Seychelles. Margot Davies broadcast to Newfoundland, Betty Warren to Australians in the Middle East and Marjorie Skill to New Zealanders, Joan Henley to South Africa. Una Marson looked after the West Indies and Jane Welch the RAF training in Canada. This was the original team and they become very popular with huge fan mail to cope with.

Vera Lynn came to be considered the one and only 'Sweetheart of the Forces' by singing in *Starlight* every night. Since this was broadcast live at 2:15 a.m. in the middle of the night, recorded and then transmitted six times more, she seemed to be almost a broadcasting station single-handed.

The two announcers of this programme, Betty McLoughlin and Barbara MacFadyean, did very well too, with their friendly manner.

Vera arrived at the Criterion Theatre every night at about 6:00 pm, just before the nightly Blitz started. She always chose the same mattress in the orchestra pit and immediately went to sleep until wakened for rehearsals of her broadcast in the early hours. Her singing programmes were so popular, her tones so even and so reassuring for the Forces everywhere, it was inevitable she would be regarded as No. 1 Sweetheart, and she deserved it. Her beautiful voice quality was unmistakable, her fan mail immense.

Anne Shelton at the outbreak of war was only 15, but her versatility and tomboyish comedy were soon apparent. She quickly moved into a No. 2 position as a Forces' request personality.

All the girls took a tremendous amount of trouble to answer their airgraphs and letters, with photos, and they soon became the most popular characters in the respective armies, supplanting the variety stars the Forces left behind

The entire company grouped round the microphone at the close of the
first broadcast of the series *Calling the RAF in Canada*.

them, who could not make the same positive contact on the air. This was a war fought with radio: radio for propaganda: radio for morale. These girls did their bit. They were friendly, they had sex appeal, they filled a need.

No-one seemed to mind if a 'Services Sweetheart' was married or had personal attachments. No-one really enquired into this and many of the letters to the pin-up Girls started frankly by saying that the writer was a married man and wondering if the recipient was married too. However in the main the thread of attraction was the male to the female and the girls got many offers of all sorts.

At the time the Nazi radios, mostly based in Belgrade, were boosting the song *Lilli Marlene* which caught on with our desert armies too, owing to its repetitious and soothing quality. We felt London should attempt a reply. As it proved impossible to agree to any actual song to repeat *ad nauseam*, our unit volunteered to put on a special programme exhaustively for the Eighth Army, creating a new Girl Friend specially for this Army, with the title of *A Date For the Desert*. Doreen Villiers, petite and cute, had a long and popular reign. When the Ninth Army had to be catered for we created *Appointment With Beryl*. Beryl Davis was pretty and full of personality. Both Beryl and Doreen were as popular with Americans as with the British.

Once a pretty wife tripped up to the microphone to speak to her husband in Libya. Said the Girl Friend announcing: "Here comes your wife, Corporal, and isn't she looking lovely. She is wearing her fur coat which you probably remember well." The wife gasped, grabbed the microphone and yelled, "Jim, it's not my coat, I borrowed it." After that I insisted on careful enquiries first!

PET

Petula Clark was ten years old when she was brought into the Criterion Theatre studio one Saturday afternoon in October 1942 with a group of children assembled to send messages to the British Forces in Iraq. This was because names had been canvassed at the other end and her uncle, a gunner, had asked for her.

The programme, which was broadcast on Saturdays, was called *It's All Yours* and was directed by Stephen Williams. My position was that of Executive Producer. We used to give the children a tea with buns, and then Stephen taught them to sing the programme's signature tune, *Yours*, made famous by Vera Lynn. After this there was usually a little time to spare when the children were asked if anyone would like to perform, sing or recite. No-one ever did.

However on this particular day a little child stepped out boldly and said, "I should like to sing," and added, "with the orchestra." It was these three words which caused something of a near panic. Jack de Leon, the conductor, was deep in a gossip and a cup of tea, and his bandsmen were engrossed in their games of cards in all corners of the stage. I was sent for from my office to witness what might happen next.

Jack de Leon routed out all his orchestra boys saying, "This little lady wants to sing with the orchestra. We can't disappoint her, can we?" Grumbling away they all took up their places unenthusiastically. "Well, what are you going to sing? What's your name dear?" said Jack. "My name is Petula and I'd like to sing *Mighty Like a Rose*." "*Mighty Like a Rose* it is, gentlemen," said Jack. This beautiful child stepped up on the rostrum, put out her arms as she had no doubt seen crooners do, and sang the song simply and with great purity, the orchestra busking. At the end the whole orchestra spontaneously applauded. The child obviously

Petula Clark,
November 11, 1945.

had something special and she was so pretty, like a little angel.

She then turned to me. "I can do impressions if you like." "Who can you do?" I asked her. "Oh, anyone," she answered, "Vera Lynn, Sophie Tucker, Carmen Miranda, Schnozzle Durante." Everyone laughed at this, and I said we would like to hear them all. It was no trouble at all and that was just what she did, with a few more thrown in. By then it was time for the programme to go on the air and we were determined that she should sing in it. Programmes on the Overseas Service were not heard in Britain, being on short wave.

Almost at once came a letter from a Sergeant Fred Monk in Malta. "I shall be glad if you will let me know the name of the little girl of ten who sang *Mighty Like a Rose* on Saturday October 16. Her Christian name was Petula. Her voice was crystal clear and sounded sweet as chapel bells on Sunday morning in England. It made me homesick. Hoping to hear Petula some more."

We arranged for her to come back again the following week. This time her father, Lance Corporal Leslie Clark, brought her and now she was an artist in her own right, along with Ted Andrews the singer, Barbara Andrews the pianist and others. It was suggested that she should sing *Ave Maria* with Robin Richmond at the organ.

After tea Petula popped into my office to explore as she was a very natural, unaffected child. She was delighted at the strip lighting and the many papers on the walls of what was the star's dressing room in a famous theatre. I told her stories of names she knew, of Vera Lynn and Sophie Tucker, the queen momma of vaudeville.

Gloria Kane, the young singer, saw Petula shiver, took off her fur coat and wrapped it round her. As she did so I overheard her say to the child "You'll have a lot of your own one day."

Petula Clark with Vera Lynn,
Arthur Askey and various other people from
the cast of *Birthday Party*

The performing couple Ted Andrews and Barbara kept telling me of Barbara's singing child at home and that they really must bring her with them some time to meet me. I confess that with one starlet on my hands I was unenthusiastic. However, she obviously caught the eye of someone who mattered, all in good time, as soon after she was being introduced nightly by Vic Oliver at the London Hippodrome and singing sweetly. She was Julie Andrews.

I decided to let Petula make her debut on the home programme in an All-Star Tenth Anniversary Broadcast on December 20 with Arthur Askey, Richard Murdoch, Elsie and Doris Waters, Michael Redgrave, Sydney Burchall, Geraldo and Vera Lynn, from the Queensberry All Services Club. I was producing this myself. It was going to be done in full stage style with stage lighting and Petula needed something special to wear. I approached a friend, Lady Marks, and asked her if she would give a dress to a brilliant child. She told me to go to Debenham and Freebody and choose whatever I liked. I shall never forget standing in the Childrens' Department with Petula's mother as Petula stood in nothing but diminutive pants while salesgirls popped dress after dress over her head. In the end I chose one in ice blue which would show up well in the spotlights.

Petula thanked Lady Marks thus:

Dear Fairy Godmother,
I call you this because I dislike calling people I like Mr or Mrs and it is really very much like Cinderella isn't it? I now have a lovely dress and shoes which I am to wear at the BBC which is more important than any ball, so I do thank you and Uncle Cecil Madden for your kindness. I know I shall sing ever so much better in that beautiful dress.

And the dress did show up well. Petula, who was billed

as 'A Soldier's Child', had a triumph in it. Everybody cheered her in the vast theatre. She was taken to the Royal Box where the Rt. Hon. A.V. Alexander, First Lord of the Admiralty, kissed her. Everyone was thrilled, including the Press. Here is the *DAILY MAIL* December 21, 1942. "Petula, 10, is a star in a night... stole the show... the BBC were flooded with telephone enquiries... shall we hear her again?"

As she was under 12 she could not be paid much more than bare expenses. I asked the BBC to appoint me as her guardian officially, so as to restrict her appearances, as she was then doing Troop Shows and was in such demand from producers she was in danger of over-exposure on the air. This led to many arguments and made me highly unpopular with my colleagues, but the wisdom may be apparent today.

The BBC had two Directors General then, (Sir Cecil Graves and Robert Foot.) I made such a fuss of Petula I suggested bringing the child to call on them. Such a thing had never happened before. They were so alarmed they did better and visited me in my Criterion Theatre office together to do so.

MacQueen Pope wrote a radio pantomime *Babes in the Wood* for the *It's All Yours* series with Petula as the Fairy Starlight, Helen Clare as Maid Marian, Gloria Kane as Robin Hood and Bennett and Williams, as the Robbers. Children of Servicemen were Robins.

Petula took part in *London Town*, a colour film with Sid Field. It was no masterpiece but she came out of it well enough. As soon as she was 12 and legally able to work she was offered a long contract with the Rank Organisation, and she soon showed she could act too, with Jack Warner, Kathleen Harrison, Anthony Newley and Jimmy Hanley in *The Huggett Family* series. One way or another she has been in the public eye ever since.

It's All Yours. The people behind the programme (left to right) Marjorie Sandford, the popular young singer; Stephen Williams, programme producer; Jane Carr; Cecil Madden, who directs the BBC Empire Light Entertainments; Ena Browne, Assistant Producer.

MY BOMB

Everyone had bomb stories during the war. This incident happened to me on September 12, 1940 and I was asked to tell it on Overseas News Reel at the time. Here is the story as I told it on the radio during the Blitz.

"My bomb? It's no worse than anyone else's bomb stories. As you know, air raids are pretty frequent in London, about six a day as a rule, so most people have some pet tale of their own experience, and pretty close to home sometimes.

I say MY bomb in this proprietary way because actually there were two bombs together, and then two more. The German above us was obviously trigger-happy thinking he was onto a good thing. Obviously the results weren't fatal or I wouldn't be here to tell you. But this is what happened to me with "My Bomb."

I was going into a house on the North Side of a famous London Common (Clapham Common), to see my mother who lived there. I was travelling in a 137 bus when the sirens started their unhappy wail. The arrangement now is that busmen can do as they like, stop and go into shelter or keep on to the end of the journey. Well, my bus elected to go on regardless, and at a certain point as the bus was going to turn left and my way was right, I had to get off. Well, I got down and then wasn't sure what to do.

Everything seemed very quiet, much too quiet, so I cogitated for a moment. Should I try to "make" a Public Shelter a long way out over open ground on the Common, or should I just go along to the house I was going to, which was some way along. Nothing ever seemed to happen to anyone one knew, so I thought no more about it and decided to walk on. I was on the pavement on the houses' side.

I'd gone just about ten steps when my mind was

quickly made up for me. I suddenly heard that devastating whine of bombs falling - not one but two - a horrid chilling noise. You just have about two seconds in hand. Well, I don't know how I made myself do it, I just dived flat to the right, all in one movement, into a garden, hat, umbrella, gas mask and all. The garden, by the way, had an exceedingly flimsy wooden fence.

A woman behind me, the only person near, saw me do it and instinctively did exactly the same. She dived right onto me and landed on top of me. Then there were two almighty explosions, a noise like all the fireworks you'd ever heard going off at once, an icy blast, and then up went the opposite pavement at an angle of 45 degrees. And what goes up must come down - well the whole thing came down on us but as she was on top of me she got most of it and I was almost all right. Actually I stuck out a bit beyond her and so I got a piece of hard pavement about a foot square in my back, but beyond being bruised I have no ill effects beyond a real old scare. And I defy you not to feel terrified in my place! The woman, who was white, literally turned black in the face from a mixture of tar and garden earth - a sort of minstrel effect. She was too startled even to cry.

I pulled her out. If we'd only known it there was an Anderson garden shelter a foot away from us - only we'd no time even to look at it - and one of the curious effects of the blast I noticed was that all the doors that were open banged shut and all the ones that were shut flew open. Quite a lot fell off altogether. The two houses nearest shared the garden we were in and when they next flew open in we popped, and in quite a mess.

I heard an old lady howling next door so we looked in and joined her. She said, "There's a time bomb in the back and I'm all alone." So I said, rather sensibly I felt, "If there really is, let's get out again quick..." But I'm pretty sure there wasn't a time bomb there, she was just terrified. This war is very hard on old people. So I rustled up an Air Raid Warden and made him look after her and also a young girl who turned up from nowhere.

Then, after picking up my own large lump of pavement – incidentally we retrieved the woman's shopping bag in the general ruins – and putting my Brick as I call it under my arm as a trophy – I've got it on the mantelpiece now – I took the woman to her home. She was a bit upset to find two houses completely destroyed on the way, but I felt then, let's go home, surely they'll never bomb us twice in one day. Luckily nor they did. Then I went on home, wiser and ready for a stiff drink.

My wife insisted on my walking her back to look at the craters and was pretty horrified at how near my shave had been. They were about five feet deep and some ten feet wide – not an atom of metal to be seen, and just the opposite side of the road. So you see, I suppose instinct helps. If I, or both of us come to that, had stood rooted to the spot, and we might easily have, well we should have been blown to pieces. The houses on our side way back from the garden were damaged and the windows didn't shatter as they might have, they just fell out in sheets! So it's not too pleasant strolling around these days during air raid alarms. I shall go into shelters more cheerfully in future. And that's the story of my bomb."

FOUR WINDMILL GIRLS

The Windmill Theatre was proud of its wartime slogan 'We never closed.' At one time it was the only theatre in the West End of London which remained open during the worst of the bombing. This theatre, which had its accent on glamour and ran non-stop revue, was financed by a remarkable lady of 87, a good friend of her companies, Mrs

Laura Henderson, and was controlled by Vivian Van Damm, the creator of *Revuedeville* or continuous revue. Although one of the side walls of the auditorium was blown out by a bomb and the whole building lost all its glass, the theatre steadily carried on, the girls making their endless quick changes without giving the Blitz a moment's thought.

Broadway made an attempt to tell a story similar to the Windmill's in *Heart of a City* by Lesley Storm with Beverley Roberts and Gertrude Musgrove, and Hollywood tried in the film *Tonight and Every Night* with Rita Hayworth and Janet Blair and later a movie called *Mrs Henderson* with Judi Dench and Bob Hoskins.

The astonishing thing about the Windmill was the restricted size of the whole theatre and stage, the cramped dressing rooms, the skilful organisation of wardrobe, music department, design, photography: rehearsal room, the company playing, the company off, and so on. The Windmill Showgirls were all beautiful. It was great while it lasted. Perhaps it was too good to last for ever.

The Windmill Nudes were entirely nude but they never moved. In Paris revues 'Les Nues' are nothing of the sort. They are usually only bare at the top, and of course can move.

Four of the Windmill girls told me their Blitz stories. They are Margaret McGrath, showgirl and actress; Charmian Innes, comedienne; Joan Jay, soubrette and dancer; and Valerie Tandy, dancer and comedienne.

MARGARET MCGRATH'S STORY:

One night (in October 1940) just after the show I went out with my friend Ann Singer to have a snack at a little café near the theatre. After we had been there about half an hour a really heavy raid started and we thought we'd better get back to the theatre as quickly as we could. Then we suddenly heard someone shouting that there was a fire at the stables down the road, and that several horses were shut up there. So Ann and I thought we'd better go along to see if we could help. We didn't know anything about horses then, but we soon learned quite a lot. We got to the stables and found two or three people standing round the gates, but nobody knew quite what to do. The stables were pretty well alight by this time, burning quite fiercely, and the flames were spreading. The horses were making quite a lot of noise – that's what got us – we just couldn't bear to hear these poor beasts neighing, so Ann and I ran up the slope and opened the gates. Inside we saw six horses, rearing about as much as the ropes from their halters would allow. We untied them and some of the other people caught them as they came out and we all held onto the ropes until they calmed down a bit in the street. I realise now that frightened horses are tricky to deal with but Ann and I were really too excited to think very much about that. Ann took three horses and I took the other three and we led them over to the fire station across the way, but when we got there the fireman said it wasn't a stable and six horses knocking about would make it very difficult for fire engines to come in and out. So we set off down the street again and there we met a policeman who wanted to know what two young girls were doing with six large horses. We explained and he told us to take them to the nearest Police Station. He showed us the way and we set off with our little rodeo round Piccadilly Circus, where we had quite a few offers of assistance from people in the street. We were feeling very courageous by then and I remember we started singing "I've Got Sixpence" – but suddenly there was a terrific whizz and a bomb burst very near. I'm afraid I didn't really notice how the horses took that

– all I do know is that we lost not only our offers of assistance but our horses as well. But we found them again eventually, they hadn't gone too far, and in about half an hour we had rounded them all up from Regent Street and Burlington Street and we marched them off triumphantly to the Police Station. The men at the Police Station were rather surprised to see us. I'll never forget the look of astonishment on the face of the sergeant in charge, until we explained. Then he was tremendously helpful and relieved us of our horses. So, having seen them to safety, we went back to sleep at the theatre.

CHARMIAN INNES' STORY:

One Saturday morning after a dress rehearsal we were all standing outside the Windmill stage door when suddenly, with no warning at all, a bomb dropped quite near the theatre. There was such a cloud of dust over the whole area that I knew some buildings must have been hit, so as I'd just passed my First Aid examination I thought I'd better go along and see if I could help. I grabbed one of the first-aid kits which were always kept on pegs so as to be handy for immediate use and, with my friend Lesley Osmond, rushed off towards Berwick Market. We got to the wreckage within a few moments of the actual explosion and asked a policeman if he wanted any help. He said he did and told us to do what we could as a doctor hadn't yet arrived. There were quite a number of injured people in the street and we guessed there would be still more under the wrecked houses. While we were attending to some of the wounded, a man rushed up to us in a demented state and asked if we had seen his wife. We told him we hadn't so he started burrowing with his hands through the debris to look for her. I don't know if he ever found her because just at that moment a policeman asked me to go and lend a hand at a nearby casualty station, where a lot of the victims had been taken. We gave all the help we could there and then went back to see how the rescue party was getting on with their job of extricating casualties from the wreckage. They were doing amazingly well; within about half an hour of the actual crash they'd got quite a number of people out, and in the meantime an RAF doctor had arrived on the scene, so I acted on his instructions and gave all the help I could until, at long last, the chief warden considered that everyone who could possibly be got out had been removed from the debris. I really don't know how long that took – I suppose about a couple of hours or so – but what I do remember is that when the job was done a policeman brought me over a cup of tea which tasted better than any other tea I have ever drunk. Naturally I was rather het up over the whole business but I think the worst part of it all was coming back to the theatre and facing a party of cameramen who had heard about what had been happening and insisted on having pictures for the Sunday newspapers. So, covered in dust and filthy as I was, they just sat me down and took pictures of me in every conceivable position, with the result that the next morning there appeared some very fine pictures of a Windmill girl looking rather like a sweep.

JOAN JAY'S STORY:

On Saturday October 19, 1940 – I have reason to remember that day – it was just after the show had closed – when Mr Van Damm, our general manager and producer asked several of us if we would like to go and dance somewhere. He used to take us out sometimes in these very hectic nights as we were all living in the theatre and looked forward to breaking the monotony of existence as often as we could by going to places which were considered fairly safe. I had promised my father that I wouldn't go out of the theatre while raids were on so I explained this and the party went off without me. There were quite a number of the company still at the theatre, among them Nugent Marshall, one of the juveniles. Well, about two hours later there was a lull in the raid – things had been quiet for quite a time – and so Nugent asked if I would risk just slipping across the road to a café. We decided that if things started to get heavy again it would only take us a moment to rush back. As I was feeling pretty peckish at the time I forgot my promise to my father and told Nugent to count me in. We went over the way with one of the electricians and we had just ordered and paid for a snack when I experienced a sensation which I can't explain. It was a sort of feeling of being pushed in the back and my throat filled up with dust – all this mixed up with a terrific smell of powder and gas, and people screaming and yelling. Then next thing I remember was knowing I was pinned down to the floor, and then I realised that Nugent Marshall was coming towards me from what seemed to be a very long way away. Actually he had been blown across the room, although I didn't realise it at the time, but I remember him trying to lift the weight that was holding me down. After what seemed an age Nugent managed to clear away some of the debris and got me out from under the wreckage. It was then be found that our companion, the electrician, had been killed outright. Nugent dragged me across the road to the theatre and he only realised when he got there that he had a bit of shrapnel in his neck which was making him feel very weak and dizzy from loss of blood. He managed to get me over to the theatre where there were quite a number of people who knew something about first aid; they gave me all the attention they could although with the bad wound I had received in my thigh they had hardly enough cotton wool to stop the bleeding. I wasn't fully conscious, it was all very hazy as a matter of fact, only I remember feeling very cold, although I was covered with as many blankets as could be found while someone was doing their best to get an ambulance to take me to hospital. That wasn't very easy in such a bad raid, as so many ambulances were being called upon that it was very difficult to find one with a spare stretcher, but our chief electrician finally put me on a stretcher and carried me down to the corner of Shaftesbury Avenue. As luck would have it he was able to stop an ambulance with just enough room for me, so I was taken off to Charing Cross Hospital, where they operated on me at once. I was evacuated to a large country hospital the next day and after three months expert treatment there I'm glad to say I was able to come back to the theatre and carry on with my work, which to a great extent is dancing. Though I have twelve scars, fortunately neither my face nor my arms were marked.

VALERIE TANDY'S STORY:

My exciting experience happened the same night Joan Jay was blitzed, but I was luckier as I wasn't actually injured, although I had a very narrow escape. I was living at the theatre, as we all did, when someone asked me to go across to the café and get an egg and tomato sandwich. I waited for a lull in the raid and then, as I always did in the Blitz, ran like a hare from the theatre to the café and asked for a sandwich. The girl behind the counter said she was sorry she hadn't got an egg and tomato and asked me if a cheese sandwich would do instead, but I would have to wait while she cut it. Being very conscientious I thought I had better make sure that the girl who had asked for the sandwich liked cheese, so I told the waitress I would go and find out. I rushed out of the café, ran across the street to the stage door and then I knew nothing more until I found myself inside the theatre lying on the floor at the foot of a flight of stairs. The blast from the same bomb that injured Joan Jay must have caught me up and blown me into the building; I was lucky to be alive to tell this story as nearly everybody in that café which I had just left was killed by a direct hit.

Hitler's war could not close the celebrated Windmill Theatre but in 1964 changes in taste of London's entertainment, attributed to striptease clubs, did so, and the Windmill Theatre was a cinema again.

ARTISTS UNDER FIRE

Many British show people went on doing their job of entertaining during the time of the enemy blitz, the V.1 robot bombs and the V.2 rockets. Some were killed and others maimed, but unless a theatre was made unusable show business earned a great record and added something to their old slogan, 'The show must go on.' Indeed I had been doing a nightly programme with the impressionist Navarre called *Not What They Seem* and read that he had been killed in a Midlands hotel by a bomb the week after.

I sought out some of the men and women who had had stirring times, mostly under the banner of ENSA. Here are just a few of the stories I collected then.

BOB LECARDO'S STORY

(Bob Lecardo was an acrobat, then in charge of the ENSA Variety Section and responsible for supplying the Forces with variety entertainment.)

It was on the night of May 10. I had been on the outskirts of London producing an ENSA show. There was a raid on and the train I travelled home in was nearly bombed twice, two near misses. Anyway they were as good as a mile to me and I was very glad when the train plunged into the subway underground. But when I got out and the escalator had taken me to the surface I found that I was in the thick of it. Bombs and shrapnel were coming down all over the place so I made my way home by what are called easy stages, short bursts of speed with intervals of lying flat in the gutter. Anyway I got home - at three o'clock in the morning - and heaved a sigh of relief. I decided to make myself a cup of tea, so I went into the kitchen and found that the glass in the windows wasn't there at all. I had to fumble in the dark so as not to show a light. I got the kettle on to boil and then went into the dining room to fetch the tea. As I returned to the kitchen the floor suddenly subsided on one side. Then there was a flash and I both saw and heard the walls caving in on me. I am an acrobat and I did an acrobatic fall. I spun round and let myself go the same way as the floor was going. Down and down I went with debris falling all around me. I felt myself going through obstructions and also felt wood tearing at my legs. And I finished up on my hands and knees. Debris was still falling all over me and I was holding it up with the back of my head. I didn't want my face to get covered for fear of suffocation. After a long time the debris and litter stopped falling. I don't suppose it was really very long but it seemed like hours. I started wriggling and working myself from side to side and I found that I could release myself, so I started scraping with my bare hands at the mound of earth and debris like a mole burrowing its way to the surface. And I came out. It was a bright moonlit night. I took a look round. The road I live in had taken on quite a different formation. There were no railings anywhere – I remember being struck by that – also by the fact that I could see right through the houses opposite. I looked round at my own house. It wasn't there. Nor were those which should have been standing beside it. They had just disappeared. The guns were still going and a plane was droning overhead. I said to myself "This is just like a battlefield in the last war." I was in the Artillery then. Well, by that time I was feeling just a little dizzy. Two girls were screaming – they were buried under the rubble nearby. I jumped up and started shouting "All right – we'll get you out." Then along rushed the A.R.P. men. By this time I was reeling about. They got me into a car and sent me off to hospital. I was lucky – I escaped with a few bruises and scratches. I learned afterwards that the girls I had heard lived in the flat below mine, and they were saved too. What worried me most was the mound of earth through which I had burrowed. I couldn't understand that. I left the hospital at daybreak and I went straight back to find out. I had fallen with the debris of my house into the bomb crater and I had dug my way out of the actual crater. And except for the bruises and scratches I wasn't hurt. That's what comes of knowing how to fall.

FRANK DEI'S STORY
(An organist,he had been touring the Garrison Theatres
and factories with his travelling theatre organ)

On a cold bleak January day on a cold bleak road in the
desolate Fen country I was moving along in my van and
I was about seven or eight miles from the town where
I was due to entertain the troops. There was nothing
else in sight, not a car, not a cart, not a living soul.
Suddenly I saw an aeroplane diving alongside of me out
of the mist only about fifty or sixty feet away. I didn't
know whether it was one of ours or not as I couldn't
see very plainly. At that time there were raids all day and
every day and I was in the worst part of the country
near the East Coast. I got to my top speed of about sixty
miles an hour, but the plane was doing much more than
that and it was flying zig-zag across my front. Then I
realised it was missing on one of its engines, and as
there had been no machine-gunning I thought it must
be one of ours in trouble and trying to land. So I
thought I'd be helpful, there was a large flat field on my
right which was interspersed with ditches: a death trap
to a pilot coming down without knowing the local
conditions. So I waved to the men in the plane
indicating the direction in which I thought they could
land safely. They managed it and I ran over to the plane
to see if I could help. It was then I got my shock, for I
suddenly saw the German markings on the plane and
then four men with revolvers climbed out. I was
thinking that they weren't very gay people to meet by
a lonely road in the Fen country but I kept on going
towards the plane, when to my surprise the German
airmen took off their helmets and threw their revolvers
on the ground at my feet. And then the plane caught
fire, which meant that we all had to run for it. Just as we

were coming up to the hedge a motorist came by, stopped, saw what was happening and drove off very quickly. However he fetched help and a few minutes afterwards a farm worker came along with a shot gun and after that a policeman. I was certainly glad to see him. Then I had quite a bit of difficulty to convince him I was not one of the Germans. In the end I satisfied him and handed over my captives, then as it was getting near the time for my show I hopped back in my car and got in just in time to set my organ up.

Another day I was giving a show for a gunsite and searchlight unit and I finished about 10.00 pm I was moving off down the road when suddenly several bombs were dropped so close to me that the body of my van, with the organ in it, was blown completely off its chassis. Even my glasses were blown off my nose and I couldn't find them anywhere, but I wasn't hurt, just a bit shocked. Before I could recover I had to move, and move quickly, because the Nazi plane started firing machine gun bullets round me. At last he got tired of that and went away so I returned to the camp where I had been performing, leaving what remained of the band where it was. The officer in charge gave me a hearty welcome and a cup of cocoa which was even more welcome. Then suddenly the alert siren went again, so the officer took me down to the command post on the actual gun site as he said it would be safe there. Then the fun started: a plane came within range and I was looking through a telescopic height finder, doing a bit of spotting for the gunners, and to my delight I was the first to get onto the target. That plane was shot down with the first shell that this particular crowd of boys had fired during the war.

ALAN BIXTER'S STORY
(Pianist and accompanist.)

One night we were giving a concert to troops in a big town when a raid started. The show was going very well when suddenly, as a background to our performance, we heard the wail of the alert siren. Then bombs started dropping - at first they seemed to be quite a long way away but gradually they came closer and closer until suddenly there was a terrific report - down came plaster from the ceiling all over the artists and audience and before we had time to recover from the shock there was another explosion. I was playing the piano at the time, accompanying the boys in community singing. The piano was literally dancing about, but it never occurred to me to stop playing, though I do remember having the utmost difficulty in finding the right keys. The audience didn't notice as they were too busy climbing out from under what remained of the ceiling.

Another time we were giving a show in a city which had been very badly bombed. A very big raid was in progress and the German planes were dropping flares all over the place. We were giving our performance in a tent serving as a temporary canteen and the officer in charge was worried in case the flares should set fire to it. The boys didn't seem to mind - it wasn't their tent. Anyway the officer let us carry on and we finished the show. On our way home we heard something whistling down and the next thing we knew the van was blown into the air. It came down facing in the opposite direction and to make things wilder, when this happened we were just between two anti-aircraft batteries and both of them let go all their guns together. The noise!!

SANDY ROWAN'S STORY
(Comedian.)

We got so used to the sirens and the alerts being a kind of accompaniment to our shows that we never paid much attention to them. But I do remember once when we were just starting a concert at mid-day. The alert had gone and we were told that danger was imminent so I asked the audience if they'd like us to pack up or whether we should carry on. The unanimous answer was "Carry on" so I put on my piano-accordion and I had just got started when a bomb dropped right behind the stage. It blew in the whole of the rock wall of the canteen where we were and the curtain and stage fittings came tumbling down, with rubble, rocks and brick crashing through the roof. After that it was a case of every man for himself, but in half an hour the All Clear signal had gone and we started to give the show again, using a great heap of debris to stand on – one of the craziest stages I have ever played.

One night there were no facilities for giving a show at a factory where we had been booked. The Nazis had seen to that before we got there. So, instead, we went to a worker's institute nearby and the workers were able to hop over in their break to meet their wives and families there. We had just got through the performance when the alert went and the gun-fire became very heavy. The police came in and asked me to carry on with community singing to try and drown the gun-fire and to keep the audience under cover. So for an hour and three-quarters we did just this, and in candlelight too because the mains had been hit and all the lights had gone out. At the finish of the raid the Welfare Officer said, "Well, you've acted like heroes so you'd better come home with me and have a bite of supper at my house."When we got to his house it wasn't there. It had been blown up in the raid.

NICK TANNER AND NORAH CRAWFORD'S STORY
(Veterans of wartime entertainment, they were touring in France in the days of the British Expeditionary Force before Dunkirk.)

When we were in France we worked all over the place and finally found ourselves right in the front line, beyond the Maginot Line, on the Luxembourg border. We were giving a show one night in a hut and while I was doing our act the Germans started a bombardment that blew out all the lights. Glass splintered all over the place. Shells were bursting all around us. It appeared we were right on the target spot. In spite of this and the noise we went on with the show until the military authorities themselves made us leave the place to take cover. Taking cover was even worse than giving the show. When we left the hut we had to cross quite a bit of open country before we got to the dugout. Although it was night time the flares from the bombardment and the bursting of the shells gave us plenty of light to see our way as we ran along, with intervals of crouching down and crawling. Norah lost her shoes and was soon barefoot.

After the evacuation of Dunkirk we went on a tour of the south coast to entertain the Forces and war-workers. Being a mobile show we were giving a performance in a field to some of the lads when a Nazi aeroplane – a Junkers I think – which was raiding came down very low and began machine-gunning us. One of our Spitfires went up and engaged him. We watched the scrap in the air and I'm sorry to say the Spitfire came down. But another Spitfire turned up and within a few minutes he'd put paid to that Nazi plane: it pancaked down into the next field to ours.

Another time we were giving a show in a seaside town further west. An air raid was going on all the time but we gave a full performance and then we got into our little van, which carried us everywhere, to drive it back to our digs. Things were pretty hot overhead and soon got hot lower down, for a German bomber dropped a sea mine which completely demolished three whole streets. We found ourselves surrounded by injured people and we realised that we had the only means of transport on the spot. We turned our little ENSA van into an ambulance, tended the wounded for the next two hours and took many of them to hospital. The rest of the night we spent there, lending a hand. Then we heard that the milkman in that district was not to be found - apparently he had been blitzed - so we finished up in the morning by delivering the milk to the crèches in the town so that the babies shouldn't go short.

FRED WILDON'S STORY
(Old-timer and concert party manager.)

We had just finished a mid-day show in a factory when the alert sounded. We were advised not to attempt to go on to another factory where we were due to perform but as we knew the audience would be waiting for us we decided to take the risk. We arrived and found that most of the audience was in shelters but there were about two or three hundred of them who considered that it was more essential to have their food than to take cover. We found them in the canteen where they greeted us with enthusiasm. I thought our concert and the noise we could make would help to drown the noise of guns overhead. I'm afraid it didn't. However the show got going and then we realised that we were the centre of the raid itself. There was no doubt about this because bombs were dropping all round us. At one moment I was singing into a microphone and the next moment the mike wasn't there – the blast hurled it about fifty yards from me, without touching or hurting me at all. Just as I was recovering from my surprise I saw that the stage was splintering all round me, and when a bullet struck the trumpet of my phonofiddle and entered the floor within two inches of my foot I realised that we were being machine-gunned from a low-flying plane. It made me think that the time had come to follow the example of the audience (who, by the way, had crawled under the tables) and take cover myself. I dived under the piano and found that my pianist was already under that piano. It was just as well that we took shelter then because at that moment the glass roof collapsed. It certainly finished the entertainment. The manager arriving from another part of the factory to see how things were going in the canteen was amazed to find that the concert had actually gone on at all. He added, "I'm afraid you won't be wanted for the midnight show!" Then one of the directors appeared on the scene and congratulated us for carrying on, because by keeping the workers in the canteen we had saved some two hundred lives as the shelter in which these particular people would otherwise have been was actually hit by a bomb and blown up. Anyway we'd finished there and the rest of the day was our own so we called in at a neighbouring anti-aircraft gun site and gave the boys a show.

GABY ROGERS' STORY
(Composer, arranger and pianist.)

My job was to organise the cabaret entertainment for the Forces and to see that they had musical arrangements. Well, having got two or three of these shows together I took one out myself. I got a company together and we had a dress rehearsal at Drury Lane Theatre. When it was over I went straight on duty as a voluntary rescue worker to stand by for the usual nightly raid. We were called out almost at once to a house which had been hit by a bomb and completely demolished. We had no sooner reached this and were starting on rescue work when another heavy bomb fell just behind us. The blast from this lifted me up bodily and shot me through a plate glass window which had escaped the blast of the first bomb. I went straight through it and was unconscious. It was some little time before I was found and then I was taken to a nearby First Aid Post where they found that a dagger-like piece of glass had gone right through my left shoulder. They performed an operation on me at once, got that glass out, strapped me up and I was able to report for work next day at Drury Lane Theatre with my left arm in a sling. My job in this particular show was to conduct the band for two hours each night and by bad luck I'm a left-handed conductor. I got through for the first two weeks, fainting every night as I came off stage, but the show went on as shows always do.

VICKI POWELL'S STORY
(Actress, dancer and singer.)

I was touring with a sing-song unit and one night we were playing at a garrison theatre somewhere in the south. We started the show during a bad raid and about half way through the bombs began to rain down all around us. One came unpleasantly near and blew up the officers mess near the theatre. Then down came the incendiaries – it seemed as if dozens dropped through the roof of the stage, and the wings and curtains began to blaze. I was in the wings and suddenly felt myself getting very hot behind. To my horror I found the back of my skirt was alight. I rushed on the stage, dropping burning bits of my frock behind me. I remember noticing the men from the front rows of the stalls already on the stage trying to fight the flames, then suddenly I realised that my hair was on fire too. Two officers seized me and buried my head in a bucket of sand while others beat out my burning clothes with their hands. They took me to the nearest First Aid Post and there I had to have three lots of stitches put into my wounds. As the local hospital was full the doctor sent me back to my digs to rest, but as most of my clothes had been burned off my back they had to wrap me up in a soldier's overcoat before they could cart me home. The very next week we were playing in a theatre up north. I looked an awful sight with what the incendiary bombs had left of my hair, and my burns were troubling me. Exactly ten days after my first experience I was just going on the stage to do my act, during a raid of course, when an oil bomb crashed down the steps leading to the stage and burst a few yards away from me. The blast knocked me flat and by the time I realised what had happened I seemed to be lying in a sea of blazing oil. Once again my clothes were on fire, but again the men came to my rescue. They dragged me out, rolled me in a curtain and put out the flames. This time my burns were even worse – I was burned all down my left side from the top of my shoulder to the heel of my foot and for a time that rather upset my stage career. Apart from trouble with my left leg and five large scars on various parts of my body which I find rather difficult to hide when I'm dancing on stage I'm all right now.

PENNISTON MILES STORY
(A musician, then 71.)

In October 1940 I was working late one night at Drury Lane Theatre on musical arrangements for some soldiers' concert parties. By the time I had finished the usual nightly raid was in full swing. Being fairly used to it by this time I walked through the barrage to my flat, which was about a mile away, to find that bombs had started fires at both ends of my street. I was tired and went to bed and despite the very heavy gun-fire I went to sleep, but not for long. I was soon awakened by a terrific crash. It was another bomb and the blast from it blew all the glass out of my windows. I thought I had better get up and, getting dressed, I went out to see exactly what had happened. A house within 30 yards of my flat been entirely demolished and the A.R.P., Ambulance Men and Fire Brigade were all busy. There was nothing I could do so I went to the nearest shelter and stayed there until five o'clock in the morning when the all clear sounded. After that I went back to bed and once again to sleep, but about two hours later a time-bomb which had been dropped during the raid went off and demolished a house three doors away from me, so I thought I might as well go down to Drury Lane and start work again. I told my little tale and some of my colleagues suggested I should sleep at Drury Lane Theatre in future, as that was regarded as one of the safest spots in London. On this very night Drury Lane itself was bombed. Six of us were sleeping in the old stalls bar which was then being used as a broadcasting studio - it is right under the pit of the theatre. Just before midnight we were awakened by a tremendous crash and to our horror we saw the nose cap of a bomb falling through the corner of the ceiling, right among us. We were covered with plaster and debris but by a miracle nobody was hurt. We discovered afterwards that the bomb had exploded at the back of the pit, having pierced the entire building. The nose cap had carried on right down into the stalls bar. It is still preserved at Drury Lane Theatre with a suitable inscription! It weighs 2.5 hundredweight. There was no more sleeping in the stalls bar that night because it had ceased to be a bar, or even a studio, and resembled a dust heap. However we got our clothes as best we could and dressed and went round to the shelter at the back of the stage to await the all clear. We were not out of our troubles yet because in the morning, somewhere about six o'clock another bomb hit the theatre. Strangely it came through the actual hole made by the first bomb. This time it was an oil bomb and it set the inside of the theatre alight. We all took a hand in fighting the flames, but the pressure of water was so low owing to the enormous number of fires in London that we could not quite get it out. However we kept it within bounds and prevented it from spreading. With the all clear the regular Fire Brigade came along and finally put it out. Then once again I got back to my musical arrangements. I'm a real cockney and it's not easy to put a cockney out.

JACK MAY'S STORY
(Comedian.)

My partner and I were playing at the South London Palace. The night before the audience had got a bit restive because they had experienced their first taste of Nazi flares, which looked very alarming, but on this particular night the Germans were dropping high explosives and incendiary bombs. When the time arrived for my wife and me to go to the theatre the raid was already very heavy and we had great difficulty to get through, because the streets were chock a block with fire engines, hose pipes and rubble. We arrived at the stage door where the manager of the theatre was waiting in a great state of agitation. When he saw us he cheered up and said 'Thank Heavens, we've only got two other acts for this evening's show.' We were late then so we dashed off to get dressed as quickly as we could, and went straight on. We went right through the act and then the other two acts went on again. The manager came over and said 'I'm sorry, Jack old boy but will you go on again as we've still only three acts. Well, Betty and I have a good repertoire so we made another appearance, giving an entirely different show. No other acts turned up so we had to go on a third time and during this I was just cracking a gag about a chicken laying an egg, and just at that moment a bomb came down behind the stage. I turned to the audience and said "I'll have that one with bacon in the morning.

Then, to my astonishment, I saw the back wall of the stage caving in and the whole thing collapsing in a heap of rubble. The theatre lights went out, but the band played on. Meanwhile we helped the stage hands to drop a black cloth over the hole in the wall. We set up a few wings to cover up the cracks so as to preserve the black-out, and then the electricians got the lights on again, so we carried on with the show. Even that wasn't the end of it. We appeared for the fourth time which should have brought the show to an end but the raid was still on and the streets all around were ablaze, so it was impossible for either us or the audience to move. We had a sing song and stayed in the theatre all night until the all clear went the next morning when we were all able to leave.

NAT ALLEN'S STORY
(Band leader, accordion and bass player.)

At the beginning of the Blitz, I was performing at a small concert in the East End when the Alert sounded. Suddenly everything seemed to happen. Bombs were crashing down all around us. The noise was terrific. Everywhere fires seemed to be shooting up. Orders came to stop the concert and make for the shelters but being a Special Constable I felt I had to get to my Headquarters in Bow Street. So I packed my accordion and set off, carrying my music stand and as I trudged along I watched the anti-aircraft shells bursting overhead and could hear the planes very clearly. After a time an old lorry came along so I got in and rode about five miles. Suddenly there was a blinding flash and a terrific roar. The road was blown up so I picked my way on. The sky was getting redder and bombs whistling down all round. Even then the Civil Defence workers spotted the accordion and shouted 'Give us a tune, mate.'

MARY BARLOW'S STORY
(Revue singer.)

I had three pretty narrow escapes. I was playing at the London Hippodrome in the Autumn of 1940 and after the show we used to invite the audiences to stay on, all night if necessary, to keep them under cover. Teddy Brown used to act as M.C, Vic Oliver was the comedian and I led the singing. Well one evening there were very few people in the theatre and at the end they all decided to risk going home through the raid. I started to walk from the Hippodrome to Charing Cross Station. On my way the raid got heavier, people crowded into the station and the bombs fell incessantly. I thought I would rather be in the open so I decided to chance another walk. When I got to Waterloo Bridge a policeman told me to go into a shelter. Eventually I got to the station to be met by an armed guard with fixed bayonets, then a bomb came whistling down. We all fell flat on our faces, then down came the bomb. Apart from shock I was unhurt.

Later I was playing in *Applesauce* at the Palladium and on my way to the theatre when the Alert went for a daylight raid. While going through Jermyn Street I heard a whistling noise and the next thing I knew I was lying on my back covered with dust and bits of brick, on the far side of the road. Somebody picked me up and asked me if I was hurt, my main concern was how I must have looked and to make myself presentable. After one of the last heavy raids on London I was playing a matinée at the Palladium and the whole cast was wondering where on earth the draught was coming from on the stage. It was not until after the show it was discovered that a parachute bomb had come through the roof and was resting on the scenery grid right over the stage.

JACK WARMAN'S STORY
(Character comedian.)

I worked in a party for ENSA, touring the provincial towns, and doing up to five shows a day. We ran into a heavy raid travelling to an Air Force Station. We all travelled together, twenty-three of us in a coach, principals and chorus girls. Pieces of shell started falling right through its roof. We gave the show that night in an Air Force hangar. All through the show loud speakers kept calling the pilots in the audience for immediate duty, we could see them getting up and going out, to go straight up and fight. My own spot was near the end of the show and I was telling a gag on the front of the platform when there was a whistle and a crash. The back of the hangar disappeared and therefore the back of the stage was wide open, so that you could see the whole Air Station. That finished the show for that night but the next night they had filled in the back of the hangar with large pieces of canvas and blankets tied up together.

Once I was playing in the East End of London, and we had a raid during the first performance. It was the fourth raid that day. I was in my dressing room and felt the whole building shake. Three bombs had dropped right at the back of the theatre. The whole of the room fell in and I flew out. I was blown right along the passage. I found the other artists and we went under the stage. Then half the stage gave way but some of us managed to scramble into the theatre vestibule which was still standing. There was a double act there, a man and a girl, both Americans. The man stayed with us in the vestibule but the girl went down into the basement of a tailor's shop next door. Five minutes later they dropped a bomb right on the shop, which disappeared completely. The girl was killed outright, with about thirty others. I got home somehow next morning, the raid had lasted eight hours.

When I was playing in Scotland, Glasgow got its first air raid. We had just finished our show and were making our way home to our digs, when bombs started dropping. We took cover under a high wall by a warehouse. Down came two high explosive bombs, the wall fell on us. Two little children sheltering there were killed, and their mother with them had serious cuts on her head and legs. The next morning my back was so painful I found I had two broken ribs.

Another raid I well remember was when I was playing at a hall in South London. I've got that experience right at my finger tips, or where my finger tips ought to be. I lost them that night. A bomb hit the hall and a falling beam caught my hand and trapped it. I got my hand out somehow, and bound the fingers up myself but eventually it was found that the tips of my fingers had to be taken off. I can still carry on as a comic and they've not blown my house up yet.

VARIETY BANDBOX

"Once again we open the *Variety Bandbox*." It was opened once a week for ten years, three and a half of those in wartime. The Americans had their own *Command Performance* and *Mail Call*. I wanted to create a British equivalent. But it needed a big place and had to be a big show.

The wartime Queensberry Club was ideal. It had been the Prince Edward Theatre, then a luxury supper place as was the London Casino. It was damaged in the Blitz, closed except to rain and wind, with a hole in the floor and a gaping roof. A group of well wishers headed by Sir Simon

Cecil Madden with US film star Ellen Drew,
at her first appeasrance as MC of the *Variety Bandbox*
programme, February 14, 1943.

Variety Bandbox, July 30 1944.
Hal Monty,resident comedian; Cecil Madden, editor of the programme;
Bertha Wilmott, singer; John Blore, British bandleader; Major Glenn
Miller; Margaret Lockwood, film star who MC'd the programme; Peter
Sinclair, aka Cock o' the North, Scottish comedian. Broadcast from
Queensbury All Services Club before a large service audience.

Marks, Mr J. Arthur Rank, Sir Adrian Dailey, and the Earl of Middleton repaired and ran it for the welfare of the Forces in London. The management included the Marquess of Queensberry and John Harding.

I proposed a Gentlemen's agreement to them. The BBC would provide a show a day, actual broadcasts, seven days a week, if the Club would provide everything else, stage staff, lighting equipment, curtains and the Service audiences. No money changed hands. Printed programmes were issued for the week and you could see side by side Australian airmen, WAC's, British Tommies, WRENS, American Sergeants, WCLAFS, Poles, Norwegians and all the other Allies.

With the help of Stephen Williams to direct I decided to call the Sunday hour-long show *Bandbox Variety*. My secretary mistyped it as *Variety Bandbox* and somehow this looked better. It was billed as 'For Men and Women of H. M. and Allied Fighting Forces.' The first was on October 11, 1941 with Geraldo, Edmundo Ros, Tessie O'Shea and Prokopieni, a Polish officer baritone. The signature tune was *I love to sing*, arranged first by bandleader John Blore, and later by Eric Winstone. It closed with *Let's Have Another One* on a song sheet.

In addition to the accompanying orchestra, I liked to have a novelty band as well. One day I felt we needed a colourful accordion band. Lew Grade had told me about Billy Reid's so I saw it and decided to book him in one Sunday. The contract concluded, I then found myself engaged in a to and fro correspondence with Billy Reid in which I tried to explain that I really wanted his accordions and on no account any more songs, as the programme was full of singers. This argument went on until we met on the Sunday for rehearsals when it flared up again. I understood he was concerned for his singer, and also it was made clear to me that her mother was ill in hospital and was hoping

Cecil Madden,
then Programme Organiser, during a broadcast of
Variety Bandbox, 1946.

to hear her daughter on the air for the first time. That singer was Dorothy Squires.

Round about then the programme was recorded as a temporary measure since there were flying bombs passing overhead and there was always a risk of wailing sirens putting a programme off the air. So it was recorded every Sunday for the next. Thus for a time we were always a programme ahead.

After endless persuasion I gave in and agreed to let Dorothy Squires sing one song with the Accordions. To my horror this turned out to be topical and semi-patriotic words set in a rising crescendo to parts of Gershwin's *Rhapsody in Blue*. I had known George well enough to know that if he had wanted words to his *Rhapsody in Blue* he would have seen to it himself with Ira, his lyric writing brother, and that this was likely to be respected by his estate now he was dead. I was told by Billy Reid that I only had to phone Chappell's and it would be alright. I knew it wouldn't but against my better judgement I let this oddity go into the recording of the programme, but as an insurance I recorded an extra five minutes music overall in case of trouble. Of course Dorothy Squires brought down the house. The service men and women loved her, she was earthy and positive, a solid personality. The applause was ecstatic, thunderous and overwhelming. But it had its sad side. Teddy Holmes of Chappell's said 'No' firmly on behalf of the Gershwin interests, threatening court action in sorrow, but no anger. There was nothing for it and after some work, we cut out the minutes of Gershwin and in went the substitute music. No one was any the wiser except poor Dorothy Squires.

This turned out to be the making of her career. She admitted it freely. The incident preyed on my mind so much I decided to do something to help her as soon as possible. I quickly booked the Reid Accordion Band again and told

Dorothy she could have a song no matter what other singers were on the bill. I also suggested she should sing 'Some of these Days" in a new arrangement. This was her moment and she grasped the opportunity with everything she had. It was a triumph and she never looked back.

Dorothy Squires was no ordinary dance band crooner. She was a real singer with punch and a style of her own, with years of hard trouping experience from dives to twice nightly variety for years. She should have emerged long before but the fates were waiting. One Sunday we needed four minutes more. I asked Billy Reid to suggest something. So he rushed up to his dressing room and on a piece of blotting paper wrote *Coming Home*, which Dorothy sang. It was exactly what the Service men overseas wanted, to come home. It sold and sold, and topped the charts of the time. Billy followed it with *The Gipsy*, a song that told a story, then *Under the Willow Tree*, *I'll Close my Eyes*, *Safe in my arms again*, *Yippy Olly Ay Ho* and *It's a pity to say Goodnight*, a great closing number.

Dorothy and Billy played as a double act at the Palladium and also appeared every fortnight in *Variety Bandbox* singing a Gershwin standard song and a new Billy Reid song. It was a great turn.

Lew Grade, who has the greatest natural flair for an artist or an act I ever met, wanted me to see the soldier comic Hal Monty, so I went out to Golders Green to catch his act. It was exactly right for its time. Originally one of the four Delfont Boys dancing team, the others being Lew and Leslie Grade and their brother Bernard Delfont, he had been in the Army and discharged, so he knew the routines of drill and could use them without being hauled into the Forces. He had stooges planted in the stalls as a Sergeant, a Captain and a Colonel and invited a real Sergeant or Captain, or Colonel in the audience to give him the words of command when he would make a fool of them very subtly and have his audience in convulsions. Woe betide the soldier who fell for his invitation. Hal Monty was always safe as he could always turn to his stooges to keep the gags moving. At once I asked him to be joint resident comedian, with Derek Roy, in *Variety Bandbox* and they alternated weekly for months on end.

Derek Roy brought in a skilful scriptwriter, Jimmy Grafton, who kept his acts topical and inventive: Hal Monty amused troops and civilians alike. Glenn Miller, who brought his Band of the AEF to appear in *Variety Bandbox*, said Hal's act was the soldier's dream: the soldier who could answer back the officers without fear of reprisals.

Glenn Miller also greatly admired Joyce Grenfell's voice, when singing straight songs. We needed big chorus ensembles to fill the vast stage and it was safest to book girls like the Arden Singers, who were factory girls, the Luton Girls Choir or ATS Girl Pipers. However there was one Service that was unlikely to be posted overseas, the Royal Army Pay Corps. Sergeant George Mitchell had organised a small Swing group with an altogether new sort of sound. This was the start of what went on to become the George Mitchell Minstrels and the highly successful Black and White Minstrel Show.

The fan mail was enjoyable to read: "I am writing on behalf of the forward mess deck of one of HM's minesweeping trawlers with regard to your grand programme which I really must say forms the highlight of our listening on board. Nearly everything on board stops except the dynamo when someone yells *Variety Bandbox* is on, washing, letter-writing and even talking stops, and the mess deck takes on such a change of atmosphere."

One idea I had was to ask a popular girl film star to be Mistress of Ceremonies. As the programme ran for nearly three years in the Club alone it featured a lot of film stars. It had the effect of surprising everyone as we never

Mistress of Ceremonies.
Leading lady, the singer Kathleen Moody,
a really beautiful girl who sang with Glenn Miller
and later married Lew Grade.

announced the names in advance. The stars were all listening in case their turn might come. Jean Simmons, Lilli Palmer, Ann Todd, Valerie Hobson and so many others all brought their own special quality. They all brought glamour, so much needed in days when nearly everyone was wearing uniform. The leading lady was the singer Kathleen Moody, a really beautiful girl who sang with Glenn Miller and later married Lew Grade and with whom I always kept in touch.

Another feature was *The Composer at the Piano*, and a hundred composers played their own music. Composers have pet tunes that never made the grades, and probably should have, and these I particularly favoured. One day an American sailor came to the stage door and modestly asked if he could come in and perhaps take part. To my surprise he was the Henry Sullivan who wrote one of the finest show opening numbers ever written, *Mona Lisa*.

The American visiting stars were always top attractions, including Ella Logan, Ellen Drew, Dean Jagger, Kim Hunter and Jane Froman, who had courageously survived a terrible ordeal in the River Tagus.

We wrapped up each edition with a service newspaper overseas, and some of the names may revive memories: The Basrah Times; General Crusader; Jambo; The North Caribbean Star; Slipstream; Teheran Daily News; Trunk Call; Victory; The Woodpecker; The Tunis Telegraph; Tripoli Times; The Rock Magazine; Boost; and Pioneer- of Diego Suarez, Madagascar.

After 3 years producing *Variety Bandbox,* when the war was over I told the BBC Chiefs I felt its job was done and it should be withdrawn as a success. It was pointed out to me that they would make the decisions. They decided to run it on to a total of ten years.

AMERICAN EAGLES

In November 1940 a group of Americans in London got together to found a club to be called the American Eagle Club in London. The premises were in Charing Cross Road and had been badly blitzed. The Club was opened with a big broadcast with Vic Oliver, Ben Lyon and Bebe Daniels, Carroll Gibbons, Claire Luce, Dorothy Dickson and Nat D. Ayer, who played his own *If You Were the Only Girl in the World* and *Oh You Beautiful Doll*. At my suggestion the BBC continued the programme weekly. It never missed a week for five whole years.

The first men interviewed were gallant young Americans who had joined the RAF. Then came the American Eagle Squadron of the RAF, and, after Pearl Harbour, the US Army Air Force. Our first helper was Mary Walsh, who later married Ernest Hemingway. The Mutual Broadcasting System asked to rebroadcast this, which it did over 170 stations, and the American Red Cross took over the Club.

I decided to seek out the then fabulous American Eagle Squadron itself, so with George Formby and his wife Beryl, we travelled in the depths of winter in bitter cold and snow to the RAF Station at Kirton in Lindsey. Squadron Leader Taylor welcomed us with Adjutant Robert Sweeny and we recorded a great concert. The Squadron chose their smallest pilot, a famous professional parachute jumper to send a message home from them all.

The interviewers were all Americans. Sergeant Dave Greger, (Cartoonist of the Saturday Evening Post and Yank), Captain Wesley Robertson USAAF (a member of the Choctaw tribe and a singer), Eugene Warner (of the American Red Cross), Virginia Cherrill (film actress, then Countess of Jersey), Captain Noel Lang, USAAF (Hollywood

General Dwight D Eisenhower,
Supreme Allied Comander
of the British and United States Expeditionary Forces, in Britain
to organise the liberation of Europe. He visited the Rainbow
Corner Club during a broadcast of American Eagle in Britain and
spoke to the men who were present. The infamous eagle
mentioned on page 000 can be seen perched next to him.

Adele Astaire (Lady Charles Cavendish)
working for the American Red Cross, Lynn Fontaine, Alfred Lunt,
Cecil Madden, Captain Ken Treadwell USAAA, assembled for a
broadcast of *American Eagle in Britain*, 1943.

hotelier), Yeoman Tom Bernard (naval editor of Stars and Stripes), Captain Gene Raymond, USAAF (film star), Captain Charles Clapp, USAAF, (author), Lieutenant Jerome Chodorov, US Army (playwright), Major Brooks Watson, Private Ed Kandel, and Corporal Kenneth Heady.

The American Army newspaper *Stars and Stripes* shared the same offices as THE TIMES where they got on famously with what they called the Rolled Umbrellas and Bowler Hats.

This great run from London to the families of the USA lasted five years. I received a letter from Edward Kelly, Executive Secretary of the Chiefs of Police in Washington DC: "It was the unanimous sense of the 51st Annual Conference Resolutions Committee that a vote of thanks be directed to you for arranging these broadcasts which contribute so much not only to the morale of our fighting men stationed in England, but also to the morale of civilians in this country."

I showed this to Bob Hope twenty years later as I always keep it on me in my pocketbook. He turned pale and hazarded that I could get drunk in every State of the Union, and the District of Columbia, without fear of arrest. However I have never put it to the test.

The American Eagle Club moved to Rainbow Corner and my main helper on the weekly broadcast there was Adele Astaire, Fred Astaire's sister and originally part of a double act with him, then Lady Charles Cavendish. Week in and week out her sense of humour often saved the day in trying conditions of flying bombs in a basement room dangerously overcrowded with GI's and actually directly under the pavement of Shaftesbury Avenue.

On March 2, 1944 General Eisenhower himself suddenly descended into our midst and spoke to the men. Some of the guests in the series were George Arliss, Alfred Lunt and Lynne Fontaine, Louise Allbritton, June Clyde,

Cecil Madden chats with Sally Elting
of the Rainbow Corner Club, from where the
American Eagle in Britain was broadcast.

Ellen Drew, Mickey Rooney, Robert Donat, Mary Brian, Major William Wyler and Gertrude Lawrence.

Maxwell Anderson presented his play *The Eve of St. Mark*, to the US Army for production in the European Theatre of Operations, and we broadcast it from the Scala Theatre, with Corporal John Sweet, who was outstanding in the role. Sweet starred again in Thornton's *Our Town* at the Playhouse Theatre. Somehow the American Forces co-opted British actress Joan Young.

On the move to Rainbow Corner I took over the M.C.-ing and production myself. The interviews were conducted by Major Ken Tredwell of the USAAF whom I leave it to a listener to describe as "especially vibrant, flexible and charming." Eventually he had to return home and I received this. "General Doolittle has asked me to thank you for the praise which you give Major Tredwell for doing effective work at Rainbow Corner Club entirely in his own time on his day off." (John S. Allard, Col. GSA Chief of Staff. HQ 8 AF).

Our great bait for the GIs and their families at home, over 3,000 miles away, was that they could say "hello" in the item called the Roving Microphone. In the warm-up I used to tell the men that it would come to about one in every ten and when this happened they had to say just two things, their name and their home town. This produced a great laugh. It was too easy. Then I said I wanted them to say their hometown first, their name second. This produced an even greater laugh. It was absurdly easy. However when the moment came and Ken Tredwell thrust the mike in front of their faces the tension was so great that many of them not only forgot where they came from but could not even remember their names.

One feature was *Purple Heart Corner* with Bebe Daniels interviewing wounded from the Normandy Front. A listener wrote, "When Bebe Daniels went into that hospital, just about everybody in the US went through with

Cecil Madden with Fred Astaire,
American Eagle in Britain, from the Rainbow Corner
American Red Cross Club in Piccadilly, 1944.

her." Ben Lyon, then a Colonel, became so enthusiastic about Bebe's item he suggested she go to US Hospitals on the Italian Front. Within hours she was flown there. That night she wandered about the forward troop positions in her usual friendly way and nearly got captured by the Italians for her pains.

When Glenn Miller arrived he offered me sections of the great American Band to be conducted by Ray McKinley. One girl singer with a civilian band fainted from the heat and was put on a stretcher in a dark storeroom like a cupboard as the broadcast went on. A drunken GI was also brought in from the street soon after, the door thrust open and he was pitched in. The girl came to in the arms of an American soldier who really believed dreams came true.

Every week we greeted a local station such as KFRD Wilkes-Barre. I grappled with names like Arkansas and obviously didn't do badly as we got this "We especially like Cecil Madden's accent. It's so different from the American voices." (Ryan, Cleveland, Ohio)

When we visited the Club as broadcasters we were always plied with peanut butter and doughnuts. On Halloween all American service units used to dunk doughnuts in competition with each other. You start with six stale doughnuts and a cup of coffee, you dunk or dip them and eat for dear life. To win you have to finish in the least time. I had to be a sport and compete so I visited the Club Chef on the quiet and found I could cunningly get served rather smaller ones than the others and piping hot, and fresh. Sadly Britain still failed to win the Donut Dunking 'Gold.'

The US War Department came out with this advice to their men:

What was funny soldier humor before is not so funny now. From time to time soldiers are used for interview purposes when they are used as mere stooges and made to appear stupid and dull when in their line of business they are far from it. Other times, the soldier's normal interest in 'girls' is emphasized and stretched to an unwholesome degree. The American soldier today is a pretty serious young man, ready to risk his life in any quarter of the globe for those he leaves behind. He is proud of his girl, proud of his country, proud of his uniform. He laughs at hardships, wisecracks at the other guy and looks for humor in every situation. We think he'd prefer it if radio reflected more of this fighting spirit to his people back home. We think his people prefer it too, for that's the way it really is.

They need not have worried. I found every GI a potential Bob Hope, wisecracking, unselfconscious and helpful.

Then the US authorities issued this excellent guide to Britain:

You will find out right away that England is a small country, smaller than North Carolina or Iowa… Keep out of arguments, you can rub a Britisher the wrong way by telling him 'We came over and won the last one.' Each nation did its share. But Britain remembers that nearly a million of her best manhood died in the last war. America lost 60,000 in action. The British don't know how to make a good cup of coffee. You don't know how to make a good cup of tea. It's an even swap. If you are invited into a British home and the hosts exhort you to 'eat up', go easy. It may be the family's rations for a whole week spread out to show their hospitality. Let this be your slogan. 'It is always impolite to criticize your hosts, it is militarily stupid to criticize your allies.'…You will have to ask for sock suspenders to get garters and for braces instead of suspenders.

We broadcast the US Army 8 Air Force show *Skirts*, the music and lyrics by two remarkable soldiers Frank Loesser and Harold Rome, with dances by Wendy Toye. This 'intimate musical in 14 scenes' was set 'somewhere in England.' Here is the title song *Skirts*, which must be something of a curiosity among Frank Loesser scores now.

Chorus:
I keep dreaming of Skirts, Skirts,
Lovely ladies in Skirts,
But the same old khaki trousers keep marching by.
I've been dreaming of Skirts, Skirts,
Through a thousand alerts.
But there is no silk or satin to greet the eye,
So if you'd like to send me something for my birthday,
And you can't decide between a cake or a pie,
Make it something in Skirts, Skirts,
That's the shortage that hurts,
As the same old Khaki trousers come marching by.

Interlude:
I don't mean a plain kilted Colonel from the Highlands
I don't mean a grass covered chieftain from the Islands
I mean something in Skirts...

Frank Loessor was to compose *Guys and Dolls*, and *Most Happy Fella*, and Harold Rome *Fanny* and *Wish You Were Here*. About the same time Irving Berlin wrote his song *My British Buddy*, which again is something of a collector's piece, together with Ivor Novello's oddity *Clear the Way to Glory*.

The Rainbow Corner Club's Art Section discovered two GI artists of outstanding promise: Sidney Chafetz and Alfred Goldman.

A listener from Redlands, California on March 6 1945 wrote:

> I think the program does more to give the Americans a friendly or right attitude towards Britain. I am imagined to be rather anti-British and there are millions like me in the US and I thought you might like to know WHY. In simple words it is because I despise the caste system. I like the British people but I hate Lords and Ladies and all titles and their attitude and mode of life. I just can't understand how the British public put up with all this clinging medievalism, living like life was a fairy story for the upper crust. I think this is the reason the American soldier feels depressed in that atmosphere and cramped. One of my Grandfathers was born near London. If this peasant Grandfather had stayed in Britain his great grandsons would have been nobodies. Because he came to America they are individuals, doing worthwhile things. I don't mean this as a slam to you. When I say your program has done so much, it is because you seem almost American.

The Royal Academy of Dramatic Art, as part of the US Army re-education programme, arranged for six US service actors to join courses with lectures from Edith Evans, Flora Robson and John Gielgud. Diana Decker, the American actress, interviewed these students and we broadcast them in a scene from Henry V.

By July we even had pickups from the American Red Cross in Berlin. To cut a five year story short the London celebrations on VE Day and VJ Day were tremendous outside the Club in Piccadilly and below in Dunkers Den.

The final *American Eagle* programme came on Sept. 9 1945.

Here is the New York *DAILY NEWS* (10.9.45) *"American Eagle* in Britain which has brought us the voices of 25,000

American Service men and woman from London closes its mikes for the last time. We shall miss it and the friendly voice of Cecil Madden." *VARIETY* of New York (12.9.45) "After beaming straight through London's Blitz and Rocket Bomb attacks for five years... as result of emceeing show Madden is better known to families in the States than he is in England, though he has been in Radio and TV 12 years. Madden producer of shoot was with it to the end and paid a gracious tribute to American talent, the Red Cross, his American audience and the American Press."

This last programme was dedicated to Abel Green of *VARIETY*, and to Arthur Schwarz, the composer of *You and the Night and the Music*, one on each coast of the USA. The two Orchestras were Geraldo's with Sally Douglas singing and the US 163rd General Hospital Band conducted by Corporal Ross Halamay. We also sped the programme to all our US Army, Navy and Air Force Censors, Liaisons and Contacts. We had given them some trying times.

Our last film star guest was Kim Hunter. The last interviewees were T5 Maurice Levine of Easton, Pennsylvania, and Lieutenant Colonel David W. Alexander, 8 Air Force, from Hot Springs, Virginia. He was wearing the DFC with cluster, the Air Medal and three Clusters, and the Croix de Guerre. He answered questions on the Ploesti Raid.

Madeleine Carroll took part from Paris with a bunch of GIs standing in the US Army & Air Forces Exposition under the Eiffel Tower. Then Phillips Carlin of the Mutual Broadcasting System spoke to us from across the Atlantic. He brought on a Mr Wells, a parent who had officially believed his son dead until months later he heard Bebe Daniels interviewing his son in our programme. Both he and his son sent us greetings in the closing stint.

VARIETY said "It was a splendid BBC service all the way through." The American Red Cross wrote "Your Title, Mr

Madden, conferred by the Forces of 'The GI's friend' has been well and truly earned."

Rainbow Corner Club closed too and the door locked for the first and last time. At the Club's opening the key was lost deliberately and a new one had to be made for the ceremony.

Brigadier General C.M. Thiele, Admiral H.K. Hewitt, Mrs Roosevelt and Mr Anthony Eden broadcast to the USA. Mr Eden said that some of the Americans had taught us and others had learned from us. If the peace of the world was to be maintained the rhythm of Anglo-American unity must not and could not again be broken.

The Club had given shelter and entertainment, to eighteen million American Service men. I believe I shook hands with them all.

SOMETHING EXTRA FOR THE BOYS

General Eisenhower had an inspired idea. As well as his D-Day invasion, that is.

It was a radio programme specially for his combined armies and for the English speaking Allied Armies (and Navies and Air Forces) of the Allied Expeditionary Force. The slogan was 'ABC American British and Canadian spells team work for Victory' and it ran from 6:00 a.m. to 11:00 pm. The proportions of presenters were to reflect the forces: 50% American, 35% British, 15% Canadian. If you add Canada to America, in voices only of course, the British said it was entirely American. The Americans said it was entirely limey.

It was geared to start on D-Day plus one. As this was a dead secret much wasted effort went into daily complete 'dry runs' but it got launched in the end. On D-Day plus one on June 7, 1944 it burst on with the statement, which also echoed over the Normandy beaches:

There is an announcement from Headquarters of the Supreme Commander, Allied Expeditionary Force. We are initiating today a radio broadcasting service for the members of the Allied Expeditionary Force. We shall call this service 'The Allied Expeditionary Forces Programme.' It is to be a service especially prepared for you, and we shall try to make it of a character suited to your needs. Its purpose is threefold: To link you with your homes, by means of news broadcasts from the United Kingdom, Canada and the United States; to give you the latest news of your own and other war fronts, and the world events; and finally, to afford you diversion and relaxation during these precious few moments of leisure from the main job now at hand. For this latter purpose, we shall bring you the best entertainment that can be summoned from our three nations. The BBC has given generously its resources and skilled personnel. The American Forces Network and the Canadian Broadcasting Corporation are working closely with the BBC, making it a truly inter-Allied effort. We shall go forward together to Victory, and on the forward road. The AEF Programme will be constantly within your reach and serving you in a manner worthy of your deeds.

There had been controversy over the name. The Allied Expeditionary Forces Programme was not enough for Sir William Haley. It was to be based within the BBC premises and he asked what the BBC got out of it? General Eisenhower in so many words said there was a war on and that should be enough. It wasn't. Haley insisted it be called "The Allied Expeditionary Forces Programme of the British Broadcasting Corporation," which with every word spoken in full and in a United States voice was quite a mouthful and took time. The American high-ups appealed to Winston Churchill, who is said to have taken a hand in the matter himself. However they all found out very firmly that the BBC was an independent body and this had to be respected. And so it was 'The AEF programme of the BBC', and it ran a whole year, a glorious year, unique in the annals of broadcasting.

A floor of Broadcasting House, which could only be described until then as a monument to respectability and stiff collars, became suddenly transformed. Pretty American girl WACs, looking like sleek air hostesses, became secretaries to all the hierarchy, leaping up and saluting every time a door opened. They were neat, charming and very cheering. American service men did most of the announcing and became familiar figures in Portland Place.

Head of the new enterprise was Maurice Gorham of the BBC, formerly Editor of the Radio Times. Next was Colonel Ed Kirby, for the US Forces. Then came Major (later Colonel) David Niven, then myself, in charge of the integrated production. David Niven had a wonderful technique at dull meetings. He was always present, always on time, and his name always minuted as being there. After about two minutes he would rise and say, "If you will excuse me, Gentlemen," then before anyone could react he was gone. The impression everyone got was that it was well known he would not be able to stay but we would be resigned to be deprived of his wise counsels.

Integrated was a great word then, and a new one. It meant that one could mount programmes with American, British and Canadian Bands, with say, an American director, a Canadian MC or any other combination desired. It was a wonderful creative time and I soon found the available resources were unlimited, if one discovered how to use them. By phoning Richard Aldrich, of the US Navy in London, the Navy Band led by Sam Donahue with Rocky

Collucio, Pianist and Dick Jones, Administrator in the Pacific could easily and swiftly be brought to the US Navy at Exeter. American sailors in white, who were really musicians, looked on me as a miracle man as they came to London - after an atoll in the Pacific where they had been led by Artie Shaw - and saw, well, Dames. *There is nothing like a Dame*, was almost a war hymn to the American Navy after the South Pacific!

USO Camp Shows would send over almost anyone requested, such as Dinah Shore, June Clyde, Marlene Dietrich, George Raft, Gertrude Lawrence. The US Army was full of bands, so was the Air Force. They all came. It was a team it would never be possible to assemble without a war to unite everyone, British artists and bands, American script writers and Canadian producers, or vice versa, all pooled, all harmonious, all enthusiastic.

American GI Corporals, who were in private life highly paid Hollywood scriptwriters, needed an outlet. A Corporal working in American Forces Network in London strolled into my office, said he had an idea for a sketch, if he could have something like Walter Rilla, the Continental actor, Broderick Crawford, the Academy Award winning actor and Marlene Dietrich. This turned out to be Vick Knight, then a Sergeant, and he wrote a great deal for individual artists, in the form of sentimental or comedy sketches.

The signature tune of the Canadian Band of the AEF was *March along, Joe Soldier*, the British Band had the SHAEF signature tune by George Melachrino. The American Band of the AEF used Glenn Miller's beautiful *Moonlight Serenade*. The Swing Sextet had *My Guy's come back* by Mel Powell. Strings with Wings had *I sustain the Wings* by Glenn Miller. The American Dance Band used Ray McKinley's *Song and Dance*, the Canadian Show played *The Time is Now*, by Fred Waring.

It was entertainment deluxe exclusively for the serving

men and women on the Continent, fighting and pushing on towards Germany. It was also unique in that the cream of all the American networks and the Canadian and British systems were all milked into one pail. As I could do the mixing, it was a joy.

Only the best shows carefully selected, no sponsors, very little speech at all, news or news headlines every hour on the hour, entertainment all the rest of the time, Bing Crosby, Bob Hope, Fred Allen, Dinah Shore, Blondie and Dagwood and all the rest, Canada's familiar shows, and the British programmes: Tommy Handley's *It's That Man Again (ITMA)*; *Navy Mixture,* and *Palace of Varieties*; my own group *Variety Bandbox,* (the British Command Performance), *Tommy Handley's Half Hour*, *Merry Go Round*, *Here's Wishing You Well Again*, *Starlight*, - to list only some of the names familiar to listeners in the UK then.

This was a chance to use our arrangement with the great Queensberry All Services Club to the full. A big show every single day. In all we brought in 149 bands. There were three house bands to schedule and what bands. The American Band of the AEF, conducted by Major Glenn Miller, some 65 strong, with arrangers like Gerry Gray, producer Paul Dudley and a fabulous new sound, even for Glenn Miller. It had 21 handpicked violinists, Mel Powell as pianist, most of Tommy Dorsey's Brass Section, Sergeant Ray McKinley on drums, Sergeant Johnny Desmond and the Crow Chiefs as singers. The Canadian Band was nearly as big, conducted by Captain Robert Farnon, with Private Joanne Dallas and Paul Carpenter as singers, Lieutenant Douglass Montgomery as Administrative Officer. The British Band of the AEF (60 strong) was conducted by RSM George Melachrino and leading the violins our old friend Eric Robinson, in uniform. There is no limit to Eric, his skill as a conductor is great, he has helped many a shaky Variety bill by his sheer experience. I have seen artists with disgraceful band parts, old, torn, sometimes nearly non-existent, full of gaps where parts have been left elsewhere on stands, some written on bits of blotting paper and old envelopes. As a producer he helped me often. I pay a sincere tribute to his versatility as a conductor, which he has plied for twenty years.

I liked Glenn Miller instantly. Modest, simple, a splendid musician and with a strange sense of fatality about him. He had brought over a vast model of the house he planned to build. One evening in the officers' mess at Bedford he showed it to me and suddenly said "Cecil, I have a sort of hunch I'll never see it." Unfortunately he was right.

When the Band arrived, Glenn Miller and his Producer Paul Dudley took a flat in Mount Royal, London. The Band was housed in a big house in Lower Sloane Street in Chelsea. Almost immediately after they got in, there were Air Raid Alerts, sirens wailing and then V1 flying bombs dropping, with buildings blown up all over the place. A number of these fell in Battersea Park, which was quite close. The Germans were trying to hit the Battersea Power Station which produced the electricity for three quarters of London in those days. There they did no harm but Chelsea was not so lucky. As this was the Band's first experience of enemy action and they were really musicians in uniform they passed a very bad night rushing downstairs into the basement in long woollen underwear clutching trumpets, saxophones and trombones.

The next day the Band protested to Glenn Miller and he protested to us for them. Within a few hours accommodation had been found for them out of London at the Co-Partners Hall in Bedford. The men were thankful to be out of London, as well they might, the building they were in - next to the Rose and Crown Public House - was bombed that night and remained a gaping hole until 1963. Bedford liked the American Band and the band liked

Major Glenn Miller, 1944.

Bedford, not only for its friendly people but because the BBC Symphony Orchestra under Sir Adrian Boult ('Boult and his Boys') was housed there. The Glenn Miller outfit contained the cream of the Symphony Orchestras of America, many from Philadelphia. In his rank of Major, Glenn Miller could ask for the ones he wanted as soon as they were called to the Colours.

The 'Queensberry' as the bandsmen called the Casino Theatre, was their studio twice a week in London. It is huge in size and could have been filled over and over again. Glenn asked for English singers and the first we supplied were Dorothy Carless and Bruce Trent. The mutes for the trumpets failed to arrive so Spam tins were used instead.

The Co-Partners Hall in Bedford, where the Band did all its rehearsing, was a bleak place but soon became a part of America. With the BBC Symphony Orchestra something of a mutual admiration society set up. When he was free Glenn Miller could be seen watching Sir Adrian Boult rehearsing. And the Glenn Miller public sessions in the Corn Exchange were full of musicians from far and wide.

The Beverley Sisters recall one of my recording sessions with Glenn Miller:"Cecil was in the control room balancing the various sections of the band, Glenn, ever the perfectionist, was darting between the band and the control room, pressing for more and yet more microphones. Poor Cecil had finally provided all the mikes that the BBC owned and still Glenn wasn't satisfied. In sheer desperation Cecil sent down to the stores for mikes that he knew he simply didn't have the resources to even plug into the system. He proceeded to position them carefully hither and thither and with his heart in his mouth they went for another take."That's much better now," said Glenn.

It was a strange sight to see a civilian queue for Fish and Chips with Glenn Miller towering among them in his draped Major's uniform. Fish and Chips in a newspaper was something that amused him very much.

In August Bing Crosby came to England under the banner of the USO Camp shows. He had once made a vow never to travel by air and in the main he travels by surface means. A ship delivered him to Scotland and he arrived at the railway Station at Glasgow in the summer of 1944 under the banner of the USO Camp Shows. A railway porter kept circling round him till he began to wonder if a button was undone. So he asked him what was up. "Bob Hope said you were a fat little man," was the answer. The girl porters wanted Bing to sing to them and they taught him Will Fyffe's great song *I belong to Glasgow*. Later Bing got Pat Kirkwood to teach him the accent. They were gaily doing it as a duet.

Bing calls me 'See-sul,' Tommy Trinder calls me 'Sissle', I suppose I call myself 'Cessel.' Bing wore the most wonderful ties then. You could see the tie coming for miles. Any attempt to move incognito in London would be frustrated by Bing's ties. There is absolutely no side about the Old Groaner. He once said "I am not a singer, I am a Diseur." His mind is so quick, woe betide anyone who tries to get a rise out of him at a microphone. The only man who dares is Bob Hope and he gets as good as he gives.

In the Band room of the Queensberry Club in London, comedian Tommy Handley ran through some dialogue we had prepared for the two of them, based on ITMA, Tommy's own comedy programme. He brought in many of the catchwords in this, which were all the funnier as every one else's lines went to Bing, Tommy keeping his own character. One 'read through' was enough for Bing. Tommy suggested a little rehearsal might be advisable. Bing was perfectly content to leave it at that. "Watch me go out there and lay the biggest egg you've seen" said Bing, but as usual his performance was perfection, his triumph complete.

His radio debut in Britain was on *Variety Bandbox*. The

Bing Crosby with Pat Kirkwood,
Variety Bandbox, 1944.

bill was Geraldo and his Concert Orchestra, Pat Kirkwood singing *My Kind of Music*, Manning Sherwin, American composer of *A Nightingale sang in Berkeley Square*, Olive Groves and Roderick Jones, the singers. Tommy Handley introduced Bing and gave him a new pipe.

A popular Music Hall gag of the time was "Praise the Lord and keep the engine running" as one of the loathsome self-propelled V1 flying bombs came past overhead. Then suddenly you heard the motor cut out, then one had ten agonising seconds in which to dive for cover. Selfishly one heaved a sigh of relief as the bomb passed over knowing it would be bound to travel on and drop on someone else. It was the luck of the Home Front and London got plenty of bad luck.

I stood on a balcony of a room at Claridge's Hotel on a Sunday with Bing, as some Flying Bombs went past looking like flying fish – his first view of this robot warfare, then we went off by car to the Queensberry Club for his first public debut on this side of the Atlantic. The crowds in the streets, despite 'alert' warnings, were immense. Even Bing, who is used to his fans, blanched knowing that mass enthusiasm can be very battering. When we got the car opposite the stage door, Bing rightly refused to get out until the American Military Police rescued us by forming a double line from the car door right inside. With the greatest difficulty we got the car door open and Broderick Crawford lead off, Bing following him, I brought up the rear. The girls screamed with joy, thrust their autograph books between the heads of the 'Snowdrops' as Bing neatly ducked all the way along with the result that the hard covers of the albums struck me like the wheels of a threshing machine, tearing the buttons off my coat.

Inside it was a song to remember, the easy naturalness of Bing's performance when he sang *San Fernando Valley*, *Long Ago and Far Away* and forgot the words of

Moonlight Becomes You' He appealed to the audience for a prompt, they obliged him. He grinned, gave the press photographers the kind of pictures they wanted, and the Tommies, WCLAFs, Wrens, GI's and Canucks the kind of time they had never experienced before. About 2,000 packed in for every normal show, and they had come to see Bing Crosby with Tommy Handley, with flying bombs going over the whole time.

After the broadcast Anne Shelton, introduced to Bing as Britain's Dinah Shore (not by me) came over and they sang a duet together. It was the fulfilment of a lifelong ambition for Anne. Anne has a tremendous sense of fun and burlesque. Joe de Rita, the American comedian, put her wise to certain standard gags so that when the questions came from Bing the answers came back pat and sharp as a needle.

It was always a pleasure to work with Anne. She was so young and I seemed so old she always used to do a mock curtsey. She did her first broadcast at 13 in *Monday Night at 8* with Ronnie Waldman, went to sing with Ambrose, who lent her to Jack Payne after which she returned to Ambrose. When Vera Lynn was sweetheart of the forces overseas in *Starlight*, we felt that any time she might go into a show and we should build up a second favourite for the boys. So Anne did a long spell of *Starlight* too, followed by *Calling Malta with Anne Shelton* and later *The Anne Shelton Show.* Malta really adopted her though her public was far wider. She sang their requests and showed her great versatility. She has great comedy gifts, but was very tied to sentimental numbers.

After the doors of the Queensberry Club had been broken down in the friendliest way, Bing was shaken but happy from his great reception, which kept up everywhere he went. We took him over to Kettner's Restaurant in Soho, where the Queensberry Club gave him a dinner distinguished by everyone making a speech, from Lord Queensberry telling his adventures in the Home Guard, to Bing's short and simple reply.

The crowds had got wind of Bing being there and congregated in the street outside, two thousand strong chanting, 'We want Bing.' It was extremely worrying for the Air Raid Precaution Wardens as V1 flying bombs were going past overhead all the time. They wanted to be friendly but they also wanted to disperse the crowds. They appealed to Bing. Bing appeared at the window and said "Good people. I'm mighty glad to be here and I want to make a little deal with you. If I sing one song will you go home where it's safer from these things." And he pointed upward.

Bing Crosby was whisked out to Bedford to record a number of songs with the Glenn Miller Band. One song was quickly arranged for Bing and the big Band, it was 'Poinciana.' This was to be broadcast in the Paris Cinema, Lower Regent Street, also a BBC studio. Glenn, not Bing, was the nervous one. He was so worried that Bing might not come in correctly he urged Bing to go through the number a few more times. With the whole complement banked up, it was a formidable sight, with a marvellous discipline as the sections rose to play. Bing was incredulous. "What, make all these boys tired? Don't worry, old friend," said Bing "I'll be all right." His timing and sureness are perfection. He is an incomparable artist and always absolutely natural.

All the time London was under constant bombardment from V1 flying bombs so conditions were very far from normal. As ever more London studios were needed, the basement of the Prince of Wales' Theatre was leased too. *The Desert Song*, in one of its many revivals, was playing on the stage and our Dance Bands caused some upset to the show. Whenever there was dialogue our bands seemed to be playing. When we were interviewing the whole stage chorus seemed to be singing.

Infuriated Cockney Riffs would be sent down in droves
by a distressed Stage Director to beg us to be quiet and vice
versa.

With GIs all over London and bombs dropping,
Sergeant Vick Knight wrote this piece which Edward G.
Robinson spoke:

"ENGLAND'S A LOT LIKE ILLINOIS"

I walked last night in Parliament Square
I saw Abe Lincoln's statue there

>Old 'Backwoods Abe' with stove pipe hat
>A long frock coat and bow cravat.

How passing strange that such as he
Should stand so close to Royalty

>A man with patches on his jeans
>Consorting here with Kings and Queens

I gazed at his face, so great and kind
And these were the thoughts that filled my mind

>Just then a moonbeam kissed his cheek
>And I heard old Abe Lincoln speak

He said 'It ever strike you, boy,
That England's a lot like Illinois?'

>I turned around with a sudden start
>A drum began to beat in my heart

For how could Lincoln be alive?
He died in eighteen sixty-five.

As dead as Adams, Tyler, Polk,
And yet, I say, Abe Lincoln spoke.

He said 'It ever strike you, boy,
That England's a lot like Illinois?'

The call sign of the service was 'Oranges and Lemons' the London song. This attracted arranger T/Sgt Gerry Gray to add to the Glenn Miller repertoire a new arrangement starring 'Peanuts' Hucko on the clarinet and Sgt. George Ockner leading the famous string section. The US Navy Band became firm favourites and once did a double session with the Glenn Miller Band, combining together in 'One O'clock Jump' a real dynamo of sound. This band also asked for British girl singers and Gloria Brent became their first guest.

The Royal Canadian Air Force joined in with their resources, the many GI bands available, Flying Yanks, Dakotas, Gremlins, as well as the British radio bands. It was exhilarating when American stars like Irene Manning or Morton Downey appeared to face the vast theatre audience in uniforms mostly unfamiliar to them, and then be accompanied by the Royal Marines Band with a Canadian Master of Ceremonies.

The song *I'll Walk Alone*, easily walked away with the popularity poll. British hits then were *Don't Say That Nobody Loves You, Journey's End, We Don't Know Where We're Going Till We're There*, and *All's Well Mademoiselle*, which the Glenn Miller Crew Chiefs also learnt as a compliment to the Composer.

The Saturday night *AEF Specials* were the big shows and a GI Sergeant Keith Jameson of Peoria, Illinois became a very popular MC, Corporal Jack Powers, seven foot Boston singer built up a big public too, singing, say an

English song, with a Canadian producer, a British name Band and the girl bagpipers of the ATS. Malene Dietrich, Dinah Shore, George Raft were just a few of the guests. They were on USO Camp Show tours and anxious to add radio contributions to their work.

Spike Jones without his City Slickers was standing by my side in the BBC Paris Cinema studio watching Bing Crosby sing with Glenn Miller's Band. He said his tour was over and the City Slickers packed to return home. I persuaded him to unpack and give just one show in London to the Forces at the Queensberry Club. I have seldom heard such laughs, their organised chaos so well timed. Before it started the drummer confidentially asked my secretary if she could provide two huge china plates, the biggest size possible. In her simplicity she borrowed these from the Queensberry Club kitchens, vast china dishes capable of holding thousands of sandwiches, under pain of immediate return after use. Imagine her horror when in the middle of their performance the drummer quietly struck these with a hammer, like a gong, smashing them to pieces with a sickly grin on his face. A memorable evening, under the *The Music Society of Lower Regent Street*, parodying the famous Basin Street series of the time.

With us too throughout was Academy Award winning actor Broderick Crawford, a favourite and a great help in sketches.

Friendliness and informality were the keynote of the day's programmes to the AEF. Starting with a prayer, it was top entertainment and news till nightfall, from 6:00 a.m. *Rise and Shine* was conducted mostly by the disc jockey trio of British AC2 Ronald Waldman, CWAC Lieutenant Charmian Sansom and Sergeant Dick Dudley. British girl announcers mixed on the rota with American and Canadian servicemen and two of the popular 'platter spinners' were Sergeant Johnny Kerr of Painesville, Ohio, with his

Marlene Dietrich,
September 17 1944, on Allied Expeditionary Forces Programe of
the BBc. She sang *Falling in Love Again,* and *See What the Boys
in the Backroom Will Have* with the AEF British Band conducted
by Major George Melachrino.

programme *Dufflebag*, and Corporal George Monaghan of Hartford, Connecticut, with his *Off the Record* programme. Their style was new and British soldiers soon acquired a knowledge of American swing bands.

On the Continent itself the team worked equally well. Whether it was the US Army Band playing in Paris, the Royal Air Force Squadronnaires in Brussels, or a real life incident within sound of the guns, everything was game for the radio bag. The varied personnel in charge included a British Naval Commander, an Engineer Major, and as producers an English Army Captain in one district, an American Lieutenant in another. Their *Combat Diary* was much listened to by the Allied troops who thirsted for war news and authentic descriptions, always, however, at tabloid length and easily heard under canteen or field listening conditions on indifferent receivers.

Vick Knight recorded combat stories in Holland, Belgium, France and Germany, besides Sgt Mickey Rooney's *Jeep Show* and Dinah Shore singing in Normandy. He told this story of Dinah. She had just given a long performance to a big crowd of GIs and was changing in her tent into her uniform with its paratrooper boots, when two American soldiers arrived, too late. They came to her tent, told her they had come a long way specially to hear her, and how about it? She changed back into her stage costume, came out and sang song after song just for these two.

Dorothy Carless had her own programme and every Sunday spoke to a GI, a Canuck or a Tommy on the Continent. The American troops got to hear our British stars, the favourite Vera Lynn, glamorous Beryl Davis, versatile Anne Shelton, Paula Green, Carole Carr and the rest.

One afternoon I was sitting in my office in the Langham Hotel on the fifth floor, an old bedroom suite with a vast white bath attached. It was during an alert with V1 bombs actually passing overhead, when the door suddenly opened and three very attractive girls, all dressed exactly alike, came in, stood in front of me and suddenly started singing. My secretary, Mrs Muriel Legge, was overcome with surprise. She went purple in the face and said "You can't allow this to happen, can you?" and I said, "Yes, we're enjoying it, listen!"

The three were sisters, daughters of a double variety act with showbusiness in their blood. They had come to know Carmen Mastren, guitarist in Glenn Miller's Band at Bedford, and he advised them to see me as their executive producer. In fact I was really the only Englishman the Band then knew.

I did not engage the girls for some time, sending them home to work and practise. Then I kept auditioning them giving them all the advice I could. I wanted them to sing fast numbers. One day they said they were ready. They also revealed they needed a good professional name. They had a list. It so happened on my desk was a letter from Greer Garson in Beverly Hills. The word Beverly on the back of the envelope looked warm, friendly and glamorous. It looked even better with an 'E.' So how about calling themselves The Beverley Sisters? This was immediately agreed upon. Joy and the Twins (Babs and Teddie) were thus rechristened in the show business world and never looked back, even their parents became Beverleys!

When they were booked for their first date they wanted some support, so they went out to the Co-Partners Hall in Bedford to find Carmen Mastren. A man came out of the gloom, and they asked him who he was. He said "My name's Miller." They told him they wanted Carmen Mastren to perform with them on their first BBC appearance, and Glenn Miller replied, "I'll do better than that, I'll give you Mel Powell." "No thanks," said the sisters, "we don't want Mel Powell, we want Carmen Mastren." They didn't know

The Beverley Sisters
in the television studio.

The Beverley Sisters,
Joy and twins, Babs and Teddie,
had made a name for themselves on the radio
when they were booked for one of the first
post-war programmes, an edition of
Cabaret Cruise in July 1946.

that Mel Powell was probably the best pianist in the world. When the actual date came, almost the whole of Glenn Miller's orchestra turned up to support them. The Beverley Sisters and I have remained great friends. I have never been able to work out which one I like the most, they are all three so charming and have gone on to all the success they have worked for and deserve, on the stage, on the air, and in TV.

Irene Kohler, the pianist, wrote to me on March 23rd, 1945: "I gave 15 recitals in 20 days to the British land forces. One of the most striking things to me was the standard of the programmes demanded. Chromatic Fantasia and Fugue, Schubert Op 142, Beethoven's Appassionata Sonata, Carnaval, Schumann. At an Anti-Aircraft site near Brussels they asked for two Beethoven sonatas. As a whole the pianos were fine but very badly tuned! I was locked out of my room at the Palace and had to share a room with a stranger since no one could open my door."

A service Pantomime called *Ali Sad Sack and the 40 Quatermasters* starred Sergeant Dick Dudley as Private Sad Sack and Squadron Leader Richard Murdoch as the Principal Boy. Private Joanne Dallas of the Canadian Army was Principal Girl and Wing Commander Kenneth Horne a visiting Air Marshal, along with Joan Young and Geraldo's Orchestra.

But tragedy was to strike the AEF Programmes. After the Liberation of Paris, the time came for Glenn Miller and the American Band of the AEF to move to the Continent. The US authorities arranged for them to go over in two Dakota aircraft. Glenn Miller should have travelled with them, but he told me he planned to go to a party, most unlike him as he hated social receptions of any sort.

Glenn Miller was packing at his hotel and I rushed over in a cab to see him and beg him not to go. "I've done my usefulness here," he said. "Be careful," I warned, "We don't want to lose you." His reply was "Well you shouldn't care, you've got 190 recordings in the bag for when I'm not here, so it really doesn't matter." I was the last civilian to see him alive. The RAF warned that conditions were bad for flying, but the Americans overruled the RAF. Glenn took off with an American Major in a two seater plane in lowering weather and was never heard of again.

Nobody knows for certain what really happened. The news was held up for a time until Christmas Eve when all the plans had been made for a link-up between us in London and Glenn Miller and the Band in Paris. It was then that the news had to be released that Glenn was still missing. People used to say that Glenn seemed to do nothing, didn't even seem to conduct, his style was so casual. The fact remains that a potential of millions of dollars vanished with him and in Paris no one could really make the Band sound the same, though the arrangers tried hard. Glenn Miller's death was a tragic loss to a world that really needed him. His lovely *Moonlight Serenade* affects me whenever I hear it. Glenn brought in a new sound, sadly he never lived to reap the benefits so many others have. He was 33.

The "AEFP of the BBC" lasted exactly a year. On July 28, 1945 it ended and the GIs were making for home.

HEADQUARTERS LAST US ARMY
APO 00001
Subject: Indoctrination for return to the United States
To: All Units. European Theater of Operations.

2a In America there are a remarkable number of beautiful young girls. These young ladies have not been liberated and many of them are gainfully employed as stenographers, sales girls, beauty operators or welders. Contrary to the current practice they should not be

Farewell AEFP, July 28, 1944.
A sad Cecil Madden is joined by Sgt Dick Dudley of Nashville Tennessee, Program Director of the American Forces Network in London, who produced many shows for the AEFP and broadcast frequently on *Rise and Shine, Dufflebag,* etc; Cecil Madden, head of the production unit of AEFP; Cpl Jack Powers of Boston, Massachussetts; Lt Doug Marshall of *Soldier and a Song,* one of the favorite Canadian announcers who took part in the daily programme, *Combat Duty.*

approached with 'How much?' A proper greeting is 'Isn't it a lovely day?' or 'Have you even been in Chicago?' Then say 'How much?'

f. Belching or passing wind in company is strictly frowned upon. If you should absent mindedly forget it, however, and belch in the presence of others, a proper remark is 'Excuse me.' DO NOT SAY 'It must be that lousy Chow we have been getting.'

g. American dinners in most cases consist of several items, each served in a separate dish. The common practice of mixing various items such as corned beef or pudding and lima beans and peaches to make it more palatable will be refrained from. In time, the separate dish system will be more enjoyable.

h. Americans have a strange taste for stimulants. The drinks in common usage on the Continent, such as under-ripe wine, alcohol, and grapefruit juice and gasoline bitters and water (commonly known in France as Cognac) are not ordinarily acceptable in civilian circles. These drinks should be served only to the those who are definitely NOT within the circle of one's friends. A suitable use for such drinks is for serving one's landlord in order to break up an undesirable lease.

j. Upon leaving a friend's home after a visit, one may find his hat is missing. Frequently it has been placed in a closet. One should turn to one's host and say 'Don't seem to have my hat. Could you help me find it?' DO NOT SAY 'Don't anybody leave this room! Some S-O-B has stolen my hat!'

k. In travelling in the US particularly in a strange city it is often necessary to spend the night. Hotels are provided for this purpose and almost everyone can give directions to the nearest hotel. Here, for a small sum, one can register and be shown a room where he can sleep for the night. The present practice of entering the nearest home, throwing the occupants into the yard, and taking over the premises will cease.

l. Whisky, a common American drink, may be offered to the soldier on special occasions. It is considered a reflection on the uniform to snatch the bottle from the hostess and drain the bottle, cork and all. All individuals will be cautioned to exercise the extreme of self-control in these circumstances.

m. In motion picture theaters the seats are provided. Helmets are not required. It is not considered good form to whistle every time a female over eight and under eighty crosses the screen. If vision is impaired by the person in the seat in front, there are plenty of other seats which can be occupied. DO NOT hit him across the back of the head and say 'Move your head, jerk, I can't see a damned thing!'

n. It is not proper to go around hitting a person of the draft age, who happens to be in civilian clothing. He might be released from the service for medical reasons. Ask for his credentials, and if he can't show any THEN go ahead and slug him.

n. Natural functions will continue. It may be necessary to frequently urinate. DO NOT walk behind the nearest tree or vehicle to accomplish this. Toilets are provided in all public buildings for this purpose.

r. Always tip your hat BEFORE striking a lady.

s. Air raids and enemy patrols are not encountered in America. Therefore it is not necessary to wear the helmet in Church or at social gatherings or to hold the weapon at the ready, loaded and cocked position when talking to civilians in the street.

t. Every American home and all hotels are equipped with bathing facilities. When it is desired to take a bath, it is NOT considered good form to find the nearest pool or stream, strip down and indulge in a bath.

This is particularly true in the heavily populated areas.

u. All individuals returning to the US will make every effort to conform to the customs and habits of the local residents, and not attempt to make new ones.

FOR THE COMMANDING GENERAL
I have left out 1, and 2b, c, d, e, i, o, and q.

No more would the Services hear "This is Corporal Saddlebags of the Allied Expeditionary Forces programme of the British Broadcasting Corporation."

THE SHOWS GO ON

Londoners went about their business as the events of the war crowded the headlines. The night raid on April 16 1941 was a nightmare. Balloons were shot down and planes were dive bombing. My mother's house was destroyed. Jermyn Street was a mass of rubble including Joan Gilbert's flat.

On April 19 the theatre list looked like this:

New Faces (Apollo), *Orchids and Onions* (Comedy), *Dear Brutas* (Globe), *No Time for Comedy* (Haymarket), *Wednesday After the War* (New), *Applesauce* (Palladium), *Nineteen Naughty One* (Prince of Wales), *Women Aren't Angels* (Strand), *Diversion No.2* (Wyndhams).

About the time our troops were evacuating Greece and Hess flew to Scotland, Chelsea Old Church was reduced to a pile of rubble. Lambeth Palace Chapel was damaged and the Archbishop said "Think of it! Seven hundred years of sacred associations blotted out in one night." A bomb went through the roof of St. Paul's Cathedral, through the floor and exploded in the crypt. Winston Churchill said "We shall defend our island, whatever the cost may be." People were cheered by the sinking of the *Bismarck*. President Roosevelt said, "Hitler must be forcibly checked now."

In June 1941 the Defence Director issued this:

CRITERION THEATRE (AND WINSTON HOTEL) A.R.P.
General Instructions:-
The following is Senior Warden: Mr Cecil Madden.
Evacuation Signal:The signal will be continued blasts
on horns. Evacuation: Staff will be marshalled into
parties and conducted either to the Paris Cinema or the
Piccadilly Tube Station.
Action by Staff: Proceed immediately to the Passage
leading to the stage door carrying the BBC Pass,
Respirator and Torch.
Air Raid Alert: Staff may, at their own risk, continue to
work in all Criterion offices.
Bugle calls would be likely to cause confusion and
must there be banned from all BBC Programmes.
(DOCD)

On August 21, 1941 Carole Raye made a hit at the
Princes Theatre in *Fun and Games*.W.A. Darlington wrote
"I defy you to take your eyes off her when she dances."
In September 1941 the theatres had what they called a
Boom in the lull. Here is the list then:
Russian Opera (Savoy), *Lyle's Cavalcade* (Aldwych),
Me and My Girl (Coliseum), *Rise Above It* (Comedy),The
Light of Heart (Globe), *No Time For Comedy*, (Haymarket),
Lady Behave (His Majesty's) *The Nutmeg Tree* (Lyric), *Chu
Chin Chow* (Palace), *Applesauce* (Palladium), Ambrose
Merry-Go-Round (Phoenix), *Blithe Spirit* (Piccadilly), *Non
Stop Varieties* (Prince of Wales), *Fun and Games* (Princes),
Ladies In Retirement (St Martins), Up and Doing (Saville),
Nuit Excitante (Stoll), *Black Varieties* (Victoria Palace),
Quiet Weekend (Wyndhams), and of course the
WINDMILL, which never ceased.
On Sunday Oct 19, 1941 it was the time of Tobruk, the

Libya stronghold defended by Imperial Forces. The War Office asked us for a special Gala programme, which we transmitted from our own Criterion Theatre. I went to see the CIGS Sir John Dill about it at the War Office. Tobruk had then held out longer than Mafeking, which held out for 186 days. General Klinecki spoke to the Polish Troops, and Sir Claud Jacob to the Indian Troops. Sir John said "By your fortitude you have won the admiration of your country, by your skill in defence and in offence you have set an example to the Army." In the big show were Arthur Askey, Tessie O'Shea and Leslie Banks.

On Nov 20, 1941 came this news. "Our second front opens. Great Empire full-scale offensive on Nazis. Navy bombards. Italians retreat and our Tanks sweep in." *DAILY EXPRESS*.

One night at 3:00 a.m. in the middle of a *Starlight* programme an enormous rat appeared at the top of a flight of steps and slowly loped its way down to the amazement of Vic Oliver playing soft music at the piano. Mercifully Sarah Churchill who was at the mike at the time had her back to it.

On Dec 8, 1941 came the Japanese attack on Pearl Harbour. "Japan declares war on Britain and the USA." (Daily Telegraph) "Japan invades Malaya, Thailand and Hong Kong." *EVENING NEWS*. On December 9 "Japs off Alaskan Coast" *EVENING STANDARD*. On Dec 10 Mr Churchill said "I have bad news for the House. HMS Prince of Wales and Repulse have been sunk." On December 12 "US declares War on Germany and Italy" *DAILY TELEGRAPH*.

In January 1942 Sir Cecil Graves and Mr Robert Foot became joint heads of the BBC. The Criterion Theatre somehow inherited a dog, Mickey, who developed a very loud bark at all bombs, blondes or bandsmen. His barking became so piercing that there was every chance of it being heard in the Pacific, the East, in Africa and North America.

The producers revolted and insisted on his removal. A member of the Canteen staff took him home to a suburb, where he only had bombs to bark at.

In February 1942, Dulcie Grey, the actress, then a member of the *Front Line Family* series asked if she could write and sing a song about Singapore, where she had lived, to broadcast to Singapore. We received this cable: "Thank you song. Please repeat. Will record." It was the last message received. "Premier announces Fall of Singapore." *DAILY TELEGRAPH*. Feb 16, 1942.

Round about March the BBC got worried at the flabby type of songs being written. They were having a drugging effect instead of making for a fighting spirit. We asked Noel Gay, who wrote ENSA's signature tune 'Let the People Sing!' but he said there was no incentive from the public. In the critical position of Burma, vocalists had to be stopped singing *On the Road to Mandalay*, *Lullaby to a Hero*, *Blue Birds over the White Cliffs of Dover*. The American music tended to live unrealistic fantasyland too, such as *Paper Doll*, and *Coming in on a Wing and a Prayer*.

March 1942 was notable for the raid on St. Nazaire and the Java Sea Epic. Then on June 12 "Britain and Russia sign 20 year pact" *DAILY TELEGRAPH*.

"BBC bans the crooners. Slushy songs to disappear' *DAILY TELEGRAPH*, July 22. The policy was: 1. "To exclude any form of anaemic or debilitated vocal performance by male singers. 2. "To exclude any insincere and overly sentimental style by woman singers. 3. To exclude numbers which are slushy in sentiment or contain innuendo considered to be offensive from the point of view of good taste and of religious or Allied susceptibilities". The Band leaders more or less agreed. The 'Slush' Committee of seven included Arthur Bliss and me. The meetings were very hilarious. Edwin Evans wrote "Don't shoot the BBC which is doing its best."

"Mr Churchill has talks in Moscow: Dramatic secret journey at Stalin's invitation." (*DAILY TELEGRAPH*, Aug 18) "Commandos back after Dieppe raid (Daily Telegraph, Aug 20). "Russians cross Volga by invisible bridges." (*DAILY TELEGRAPH*, Sept 25). George M. Cohan dies: "Actor, Dancer, Producer, Manager, Composer, Lyricist, Film personality. I rate him unique." (Charles B. Cochran). He wrote *Over There* at 64.

In our *Anzac Hour* series from the Criterion Theatre studio the producer David Manderson achieved another first for our Unit by giving out actual money in a 'cash quiz'. We called it 'Double or Quits.' It caused great heart searching at Broadcasting House and was cheap programming at £3-15-0 for a quarter of an hour item. Roy Rich was question master. Others who handed out the BBC's largesse wore such varied personalities as Will Hay and Dr Charles Hill. It was a start towards a broader outlook. I also persuaded the authorities to put the letters 'BBC' on microphones for the first time. They only agreed if a microphone was likely to appear in a photograph and insisted that they be very small.

Anzac Hour changed title to *Australian Magazine* and *New Zealand Magazine*. Then both changed to *Middle East Merry-Go-Round*. Out of this sprang three series in their own right, Charlie Chester in *Stand Easy*, Kenneth Horne and Richard Murdoch in *Much Binding in the Marsh*, and Eric Barker in *Singing on the Ooze*. These covered the three services as gaily as possible and lasted for years after.

On Nov 30 the Home Security Ministry revealed that in London more than 1,000 people were killed in each of the three biggest air raids of the Blitz. 190,000 bombs were dropped on Great Britain, 43,661 civilians were killed, 6,000 being children.

Comedian Tommy Handley was broadcasting in *ITMA*

The Theatre Under Fire,
broadcast in the BBC's Overseas Shortwave Service.
September 3, 1942. W. MacQueen Pope, the celebrated theatrical
historian and manager tells the story of the theatre from the actual
places in the bombed building to Cecil Madden, BBC Empire
Entertainments Unit. With them is Jill Allgood, a producer in the same
unit. They are standing near the wrecked stage entrance.

(It's That Man Again) every week. We wanted him to do another series especially for the Forces Overseas, so this was called *Tommy Handley's Half Hour*. He was supported by Jack Train and Dorothy Carless, both endlessly versatile. Edward G. Robinson guest starred in a memorable gangster sketch with Tommy and the company.

Having studied a lot of overseas mail I had to direct my own producers to these points as we were our own censors:

> Avoid any suggestion their girls or wives might be getting off with Americans, Poles, or Free French. Reference to leave which some men have not had for 10 years. Suggestions that people at home are having a gay time and spending a lot of money. Alarming air raid stories.

"Churchill meets Roosevelt in French North Africa" (*DAILY SKETCH*, January 21, 1943). Greer Garson, a good friend and Godmother to my daughter Mardie, won the 1942 Oscar for *Mrs Miniver*. "British Air liner shot down by Nazis. Leslie Howard among 17 lost" *DAILY TELEGRAPH*, June 3. "Mussolini resigns. King of Italy as C. in C. *DAILY TELEGRAPH*, June 26. "King Boris of Bulgaria died at his Palace in Sofia from a mysterious illness only a few days after returning from an urgent conference at Hitler's HQ" (*DAILY SKETCH*, Aug 29). Eisenhower's promise to Italians: Help in throwing out Germans" *DAILY TELEGRAPH*, September 19, "Geraldo and the whole of his Band are going to entertain Middle East Troops" *MELODY MAKER*, September 11. "Heart of Berlin paralysed" *DAILY TELEGRAPH*, November, "Teheran agreement for War and Peace. Churchill, Roosevelt and Stalin decide." *DAILY TELEGRAPH*, December 7.

I put forward a suggestion to the Director General of the BBC in November 1943 urging him to buy an option on

Greer Garson, Godmother to our daughter, Mardie.

one of the many vast bomb sites in London itself, for the return of television, to avoid a return to Alexandra Palace, so far and unhandy. It got nowhere and only came to light again when I retired in 1964. It could have saved time, energy and many millions.

Another memo of mine that fell on deaf ears at the declaration of the war, was to keep on the TV Film Unit, then just one oldish man, to film the BBC at War. We had cameras and equipment. As a result nothing visual exists of the BBC's great war story.

Suddenly the BBC decided to switch the Overseas Programmes entirely to the Forces Programmes. THE SUNDAY CHRONICLE said "Who's behind all this? BBC newcomer and strong man 42 years old, slim, silent, slit-eyed journalist W.J. Haley, behind him tall willowy Cecil Madden, dark saturnine Overseas Controller J.B. Clark, dark plum-voiced Norman Collins, General Forces Programme Manager." THE DAILY EXPRESS, February 7, said "BBC man responsible is ex-TV Producer Cecil Madden "underground showman working in a basement theatre in London. He has sent out overseas programmes for the last four years." It was not accurate but in the event brought our *Variety Bandbox* and *Merry-Go-Round* onto home air and a lot of other programmes besides, saving a lot of money in the doing.

The Germans dropped illustrated propaganda leaflets on British lines in Italy thus:

While you are away the Yanks are lease-lending your women. Their pockets full of cash and no work to do, the boys from overseas are having the time of their lives in Merry Old England and what young woman, single or married, could resist such a "handsome brute from the wide open spaces" to have dinner with, a cocktail at some night club and afterwards. Anyway so numerous have become the scandals that all England is talking about them now. Most of you are convinced the war will be over in four months. Too bad if it should hit you in the last minute.

"German rout in Crimea" (*THE TIMES*, March 1944), "5 Army free Rome" (*DAILY SKETCH*, June 5), "The Great Assault going well. Battle for the town of Caen." (*THE TIMES*, June 7) "The New Air Weapon" (*THE TIMES*, June 20) "Pilotless Planes now raid Britain." (*EVENING STANDARD*, July 6) "Flying Bomb Attacks" (*THE TIMES*, July 7).

From the BBC "Will you please see that NO gags or jokes are made in connection with flying bombs, as this is far too delicate a subject to be treated in a flippant manner."

"General de Gaulle Enters Paris. German Community yields." (*THE TIMES*, August 26),"London's 80 day ordeal. Toll of Flying Bombs. The Battle is Over." (*THE TIMES*, September 8). Then this, "V2 attack on England." (*THE TIMES*, September 9). President Roosevelt on January 6 said "1945 can be the greatest year of achievement in human history." "Victory plans drawn up in Crimea." "The Conference of Mr Churchill, President Roosevelt and Marshal Stalin held at Yalta has drawn up military plans for the final defeat of Germany." (*THE TIMES*, February 13, 1945). "We are over the Rhine." (*DAILY SKETCH*, February 13). "Television may cost you 30/- a year." (*DAILY SKETCH*, March 9). "Collapse complete." (*DAILY SKETCH*, March 29). "Death of President Roosevelt." (*THE TIMES*, April 13). "Mr Truman sworn in as President." (*THE TIMES*, April 13).

On April 25, 1945 the theatre list was strong:

Desert Rats (Adelphi), *Tomorrow the World* (Aldwych), *Sweeter and Lower* (Ambassadors), *Private Lives* (Apollo), *A Night in Venice* (Cambridge), *See How they Run* (Comedy), *Is Your Honeymoon Really Necessary?* (Duke

STARLIGHT DAYS The Memoirs of CECIL MADDEN

of Yorks), *Blithe Spirit* (Duchess), *Madame Louise* (Garrick), *While the Sun Shines* (Globe), *Hamlet* (Haymarket), *Perchance to Dream* (Hippodrome), *Irene* (His Majesty's) *Love In Idleness* (Lyric), *Sadlers Wells Ballet* (New), *Gay Rosalinda* (Palace), *Happy and Glorious* (Palladium), *Another Love Story* (Phoenix), *Appointment With Death* (Piccadilly), *Lady From Edinburgh* (Playhouse), *Strike It Again* (Prince of Wales), *Three Waltzes* (Princes), *The Wind of Heaven* (St James), *The Shop On Sly Corner* (St Martins), *Three's A Family* (Saville), *The Assasin* (Savoy), *Arsenic and Old Lace* (Strand), *Laugh Clown, Laugh* (Stoll), *No Medals* (Vaudeville), *Arthur Askey* (Victoria Palace), *Yellow Sands* (Westminster), *When Parents Sleep* (Whitehall), Leslie Henson Gaieties (Winter Garden), *The Years Between* (Wyndhams), Revuedeville (Windmill).

"London's ordeal of V2's. 2,754 killed, 6,523 injured, total of 1,050 Rockets."(THE TIMES, April 27, 1945). "Russians pouring into Berlin"(THE TIMES, April 27) Americans join Russians on Elbe" (DAILY TELEGRAPH, April 28), "Himmler includes Russia in new surrender" (DAILY SKETCH, May 1) "Hitler is dead" (DAILY SKETCH, May 2). "War in Italy ended"(Daily Sketch, May 3),"Donitz group arrested" (THE TIMES, May 24. "This is VE Day" (May 8).

May 8, 1945. "Today's Victory is one in which everyone in the BBC can feel he or she has played a part. Broadcasting is the newest of the great instruments of peace which can also be used to wage war, and at home. Overseas, and in the enemy and enemy-held countries, we have used it as well, efficiently and as vigorously as each one of us knows how. Tomorrow we must turn that same energy to the problems of peace. But today thanks."

W. J. HALEY
Director General.

"Unconquered soul of London. People's long ordeal of Bombs and Rockets."... "A Battered but cheerful Capital." (*THE TIMES*, May 12,1945). "Signing of the World Security Charter." (*THE TIMES*, June 27). "British in Berlin." (*THE TIMES*, July 5). "Lights of London go Up again" (*DAILY SKETCH*, July 16), "Mr Churchill's tour of Berlin." (*THE TIMES*, July 13) "Truman presides at Potsdam. The Big Three Marshal Stalin, Mr Churchill, President Truman." (*THE TIMES*, July 18). "Attlee Prime Minister." (*DAILY SKETCH*, July 27) "I lay down my Charge" (Mr Churchill to the People): "First Atomic Bomb hits Japan." (*THE TIMES*, August 7), "Japan Surrenders", "V.J. Day" (*DAILY SKETCH*, August 5, 1945).

"Peace has come again to the World, let us thank God for this great deliverance and his Mercy." Mr Attlee, August 15 1945.

"An Angel with a Trumpet said
Forevermore, Forevermore
The Reign of Violence is over."
LONGFELLOW

In September 1945 the Criterion Theatre was handed back to Wyndhams Theatres Ltd. It reopened with Edith Evans as Mrs Malaprop in *The Rivals*.

Cecil Madden
on the roof of the Criterion Theatre in Piccadilly,
with helmet and gas mask, October 12, 1941,
broadcasting for *Something Going on in Britain Now.*

5

PEACE

TV STRIKES AGAIN

On Friday June 7, 1946 television service resumed. Alexandra Palace Studios had survived the bombings, and the television equipment was kept in perfect condition by Pafford, an Engineer.

At the reopening the Postmaster General, the Earl of Listowel, did the honours, then Margot Fonteyn danced. David Low drew Colonel Blimp and told us how Blimp had survived the war and was watching from his bath. Then came Walt Disney's Cartoon film *Mickey's Gala Premiere*. This was the cartoon that was so rudely interrupted by the coming of war on September 1, 1939. I had always joked about restarting the television service right in the middle of the cartoon, but was overruled. This time viewers saw it all.

Eric Fawcett produced a Variety party based on Mantovani's orchestra, George More O'Ferrall produced Bernard Shaw's *The Dark Lady of the Sonnets*. The announcers were Jasmine Bligh, from the old team and two new ones, Winifred Shotter, actress from the Aldwych farces, and McDonald Hobley. In the evening came Geraldo and his orchestra, Michael Barry produced a war play, Vercors' *The Silence of the Sea*, about France under the occupation. J.F. Horrabin showed maps illustrating the progress of the war from 1939-46 and to end there was Pouishnoff at the piano.

On the Saturday came the great Victory Parade. Later viewers saw a fashion show, films, and Koringa with her new crocodiles. She lost all her former ones in Germany. Then came zoo animals, the RAF Squadronnaires Dance Band and my own production *Cabaret Cartoons*. I revived it only to help out a small staff and to get my hand in again. Beautiful Kathleen Moody made her TV debut as did the Beverley Sisters. The Windmill Girls completed a big bill. It was the last programme I ever directed.

The new head of TV programmes Maurice Gorham could not contemplate his Planner also producing programmes and said so. Denis Johnstone was appointed programme director but was unable to come in time for the reopening date, so once again it fell to me to organise the resumption, as I had for the original opening in 1936, exactly ten years earlier. I was then told to stick to the offices and not haunt the studios.

Denis came later and we agreed that he would handle the detail of the Drama policy whilst Variety and the Planning would be for me. Meanwhile I constructed a pattern of a TV week which survived for many years to come. Denis had great Irish charm and easy-going ways. Once we were both sent to represent the BBC at a meeting about raising TV Drama fees. It was overdue but there was something amusing about sending two playwrights, both on both sides of the fence. Denis wrote a lot for TV, his plays suited the medium. He resigned soon after and went to live in America. This paved the way for the coming of Cecil McGivern, then in the film industry.

The service restarted with obstacles on all sides. People were suddenly afraid of what television could do. Sports promoters, music publishers and variety circuits all suddenly imposed bans. Ivy Benson's Girls' Band and Harry Roy's were at once stopped from billed appearances. All these setbacks made headlines and in these days we had no films or recordings to fall back on and little programme money at all. The British Film industry had never allowed us to show any feature films, but they had allowed newsreels before the war, now they refused even those. The removal of all Chappell-Harms music from all specialty acts was tedious and wearing on everyone, and tended to throw performers: the substitute music was disturbing to routines when an acrobat was balancing on a finger on a bottle high up in the air.

Before the war only 'fades' had been possible between one camera and another. After the war it was possible to cut in action. No recordings had been possible till now but in November 1947 a method of filming off the TV tube was devised. It was crude but it was a beginning.

I had been very disturbed by an old actress forgetting her lines in a play and though another old actress saved her, it made me think some method could be devised for prompting in television. A child could have thought of it. It resulted in a pear shaped press button going straight to the control room by a flex, cutting off the sound only. In this way the line could be given loud and clear without the viewers hearing. Nor could anyone detect this. An example came up soon after. We took over a play and cast from a small theatre. Unfortunately one of the key actors in a small cast could not come. Someone else had to be booked. When I heard who that someone else was I said to the producer, "But he is one of the worst studiers in the business, so see you have the cut-out switch handy." He replied that his actor was ideal in appearance and manner.

After an agonising day of rehearsals with dry-ups all along patiently borne by the others in the cast, I watched at home. Next day I congratulated the producer on his choice and for getting through without a hitch. "We used your cut-out switch four times," he said.

The biggest event in 1947 was the wedding of Princess Elizabeth and Prince Philip. This gave the sale of sets a spurt. On November 5 Maurice Gorham resigned and Norman Collins succeeded him.

Richard Afton, who produced his *Rooftop Rendezvous* and other *Top Hat* series of variety shows with plumed girls coming down the staircase in Oo-La-La style, once booked a touring ice show, with a portable ice rink. This was duly laid in Studio D and the heavy generating plant hauled up from the scene dock to the studio level, a considerable height. This had put a great strain on everything and obviously upset the mechanism as it refused to function and so the ice started melting. At rehearsals the skaters began to protest as they were getting splashed by water and the studio lights had to be turned off as they were adding to the general thaw. If we were not to cancel there was nothing for it, Afton had to go off in his car buying ice from all the fish shops in Wood Green to keep the little round rink frozen, and it was none too good a surface at that.

In my eternal search for new talent I had always haunted the Windmill Theatre and on their glass stage there was always new talent. However one had always had to brace oneself for endless arguments with Vivian Van Damm who ran it dictatorially and produced the shows too. He not only insisted on credits outside, which was only right and fair, but disliked it if his discoveries became popular outside the Windmill. However show business is a series of changes and the discoverers of talent seldom enjoy anything but personal satisfaction.

Jimmy Edwards was playing his trombone in the intervals of tableaux of nudes and Harry Secombe was doing an act he called *Shaving*. He used to shave in public five times a day using a cut throat razor and real soap and probably destroying his skin at the same time. Robert Lamouret with his duck Dudule told me his secret was to wear a Gabardine dinner suit and used ice cream for his comedy shaving act where the duck covered his face and clothes with soap suds. Harry Secombe's charm, good humour and kindness are a beacon in show business. We always used to greet each other with "Real soap!' as a reminder of that old act of his.

Soon after came *The Corn Is Green* with Richard Burton and Mary Newcomb, and Eleanor Summerfield as Bessie Watty. It was directed by John Glyn-Jones.

One of Eric Fawcett's productions was the American play *The Gentle People*, set in New York's dockside. It called for a boat as the characters were two old men who used to go fishing together at night. A gangster was extorting protection money from them and when, after further provocation the gangster casts his eye on the daughter of one of them as well, the old men decide to lure him into their boat and kill him. Fawcett insisted that the boat must float, to give authentic atmosphere. Tarpaulins were laid and tons of water pumped in to the studio for a most realistic result. The boat floated all right but water seeped through the floor into the transmitter room below to the rage of the engineers.

I had seen a submarine play *Morning Departure* produced on a Sunday night by the Repertory Players. I got hold of the script and brought it to television. It was produced by Harold Clayton at Alexandra Palace with Nigel Patrick. A year later it was revived with Michael Rennie. Stoker Snipe was played by Leslie Phillips.

Royston Morley directed the whole Eugene O'Neill

The outside broadcast cameras went to the wartime fighter base, North Weald aerodrome north of London, during Battle of Britain week in September 1949. Flanked by a Mk.16 Spitfire from 1943, Richard Dimbleby talked to three Battle of Britain pilots including (r) the legendary Group Captain Douglas Bader.

Mourning Becomes Electra, with Mary Newcomb, Marjorie Mars, Mark Dignam and Basil A. Langton as the Mannons. Revived a little later Andrew Osborn played Orin Mannon and Kenneth More Captain Niles. Revived yet again Catherine Lacey was Christine Mannon with Patrick Macnee as Captain Niles.

Rope had a long television history. First played by Ernest Milton revived with Elwyn Brook-Jones it had David Markham and Dirk Bogarde as Brandon and Granville. Revived again with Alan Wheatley this time Granville was Patrick Wyngarde. Andrew Osborn played *The Wandering Jew* with Leueen McGrath as Jeanne de Baudricourt.

An interesting American play I got from a Hollywood

Anna Neagle
was an occasional guest on *Television Dancing Club.*
With her in a March 1949 programme was Victor Sylvester,
who provided the music with his ballroom orchestra.

author called *Cry Havoc* caused quite a stir. With an all-women cast it was about nurses on Bataan, and was described as a female *Journey's End*. Joyce Heron, Sally Rogers, Joy Harington, Margery Pickard, Deryn Kerbey and seven other clever girls so impressed everyone it was transferred to the theatre, when Mary Kerridge joined and led the cast at short notice.

Jay Pomeroy, who was then running the Cambridge Theatre with popular Operas, offered us this theatre which we took over for "La Boheme" with Daria Bayan as Mimi, Lester Ferguson as Rudolph and Ian Wallace as Schaunard; decor by Alexandre Benois with Alberto Erede conducting. This was followed by *The Barber of Seville, Falstaff, Tosca*, and *Don Giovanni*.

Sir Seymour Hicks and Dame Irene Vanbrugh came to add to the sparkle of Congreve's *Love for Love*.

We had among us an American director Joal O'Brien who asked to do more American plays. His mother had been concerned with the start of the Provincetown Players in Eugene O'Neill's early days. I had heard of an American play by Arthur Strawn, which I retitled and somewhat rewrote, called *The Soul of Anthony Nero*. In this John Slater gave one of the finest performance of his career playing two parts: Anthony Nero and Judge Young. Stanley Maxted was remarkable as the Angel Gabriel, played realistically in an old mackintosh with a battered trumpet in his hand.

Another American play, Elmer Rice's *The Adding Machine* provided Stanley Maxted with another fine role as Mr Zero. The ubiquitous Joan Young was brilliant as Mrs Zero. Mildred Shay was exciting as Judy and Alan Tilvern who has done everything in television since, was Mr Five.

Jean Cocteau's *The Infernal Machine* made surprisingly good television with Sydney Tafler as Oedipus and George Bishop as Creon. Ian Atkins made a memorable event of his production of Laurence Housman's *Victoria Regina* with Pamela Stirling as Victoria, Geoffrey Toone as Prince Albert and Ernest Milton as Disraeli. Denis Johnston produced his own *Death at Newtownstewart* reconstructed from the records of the Ulster Assizes.

The *Inventor's Club* caught on. Philip Harben became the postwar TV Cook. Victor Silvester started teaching dancing on television. Henry Caldwell was getting into his stride as a finder of foreign acts with *Café Continent* which, basically, was just that, tables round the edge of a floor. He had unorthodox methods and argued well, that in an unorthodox situation one had to be flexible. Continental artists do not much like cheques since they move on immediately and much prefer to be paid on the spot in cash for a performance. This is what they are used to and as a result enormous sums in notes were floating around in secretaries' handbags or Caldwell's pockets, to the horror of accountants. Henry presented Josephine Baker and Maurice Chevalier, both when they were at their best. Maurice's great concern was always about his transport arrangements.

In 1948 we gaily televised *No No Nanette* with George Gee, Adele Dixon, Charles Heslop and Lois Green. Hattie Jacques was Flora. There was some query as to whether we really had any right to think we had the rights and we were never allowed to repeat it as planned, to be on the safe side.

On the subject of dramatic rights we did a very fine production of *The Scarlett*. It was three hours long, our biggest effort to date, and we'd spent an awful lot of money, so we decided to film it. We put a film camera in front of the monitor and filmed it all. It wasn't satisfactory, because of course you could see the lines, but it was something. The following morning I got a phone call from Sir Alexander Korda, who said "I understand you have enfringed my rights by making a film of the *Scarlett Pimpernell*." I assured him that no one was going to use it, it was just for the record, but he swore that his mechanical rights had been enfringed and he was ready to sue the BBC. He further said, "You will take your negative, and your positive, out into the open air in front of Television Centre and you will burn them, and you will film them being burned so that I will know that you have done it." And we did it.

Musical show highspots are what people most remembered, such a Eric Maschwitz's *Balalaika* (1948) with Carole Lynne, Dennis Bowen and Harry Welchman, and *Carissima* (1950) with Eugenie Castle, Barbara Kelly and Norm Lawrence. This one we televised again a lot later with Ginger Rogers and David Hughes. They were full scale productions using two studios. However with only one orchestra, musicians were grabbing their instruments and running between studios A and B to accompany the songs. The use of inserted film of the canals of Venice gave it much of the quality of a musical feature film.

Another Operetta produced was *Gay Rosalinda* starring Jack Buchanan. He was exhausted at the time and should never have agreed to do it at all. I feared it might have shortened his life, but the subject attracted him and as usual his personality illuminated the work. Isabel Bigley from the *Oklahoma!* Company at Drury Lane Theatre played Adele. With them were Peter Graves, Lester Ferguson and Bernard Clifton, who used ably to support the two Astaires in earlier stage days.

To expand out of the London area, television had to move up into Britain. It also had to get abroad. It did both, almost simultaneously. In 1949 the Midlands transmitter opened. In 1950 came the first programme from Calais. This paved the way for Eurovision, covering all the European countries and later for Intervision into the Iron Curtain countries. Television came to the North in 1951, Scotland in 1952, then to Wales and the West. In 1953 television arrived in the Isle of Man, 1954 the Isle of Wight. Certain other technical advances were exciting when new. 1950 saw the first aerial TV; 1953 the first broadcast from a ship at sea; 1955 the first TV from an RAF bomber; and 1956 the first TV from a submarine.

Until now if we wanted a whole show from Paris we had to bring the show to Alexandra Palace Studios. So we engaged the whole Lido Cabaret in Paris called *Confetti*. We somehow persuaded Messieurs Guérin and Fraday who ran the Lido, to drop a whole night and fly over the entire show. The organisation was splendid. The whole company, stars, girls, and speciality acts with Chaz Chase, Josette Bayde, Les Charlivels, Gillette and Richards, Les Debonnaires, Le Quatuor Ben Yost, Violons on Parade, Les Bluebell Girls, and all, finished their last very late night show in Paris in the early hours, packed up costumes and feathers and made for the airport and flew to London, props and all. Out at Alexandra Palace all day everyone rehearsed for the cameras, at night they gave their show. The basic scenery had of course been reconstructed and built in London. The big props, huge mechanical swans which moved by their own propulsion were seen to great advantage. It was a colourful, sexy and funny show. It ended and everything was set for the company to return to Paris. Then the fates took a hand and and fog descended on London. The last plane that got off to Paris carried only the motorised swans, no people. All the artists, all the acts, all the girls were left behind, lost in thick fog. Many got to the airport with great difficulty and had to be got back to London again. The phones to Paris burned with the news, the show couldn't get back to Paris and all seats at all the tables booked for the next night had to be refunded. It cost another million francs and the publicity made headlines all over the world. Money aside, in overcrowded London, to find hotel accommodation for a hundred performers, all to be housed according to their station on the bills was a huge task, executed in thick fog, making all movement dangerous. This fell to Imlay Watts, who was used to such mad situations. Certain acrobats hated other acrobats and would not be housed in the same hotel, fog, or no fog. The Bluebell Girls, mostly English, were much easier to handle. They were all put in somewhere. Eventually they were all got off back to Paris by train and boat, but another day later. Everyone heaved a sigh of relief.

Being gluttons for punishment, on Bastille Day we brought over another all French star bill to Alexandra Palace. Led by film actress Annabella, there came George Ulmer, the comedian, Yvette Chauvire, the Ballerina, Les Fratellinis, the Clowns, and the Ballet Avila, to do their popular Can-Can. Why was the Can-Can so successful in the great days of the Moulin Rouge? The music is wild but it seems that when the Police were not looking for trouble the girls wore none of these picturesque white underclothes in the Lautrec posters. A summer revue at the Folies Bergères in the early 1900s was "Sans Culottes Mesdames!" With this splendid company came Ande Luguet and Francois Porier, the French stage stars, in the tea cup scene from Sartre's *Les Main Sales*. When produced in television in English in 1949 it was called *Crime Passionel* with André Morell and Michael Gough playing these parts. It was done again later by Bernard Leo and David McCallum.

There is a thrill about great talent. One day we had together in our studios Benjamino Gigli, the great tenor, Rosario and Antonio, the Spanish dancers who are cousins, the entire company of the Comédie Française in *Othello*, besides the two Hulberts. Gigli told me he had in his repertoire sixty-three Operas, many in several languages.

One day there arrived on my desk the script of a play apparently from no one. It had no covers, was drenched in tea stains and grease and was in such a mess, it actually smelled. One's only instinct was to fling it far out of the window. My room then was on the 5th floor at the top of the tower. These loose pages had a title somewhere inside: *The Happiest Days of Your Life*. I sent it in an envelope to producer Stephen Harrison. He sent it back smartly with a note saying it was too long, so quickly that I was certain he could not have read it at all. So to call his bluff I asked him if he wanted a date reserved for it at a short length. He at once asked for it back. I was thankful to get rid of the script.

After much to-ing and fro-ing it was indeed scheduled. And Harrison produced the farce starring Hermione Baddeley, in a week which had another unproduced and therefore new play, biblical at that and therefore some contrast, *The Little Dry Thorn*. This could be called a critics' piece. And so it was. *The Happiest Days of Your Life*, the school farce about a mix-up in billeting two schools in wartime, a boys' and a girls' school in the same building, caused no comment, the serious play was hailed by the critics as a masterpiece. So much so that shortly after it was presented at the Lyric Theatre, Hammersmith, where it pleased a second lot of critics again, and expired instantly.

However there is a sequel. I felt the potential in the *Happiest Days*, so I wrote to my old friend Harry Dubens, who had been impresario of the *Sweet and Low* revues, suggesting he should think of staging it. He thanked me profusely but I fear he forgot it. Next John Dighton, the author, thanked me for trying on his behalf. Anyway nothing happened. Some months later one of the actors in the television production took the play to the Repertory Players, the Sunday play producing organisation. It was an electrifying night and a great success. As a result it was bought by the Tennent firm and the rest is history. They changed the cast again and it ran for two years in London

George Cole (left) and Alastair Sim
appeared in January 1949 in The anatomist, a play about
the Edinburgh body snatchers, burke and Hare.

and elsewhere and was also made into a film.

Leslie Banks and Daphne Arthur played *Jenny Villiers*. George Hayes played *An Inspector Calls*, Valerie Taylor and Clement McCallin *The Long Mirror*, all Priestley plays.

Chekhov's *The Seagull* was played by Luise Rainer as Nina, Tatiana Lieven as Masha and Jeanne de Casalis as Madame Arkadina. In the cast were Allan Jeayes, Geoffrey Keen, Michael Rose and Michael Hordern.

Jack Hulbert and Bobby Howes brought their Saville

Harry Secombe had yet to achieve national recognition as
a Goon when he sang in *Rooftop Rendezvous* in November 1948.
A rival to *Café Continental* it included Jack Jackson
and the Rendezvous Orchestra.

Theatre Revue, *Here Come the Boys*. Next came the
Hulbert Follies, Cicely Courtneige with Thorley Walters
Under the Counter, and Leslie Henson in *Bob's Your Uncle*
with music by Noel Gay. Jean Kent was at her finest in A.P.
Herbert and Vivian Ellis' musical *Big Ben*.

In the special television performance of the Cambridge
Theatre Revue *Sauce Tartare*, there was a girl in the chorus
with exceptional looks and personality, Audrey Hepburn.
She became a popular favourite in TV revues at Alexandra

Palace. Rumour has it she went to Hollywood.

Anouilh's *Antigone* was notable for Irene Worth in the name part with George Relph as Creon. *John Keats Lived Here* had Rene Ray as Fanny Brawne and Denholm Elliott on the Sunday and Michael Warre on the Thursday. Everyone watched it twice. Pinero's *Trelawny of the Wells* was played by that grand man Bransby Williams as James Tolfer and Sheila Shand Gibbs as Rose. Bransby Williams, despite his great age, also later played Sir Henry Irving's great role in *The Bells*. He told a story of his early days playing Armand in *The Lady of the Camelias* with a stock company. He was suddenly told he would have to go on as Armand's father as the actor was drunk somewhere and had failed to arrive. He was busy changing wigs and coming on and off haunted by the moment when father and son would have to meet face to face in the great confrontation scene. Alas Bransby is no longer with us to finish the story.

Fred O'Donovan revived Dickens' *The Only Way*, originally written as a play by Lieutenant Colonel the Rev. Freeman Wills and the Rev. Canon Langbridge for Sir John Martin Harvey. Andrew Osborn was Sydney Carton, Harold Scott Doctor Manette, John Arnatt Boulainvilliers and Geoffrey Steele the Compte de Fauchet.

In Max Catto's play *Kid Flanagan*, Sidney James was Sharkey and Michael Medwin was Johnny. Sidney was also in *The Front Page*, with that great star of the original *Broadway Melody* musical film, Bessie Love.

The first TV *Alice in Wonderland* was Ursula Hanray, James Hayter was the first *Toad of Toad Hall*.

Here are a few notes of interesting casting: Andrew Cruikshank as General Burgoyne in *The Devil's Disciple*, Bernard Miles as Lickcheese in Bernard Shaw's *Widowers' Houses*, Barbara Mullen in *The Kingdom of God*, Harry Morris in *The Trial of Madeleine Smith*, Roger Livesey and

Walter Fitzgerald in *The Winslow Boy*, Luise Rainer and Robert Flemyng in *By Candlelight*.

There were changes at the top. "Controller of Television. Resignation by Mr Norman Collins. The BBC has created a new post of Director of Television. Mr George Barnes has been appointed." (*THE TIMES* Oct 14, 1950)

The Queen had paid a visit to the Alexandra Palace Studios as Princess Elizabeth with Prince Philip. She later visited Lime Grove Studios as Queen, with the Duke of Edinburgh, knighting George Barnes in my own office, which had its pictures quickly removed and was transformed into a kind of Palm Court. At the Variety programme after the ceremony some gold chairs from the Prop room had been cleaned up and placed on a dais for the Royal Party, when suddenly in the middle of an act the new Knight's chair, next to the Queen's, collapsed right to the ground. The Queen looked rather apprehensive in case woodworm had got into hers too.

FOR THE CHILDREN

In 1950 I was suddenly asked if I would like to start Children's Television for an hour a day, a new challenge. I was tired of planning. It was soul-destroying and one had to contribute many ideas oneself, if not so many were forthcoming, and the total programme money was still absurdly small. Besides, the journeys to Alexandra Palace and back were wearying. It was a chance to start TV at the newly acquired Lime Grove studios.

Lime Grove studios had been the scene of many famous films such as *The Wicked Lady*. Studio F had a huge tank let into the floor. The ground floor office suite had been occupied variously by Michael Balcon and Sydney Box. The Madden Unit was put on the roof, in what had been the dressing rooms.

After eight years at Alexandra Palace to see shops again and work in a relatively civilised district like Shepherd's Bush was quite a joy. Certain of us had had a slight hand in urging the BBC to acquire the studios which had been closed and were on the market. In fact they nearly became a biscuit factory.

It failed as a film studio for the very reason it might succeed as a TV studio. All film studios are on ground level. Lime Grove had studios on floors on top of each other to the roof. It raised problems of scenery haulage television did not have. Film sets are solid. Television sets are not. Often they can be created by lights alone, so that imagination plays a part.

So after pioneering Alexandra Palace Television I found myself an executive in pioneering production at Lime Grove Studios, and – by an accident which came later – at Television Centre too, which was then only an idea and not even a hole in the ground.

At that point there had been little beyond the delightful *Muffin the Mule* and I was determined to get it out of the Princess and the Pea mentality to something robust, for boys and girls to be keen on and if possible parents too. Luckily I had a fine staff and designers of taste in Laurence Broadhouse and Richard Henry. We scheduled 60 minutes a day and in September 1950 we were doing it.

One day this letter came. Who could resist an invitation from Hugh Beaumont, Managing Director of H.M. Tennent Ltd and much besides, thus, "Noel Coward would be deeply grateful if you would support him by being present in the West End Managers Audition Tent." *THE DAILY TELEGRAPH* said that, "The Managers' audition was second in popularity only to the refreshment tents." This was, of course, the Actors' Orphanage Theatrical Garden Party. The jury consisted of all the Theatre Managers in London and a very distinguished lot had been assembled. Anyone could pay 5/-

and perform anything to a captive audience. Many did. However one old lady kept coming on and reciting all the great male Shakespearean speeches, Hamlet, Othello, and some of the Kings. It seemed impossible to stop her if she paid enough. However the Managers solved it by diving out for tea, while I sat on. Suddenly two young and very pretty girls came on and spoke some poetry. They were, I found out from them, Susan Stephen and Norah Gorsen. I noted them for their looks and enterprise. They told me they were doing Louisa M. Alcott's *Little Women* at the Royal Academy of Dramatic Art, of which I was an Associate Member, and would I come to a performance? There I also found Sheila Shand Gibbs and Jane Hardie. With four such delightful girls I resolved to start *Little Women* as a TV serial, directed by Pamela Brown, herself a writer of children's books. Apart from Wensley Pithey, who went on to be a popular TV Detective, the cast also included David Jacobs as Laurie and Alan Bromly as John. David Jacobs later became well known as a disc jockey and Alan Bromly was a brilliant light comedian I had first seen in Harry Hanson's repertory company, of *Up in Mabel's Room* the American farce at the Grand Theatre, Clapham Junction.

This was followed by *The Railway Children* produced by Dorothea Brooking, an actress, and *Treasure Island*, produced by Joy Harington also an actress.

On Saturdays we ran two Magazine programmes, *Telescope* produced by Jill Allgood, and *Whirligig* produced by Michael Westmore. *Telescope* was deftly compered by Cliff Michelmore. He had to interview children, and if you can do this well you can do anything. This was where he learnt his groundwork as he proved so well years later in *Tonight* which gave a new way of life to magazine programmes. Valerie Hobson ran *How to* - Kitty Wilson taught cookery to children, Elizabeth Cruft showed puppies, Lionel Marsland Gander demonstrated chess

Cliff Michelmore
was involved in a number of television programmes
in the early 50s including *Telescope* for children.
With him in May 1951 was Elizabeth Cruft, great
granddaughter of the dog-show founder in an item
Your Puppy.

Muffin the Mule
was the first television character to become a national
children's favourite. With Annette Mills and the puppetry, generally,
of Ann Hogarth, Muffin first appeared in October 1946.

Valerie Hobson
had appeared in a number of films and on the stage when she
became a presenter of *Telescope*. With her in a December 1950 edition
were 'Timothy Telescope' and 'Cactus the Camel'.

problems, Doris Langley Moore explained old silver and costume, Hugh Gee made a model theatre, there was 'Timothy Telescope' a puppet, a child musician, children from other countries, Francis Coudrill's cowboy puppet 'Hank'. There were request items and a Competition every week. We were overwhelmed by the response. Whirligig had Humphrey Lestocq and 'Mr Turnip.' There were *Men of Action* and *The Junior Wranglers* produced by John Irwin.

Our child announcer Jennifer Gay got chicken pox. It so happened at lunch at Denham Film Studios at the next table was a child of 12 in pigtails sitting with her father. I asked who she was and the American Director Henry Koster said, 'She is the best child actress I've ever known.' The stars of the film she was making were James Stewart and Marlene Dietrich. The child was Janette Scott and I booked her at once as Announcer for Childrens' Television. She made many new friends, was stopped in the street and soon had nation-wide publicity. Her mother was the well known actress Thora Hird.

Among my film purchases the best was *Renfrew of the Mounties*. Set in Canadian scenery it had an amusing basic idea. Renfrew was a Sergeant and his sidekick a Corporal. In his assessment of any situation Renfrew was invariably wrong and the advice his Corporal preferred, which was never taken, was always right. If a girl entered the story she always tricked Renfrew. Women were never to be trusted. Besides all this there was no old-fashioned nonsense about pursuits on horses. Renfrew moved in helicopters and motorized canoes. And there was good old *Hopalong Cassidy*, whiter than white versus unshaven villains in old hats on black horses.

Alan Bromly produced *The Powder Monkey* a story of Nelson. He cast Jeremy Spencer as the boy and Philip King, the playwright, as Captain Hardy in this story of Trafalgar. As money was scarce Nelson had to fall on the Quarterdeck and not on the Poop Deck. Powder monkeys were boys who carried cartridges from the magazines to the guns during action, and many got killed. Bromly's research revealed that the wheel was shattered and the Victory had to be steered by the tiller and the efforts of 40 men. There were 800 men in the Victory at the time, amazing considering the small size of the ship. Its sequel *Midshipman Barney* starred another boy actor Sean Lynch.

Richard Findlater in *PUBLIC OPINION* wrote, "A square deal for children. They now fill a quarter of the weekly viewing time and fill it very well. With their own newsreel, announcers, serials and magazines young viewers can feel and do feel they have a personal share."

By various competitions and advice we had every child keeping diaries and 250 budding playwrights a week from Frank Coven's *Write it Yourself.* Thousands of drawings poured in from the competitions.

I went to the top talent in the country and found they would all work in children's time. Robert Morley, who had refused all television so far, cooperated at once, suggesting a series *Parentcraft, or How to Handle Parents*, with himself starring, which he would write too. To play in it came William Mervyn and Janet Burnell as Parents and two clever children William Fox (now called James) and Shirley Eaton, later to star in *Goldfinger* the James Bond movie. Both have done pretty well since. Children are always hungry and these two used to eat all the property food, real food which invariably goes bad under the lights. Robert could never understand why the children kept being sick and accused us of providing bad food. It started good, went off, and should have been left strictly alone as 'props.'

Robert Morley was then appearing in the play *The Little Hut* and William Mervyn in *Ring Round the Moon*, both French plays. Robert devised for himself the part of R.

Cressington Tallboy and William Fox was Irving. Robert Morley is reported as having said, "I think I simply do not know how to be a parent." Nevertheless he is always reassuringly Robert Morley.

Just William began its lively career in television with Andrée Melly and Jill Fenson. Naomi Capon produced Macgregor Urquhart's children's play *The Little Swan* and *Sara Crewe* as a serial, and in ballet Alan Carter's choreography with *The Lillipops* and the work of Peggy van Praagh, now in Australia.

Two young writers joined the enterprise, Hazel Adair and Peter Ling. They went on to create the serial *Compact*. A child actress of promise and good looks made her debut, June Thorburn. We ran *Puck of Pook's Hill* as a serial and cast Wee Georgia Wood in this.

Not many recall the work of Talbot Baines Hood who wrote the once famous *Fifth Form at St. Dominic's* and *Tom, Dick and Harry*. John Fitzgerald discovered a pamphlet Baines wrote 60 years earlier for the Religious Tract Society called *A Night with Crowned Heads*. It was written in the first person. A father gives his son ten shillings for winning a history prize. He spends it visiting places of interest in London, reading at Madame Tussaud's where he falls asleep, exhausted, in the Hall of Kings. He then dreams that all the people in his history paper come to life and have him arraigned on a charge of malicious libel. He protests that what he wrote was true. They didn't see it that way. King William I did not agree that he was a cruel tyrant and King John was upset at getting no credit for granting England liberties (Magna Carta and all that). The boy is saved from dreadful death at the hands of Marwood the Executioner by being woken up by an attendant. Talbot Reed included all six wives of Henry VIII and assorted historical types like Oliver Cromwell and Hereward the Wake. Because of money we had to cut out many Kings and almost all the Queens, but we saved the Empress Matilda. She tried so hard to get into the history books, with so little success, we all felt we should give her a small whiff of glory in *The Trial of Andy Fothergil*.

A delightful series of puppets, *Vegetable Village* by Rita Pope, had a run produced by John Warrington. I had always loved puppeteers, who are all charming, and as a child had my own puppet show with my own sketches. It was an introduction to handling audiences. I recommend it to any child. It helps one to lose self-consciousness, which besets so many, because you are hidden while you speak the parts in character voices, and in my case several languages too.

John of the Fair produced by Vivian Milroy was an 1812 story by Arthur Groom. This was our biggest effort with a very big cast. It was later made into a film.

One of the liveliest comedy series was the *Mick and Montmorency* show, one tall and thin, the other short and plump. Ending in slapstick and soap suds the small one became better known as Charlie Drake.

After less than a year, aged 48, I was told I would be replaced by Freda Lingstrom, then 58, Assistant Head of School Broadcasts, and I would be transferred to other work. It caused quite a stir in the Press.

I had planned *The Odyssey* in detail as a serial and many other ideas which were never done. I only mention this to explain why I did not go on with the childrens programming. It was a great sadness to leave it.

SURPRISES

On July 5, 1951 I was appointed Assistant to the Controller of TV Programmes, who was Cecil McGivern. It was politely called being 'kicked upstairs.'

The DAILY EXPRESS (July 7) was pleasant enough to say, "Madden gets job as Mr Ideas." On being asked how he got the ideas for his plays Bernard Shaw was reported as saying "I am full of ideas, but I have been keeping them out of my plays all my life." George Campey on July 23rd in the *EVENING STANDARD* said "Mr Talent. The man from Mogador has a new job - to freshen British TV. What are his chances? Madden has the reputation for not being satisfied and he will work his producers keenly. He will admit he is not the best loved man at the BBC and nobody would expect him to be. He has often been in conflict with his bosses and the bosses have sometimes been out of patience with him. But he will defend his staff to the death and they, in their turn have acquired an admiration for his talents."

A Cairo newspaper wrote "Madden is Controller of the BBC." On the Savoy Hotel bookstall I had once seen a New York newspaper headline "Madden goes back to Sing-Sing." It gave me a turn but it was the late Owney Madden, a US citizen.

'Freshening' television was a hard mandate to live up to and McGivern was far from well. I felt that what television then lacked was topicality and trailers, so once again I asked for the opportunity to pop in surprise items at any junction of programmes. One of the first was to get Captain Carlsen who had hit the headlines and captured the world's imagination by refusing to leave his stricken ship, The Flying Enterprise, where he stayed on alone, drifting helplessly in heavy seas. Daily aerial photographs had endeared him to the public but in the end he had to give up when the ship was about to sink. To his own surprise he found himself rushed in front of the TV cameras as soon as he set foot in the South of England.

The surprise items were so contrasted they always came as a surprise. Here are a few in a sample day: Lennox Robinson, the Irish playwright of *The White Headed Boy*, Hollywood starlet Margaret O'Brien, Anthony Eden on his impressions of the USA, and Artie Shaw, star of the clarinet.

It was a kind of magazine but spread through an evening.

Informality and some of the early spirit of dash came back to the service. A newsreader had once said at the end of the war, "and a cracking good bulletin it is too!" Mary Malcolm had such a bad cold she said 'Oh dear if I go on like this I shall be able to sing bass at the Albert Hall.' Joan Gilbert complained to viewers that sinus trouble was affecting her audibility as an interviewer. It could not happen now with tighter timing, but it suited the informal fifties.

From the surprise item I felt the next step was to solo performances. The only logical thing that adequately fills a small TV screen is a face. Faces tell you most of what you want to know about people.

Emlyn Williams set a pace as Charles Dickens. He was followed by Donald Wolfit, Michael MacLiammoir, Bernard Miles, Marius Goring, Alastair Sim, Sam Wanamaker, Burl Ives, Marie Ney, Margaret Rawlings, Godfrey Tearle and Bransby Williams. John Slater and Anthony Oliver made a name for themselves as storytellers and Tony Richardson did some effective productions dramatising short stories. THE TIMES called it "The Glittering Eye: Story Telling on Television."

Another splendid solo was by Fernandel, the French comedian, who I had seen in variety in Marseilles as a young man. He had just played six parts in one film and by trying on a series of hats from the BBC wardrobe and creating laughter out of such simple material. He has never learnt English outside the cogent words 'Yes' and 'No.'

Another distinguished French visitor was Sacha Guitry, who came to London to appear in a play of his and so was coaxed into a television interview. He came with a box of hairpieces which all made him look very distinguished but all slightly and subtly different. He seemed to change moods as he tried them on. He never could quite make up

Fernandel
(second from left), the celebrated French stage and film star,
who appeared in a television programme on March 25, 1955
is seen here with (from left) Adalbert de Segonzac (interviewer),
Cecil Madden and Alan Sleath, the producer of the programme.

his mind which to choose. He confessed he was unhappy away from Paris and his fabulous picture collection. He was then married to Lena Marconi. One of my finest theatre recollections was seeing him, with his father, Lucien Guitry, and Yvonne Printemps, then his wife, in his own play a skit on the Ruy Blas type of costume piece with a very amusing backstage scene signing receipts and duelling at the same time. He illuminated the Paris boulevard theatre with his wit, gaiety and output for so many years.

The best woman interviewer at this time was Jeanne Heal and one of her most interesting subjects was Maria Callas.

Baron, the photographer, deserves a chapter. He had a television personality. There were three subjects on which people spend vast sums, not reflected then in our programmes – Photography, Holiday Travel and Popular Art. Baron got everyone with a camera in his hand and brought in guests. He died suddenly and no one has taken his place.

Reginald Pound in *THE LISTENER*, Jan 3rd, 1952 said:

Television's business is not with mere shadows but with life itself. For this reason it is worth passing on word that the documentary activities of BBC Television are to be centred in a single Department, a task of organisation entrusted, one understands, to Cecil Madden, whose enthusiasm for television is balanced by temperate judgement and, one would wish to add, by good taste. Bringing pictures of events into the home as they occur, television news and factual programmes will be likely to sweep the board of all possible rivals. Cecil Madden takes on what may prove to be his heaviest responsibility in a career of effective and unassertive work in the backroom of both kinds of broadcasting. He deserves our good wishes.

When *This is Your Life* with Eamonn Andrews started in
July 1955, the BBC had reservations that its audience
would not approve of the intrusion into people's private lives.
Vera Lynn was the subject in October 1957.

It was true, I was to run documentaries as a group. Making a group of individualists into a department was a challenge. Cecil McGivern, himself a documentary producer in the war, was deeply interested, but was now ill, and Seymour de Lotbiniere was deputising for him.

Taking them separately Robert Darr specialised in social subjects like *Dangerous Drugs* and the police series *Pilgrim Street*. In one of the anonymous casts was Vincent Ball, and Bernard Hopton as 2nd Ratcatcher. Stephen McCormack ran *London Town* and *About Britain,* Miss Caryl Doncaster handled youth in "The Rising Twenties", subjects such as '*The Call Up*, *Sales Girl*, *Factory Girl* and Ted Willis *The First Job*. Duncan Ross led a strong writing team with Arthur Swinson and Anthony Steven. Gil Calder was then the 'maid of all work.' He took on all the novelty items.

1953 was full of royal events. On March 25, "Death of Queen Mary" (*THE TIMES*). June 3 "The Queen crowned at Westminster." "Historic Event in Television" (*THE TIMES*) "Television's Finest Hour" (*THE SUNDAY TIMES*, June 7). Now TV sets really sold.

On Dec 2, 1953 at lunch my colleague Robert McCall, then Deputy Director of Television casually said that if we were in Australia we would have a weekly Sports programme. I suddenly wondered why we had waited ten years for such a simple idea. The greatest ideas are always the simplest.

At once I went to Seymour de Lotbiniere's office suggesting the idea and to lay a claim to starting it. He replied on paper "I am certain there is room for a weekly Sports programme." Six days later I held a meeting with all the Departments interested and reported the result. De Lotbiniere wrote to Peter Dimmock asking him to be the central figure adding "I know you would hate the publicity." Thus *Sportsview* was born.

Bandleader Edmundo Ros
with explorer Michaela Denis, 1955.

In my quest for exciting documentaries I was lucky enough to be phoned one day by David Jones, then at RKO, to tell me that Armand and Michaela Denis the explorers and animal photographers were in London and would I like to meet them?

They made the colour films *Savage Splendour* and *Below the Sahara*, and their great sequence of a native gorilla hunt was hair raising on a big screen. They never touch a gun and the most menacing of wild animals seem almost literally to eat out of their hands, they have a rapport which is rare.

In 1954 Armand and Michaela Denis came to Lime Grove Studios and appeared in their first programme in London with their own film clips. Huge crocodiles seemed to dive straight at the camera, a rhinoceros charged and overturned their truck. They made an instant impact and became celebrities overnight. Michaela, with her pink hair, long silver fingernails, and shapely trousers, certainly added a touch of glamour to the jungle scenes. She and Armand had met when she was out on a South American expedition to Ecuador where she ran into Armand running an expedition of his own. They teamed up, first for practical reasons, then for personal ones.

I took them to Whipsnade where Michaela distinguished herself by riding the three ton rhino and handled all the snakes with gay aplomb. Armand talked to a Bengal tiger and soothed him to a standstill. The Denis's have since been all over Africa, Asia, Australia and the Americas for television, and the result has been many years of Armand and Michaela Denis *On Safari* for television. The programme is illuminated by Armand's great curiosity and intimate knowledge about everything in nature, particularly such special oddities as the okapi, the vicuna, the aardvark, or the monitor lizard.

I shall never forget a snake's raid on a bird's nest or one episode in which many buried crocodile eggs were raided and nearly all eaten. The little ones that managed to hatch out and swam into the river had many hazards still to meet so only a few ever survived at all. Personally I find crocodiles sinister and dangerous, but not Michaela, as the last hatchling struggled out, "Good luck little crocodile," she murmured. they became very good friends of mine.

From the world of animals my thoughts, on behalf of BBC television, turned to water, which to me is the most beautiful substance television cameras can look at, with its endless changing patterns of light. I sought out Hans and Lotte Hass, who swim so gracefully underwater with their cameras in front of them. We have now all shared their exploration of the Maldives coral reefs, and the Nicobar islands, a sunken mountain chain. Their story of the shark infested wreck of the Elphinstone and the Arab silver ship which was wrecked on Kendera, and how the hoard of silver returned to Mecca, are now known to ordinary people who probably cannot even swim, but can now dive under the sea without effort in their own living rooms. As Hans says, "Two thirds of our globe are covered by sea, two thirds of our globe are still unexplored."

Charles and Elsa Chauvel were pioneer Australian filmmakers. They made the first *Mutiny on the Bounty* with Errol Flynn. A later film called *Jedda* was the first feature film to be made in colour in the Australian outback. This had a tremendous fight between an aborigine in a river with a 14 foot crocodile. I saw this film and wanted to meet the Chauvels so as to show these scenes on TV screens. Ultimately they made thirteen half-hour films of Australia.

These were an introduction to the dramatic seasons from the "wet" to the "dry" and back again, simple things and simple truths which give comfort and strength. This sincerity and naturalness were the essential quality of the Chauvels.

The Tribal dances, the Aborigine rock drawings on cliffs, talking to a 90 year old aborigine who remembered the first coming of the white man with his sheep, the Picnic races, the antbed country, the vampire bats, a crocodile hunt, these are epic stuff. It appears that a crocodile's air passages do not connect with its throat, instead they travel through the snout to the back of the head, sealed off by a valve. That is why it can pull its victim under water and still keep its jaws closed.

All very different, you will agree, from life at Shepherd's Bush, London, W. 12.

A decision went forth in the BBC that on March 19 1954 the Alexandra Palace studios would be declared officially closed, having done yeoman service since 1936. It would be called *Farewell Ally Pally*, and as I was the first producer in and always imagined to be nostalgic about the old place, on top of everything else I then had on hand, topicality, documentaries, liaison with the theatre world and the film industry, I was also appointed Editor of this night. It was expected to be warm, as we were enduring a minor heatwave. In fact it started to rain, the approaches became mud, made worse by the influx of guests in large cars. It got so cold during that programme, some of which was outdoors, that it actually snowed. It was scheduled to end about 11pm with a party held in the Canteen, opposite the transmitter room. In the event, owing to the merriment, the Farewell not only overran but went on far into the next day, probably a record. And of course the studios never closed at all.

Another decree went out from on high that there were again to be afternoon television programmes, with myself in charge of the afternoon hour, but without dropping any other work. They were presumed to be for housewives and shiftworkers.

I took on the job and determined to make them

glamorous. So I found all the clever attractive girls I could: Vera McKechnie, Cherry Huggins, Pauline Tooth, Ann Valery, Elizabeth London, Ann Joliffe, Patricia Hughes, Gwen Evans, Brenda Beith, Susan Franks, Jane Hardie, Rosamund Waring, Gay McGregor, and Elizabeth Havelock. *THE SUNDAY EXPRESS* of Oct 30 called them "Cecil Madden's young ladies. Ultra pretty announcers known officially as Afternoon Hostesses." In addition there were Sylvia Peters, Nan Winton, and Peter Haigh, an experienced team.

I demanded one thing only as a condition of taking on the job, an Outside Broadcast Unit on the first day. Something striking was necessary to tell viewers about the new afternoon programming. I thought of a giant televised tea party to be given in the Scene Dock of the new Television Centre on September 26, 1955. I sent out 1,500 letters of invitation and waited. Perhaps no one would come at all? All the Producers from Lime Grove studios were dragged in to help as hosts. A dance floor was laid on the concrete. After agonies of worry on my part the first guests came. Then more and more. Car parks became jammed, all street approaches were clogged. Buses could not get through. There were queues for a mile. Nearly everyone brought a friend and 2,500 people turned up. I shook hands with everyone at the door and introduced the hostesses.

Petula Clark and the Beverley Sisters sang and there was Edmundo Ros with both his Bands. Show people met who hadn't seen one another for years. Josephine Douglas and Berkely Smith did interviews here and there. Harry Secombe danced with Sabrina, guests included Sally Ann Howes, Margaret Leighton, Hermione Gingold, Diana Docker, Terry Thomas, Yana, Stanley Baker, Freddie Mills, and Dave King to pick out a few at random.

Most of them never even got a cup of tea or a piece of seed cake but all seemed to enjoy it. I am sure it was shocking television but it hit the target. James Thomas in

Petula Clark
In 1950 at the age of 18, Petula Clark (right) became
'Woman Television Personality of the Year' In 1952 she
had her own television series *Pet's Parlour.*

In a February programme her guests were (left to right);
Joe Henderson her accompanist;
Denis Goodwin, comedian and scriptwriter;
her sister, Barbara;
Bob Monkhouse comedian and scriptwriter.

the *News Chronicle* wrote on Sept 27 "£30 of tea draws £75,000 of Stars."

The afternoon programmes were certainly different. The pretty hostesses really entertained and even gave information on subjects such as new books and clothes and food and took part in each other's programmes. The staff of afternoon programmes thought they were home and dry for a very long run. Philip Phillips in the *Daily Herald* on Nov 19 said "Cecil's big gamble comes off."

Weekly items included *Sculpture for all, Keep fit with Freddie Mills, International Cookery with the Cradocks*, Elkan Allan's *Armchair Traveller, Storyteller, Meet the Services, Fabian of the Yard, Musical Personality Parade* (Wilson, Swann, Slade), and *Film Time*. Romney Wheeler of NBC supplied us with a now long forgotten Telefilm series *The Visitor* with two sinister anonymous feet, which started and ended every episode and haunted everybody.

Afternoon programmes were able to present a two-hour spectacular in the Vanbrugh Theatre. Two schools, the Royal Academy of Dramatic Art and the Central School of Arts and Crafts combined to stage *She Stoops to Conquer*. RADA provided the actors and actresses for *The Mistakes of a Night*. Central designed the scenery and costumes, which the art students made for the drama students to wear. My daughter Mardie was then a Stage Design student at the Central School of Arts and Crafts and she made the costume for Hastings. Richard Burnham, who had walked on in a play of mine at the Birmingham Rep., and himself a Bancroft Gold Medallist, directed. Alan Sleath, a former RADA student, presented the TV side with the cameras. This was public television and the students were thus making their first professional public appearances and all got Equity fees. Of the 20 parts it is perhaps invidious to pick out Albert Finney, Roy Kinnear, Keith Baxter, and Richard Briers. The experiment was never repeated.

Cecil Madden with daughter Mardie at a film premiere, 1955.
And (below) with Benny Hill.

1955 Portrait of Mardie Madden
by Tony Armstrong Jones, later to be Lord Snowdon.

In the event, nothing mattered as Sir George Barnes needed a large lump sum to buy a package of old American films. The easiest thing to do was to axe the whole budget of afternoon time, and so it vanished overnight with all the promise along with it.

In 1955 my Surprise items had turned into *Sunday Night Interludes*. The Controller wrote to me "The Service is grateful to you for these." But there was a long way to go before the overdue reorganisation of the News in TV.

In June I created an experimental magazine which Alan Sleath directed called *Now*. So you don't have to take my word for its quality I quote Reginald Pound in the *LISTENER* on June 23:

A programme called *Now* laid hold of the doctrine that the business of television is with contemporary living. It introduced a Barrymore granddaughter because she was over here to sing; Bessie Love, a film star because she has written a book; Betsy Blair, because she is Clara in the film *Marty*, and Robert Fabian with Bruce Seton. *Now* is one more television magazine, but with its sense of immediacy, its production deftness, its smart three-dimensional captions, it might become a valuable asset to a service which is bound to be increasingly responsive to the world around us. Watching it, I thought I saw hovering faintly behind the programme the shadow of Cecil Madden. It is one of his many chores for television: we may expect to see *Now* back again. No one is more capable of steering it safely through the shoals of experiment, particularly BBC experiment. The television version of *In Town Tonight* is another side of his labours. Last Saturday he could boast of a great coup in that programme, Tyrone Power, 'Little Mo' and Hoagy Carmichael one after the other, just like that. Earlier in the week he had brought before

Eartha Kitt, cabaret singer and actress.

us the woman survivor of the recent Sahara tragedy, Barbara Duthy.

I hoped in *Now* to start a new magazine with some edge and cover the sort of ground that four years later would be called *Tonight*. But it was not to be as it fell foul of internal TV politics. The powerful Outside Broadcasts Department suddenly wanted the title *Now* for its outside visits to places. After endless memos to and fro I was made to drop the title and without this title, which was clearly mine, I refused to go on with the magazine, so *Now* died stillborn.

I felt there was a television dramatic actress latent in Eartha Kitt. Through Harry Foster I got her interested in a one act play *The Valiant* that I had once produced. We conceived the idea of reversing the sex of the main character to make it a part for a girl. Eartha Kitt came over and played it. Later she played *Mrs Patterson* too, which she had done as a stage play. Later still a third vehicle was specially written for her in which Richard Todd co-starred.

The Film Industry's sustained weekly run of its product on British TV Screens called *Picture Parade* started under my aegis in 1955 and ended nine years later, in 1964. It had Peter Haigh and Derek Bond at the helm. It seemed to fill a want and was a shop window.

There were, besides, film Profiles of Stars and Directors, such as Cecil B. de Mille, Richard Burton, Fred Zinnemann, and two by Stanley Kramer, which he boldly called 'My Successes' and 'My Failures.'

The Pinewood Story, *The Elstree Story*, *The Warner Brothers*, *Tribute to Sir Alexander Korda*, *Romulus and Remus*, and *Columbia Cavalcade* produced many attractive clips and sensational line-ups of stars in person.

Probably the most simple star of all to visit the London studios was Ingrid Bergman, the most cooperative Cary

Mr and Mrs Miller arrived early to avoid the crush of spectators.

FIRST NIGHT OF A NEW VENTURE

Authur Miller's play *A View from the Bridge* has sent the New Watergate Theatre Club off to a successful start at the Comedy Theatre. 1956

Marilyn Monroe and Athur Miller (above) were sitting directly behind us in the third row of the stalls at this.

We went to a lot of Theatre first nights and film premieres together in the 1950s. My mother was not so keen and I loved going to everything.

PHOTOS THE SKETCH OCTOBER 24, 1956

Mr Cecil Madden and Miss Mardie Madden.

Grant, the most natural Doris Day, the most straightforward William Holden, the most delightful Julie Harris.

The date of September 22, 1955 changed the face of British TV: it was the start of commercial television, with its own Independent Television Authority. Overnight it doubled the work for artists, musicians, writers, producers, directors, designers and costumiers, not forgetting the press correspondents and critics. It brought competition without sponsorship and makes dollars from exports. It was a healthy breath of fresh air. Lew Grade asked me to join them but I felt I must stay with the BBC as I had been there from the beginning.

TV really started at a Radio Show, in 1936. Twenty-one years later, in 1957, I was asked to be the host and thus run the BBC's *Celebrity Stage* at the Earls Court RIC Radio Show and I continued to do this each year until 1962. My method was to invite all the show people of stage, films, TV and Radio I know to come along and make personal appearances. And they all came. In 1961 we had colour TV studios as well with live appearances all day, interviews and performances. It showed us how much can be done with imaginative use of colour in clothes and in background design. Twelve hours a day of crowds, fans, autographs, stars, singers, celebrity personalities, bands, groups and noise. It all added up to a lot of gaiety and looked good in the hundreds of closed circuit receivers controlled from the TV cameras directed by Chris Doll in both colour and black and white.

In August 1958, five Radio Italiano producers visited the BBC Television studios to study British methods of television. Cecil Madden, BBC Assistant Controller Television Programmes, (second right), is seen discussing details of the programme with the Italians during a break in rehearsal in Studio G, Lime Grove.

BELLS WERE RINGING

One of the great freedoms of working for the BBC was that one could often originate one's own conception of work. The enterprise of the English Stage Company at the Royal Court Theatre under Chairman Neville Blond, starting with five failures, was at a low ebb. Tony Richardson's 1956 production of John Osborne's *Look Back In Anger* was in its last days. It was a new kind of play, of protest in its way, with Kenneth Haigh, Mary Ure, Alan Bates and John Welsh. I was determined to try to help it with television. The producer then responsible for outside relays thought it unsatisfactory and said it would not make good television.

In a way he was right. Cecil McGivern, then Controller of Programmes, said he could not help, but admitted my enthusiasm for causes and suggested I find a way to help myself. I got a script from the theatre and with my Secretary we could only find 15 minutes then considered suitable for a family audience, mainly the scene where the father visits his daughter in the attic where she is living.

An Outside Broadcast Unit was in fact standing by against a political emergency: I also knew that I was running a film industry programme *Picture Parade* for 45 minutes every week of film clips, star interviews and so on. So I decided to steal 20 minutes off this without telling anyone outside, to give 15 to *Look Back In Anger* and five to an introduction.

I received a furious phone call from John Osborne telling me I was presenting his play as a drama when it was really a comedy. I got rid of him by saying I would speak to Tony Richardson who had been a BBC producer and in my own group at that, doing dramatised stories. Tony Richardson was just as furious saying we were presenting his production as a comedy when of course it was really drama.

I protested that I was only trying to help my old friend Neville Blond who had appealed to us. He had said he saw no way to go on, funds were at such a low ebb. I replied that if they all wished to withdraw from what I was trying to do, no one would care at all and *Picture Parade* which was overwhelmingly popular would revert to 45 minutes. This soon put a stop to the argument and with very bad grace all decided to shut up and stop biting a hand trying to feed them.

We were taking over the theatre on the ninth day before it was officially coming off and with little time we also had to find an audience. We gave tickets wholesale to BBC secretaries, the actors got a TV fee and the author his royalty.

It was not the producer's best effort, he had no heart in it and far too much was in long shots. In the BBC marking system he estimated it would get a low rating of 43. He was right. Anything under 50% was considered disastrous. People in the audience could even be seen rising, going to the lavatory one presumes. Anyway they saw the whole play free, as was the custom for invited audiences on such television occasions.

Bells started ringing in the Box Office, unmanned at that late night hour and they continued ringing. Next morning they went on ringing and all round Sloane Square there was a queue of people, waiting to book seats. George Fearon, Press Representative of the theatre phoned me, "We don't know what hit us." Neville Blond also phoned "Cecil, thanks to you a miracle has happened. There isn't a seat to be had for the rest of the run. I've taken the Lyric Hammersmith for three weeks to take care of the overflow and then we'll bring it back."

The rest is history. Run after run and a film with Richard Burton. John Osborne completed *The Entertainer*. This was played at the Royal Court, transferred to the Palace

Theatre and to New York and also filmed. And so on, to *The Kitchen* and the rest of the Royal Court authors and directors. The newest medium came to the rescue of the oldest.

Here is what THE TIMES had to say:

The Royal Court Theatre. Originating in the minds of Lord Harewood and Mr Ronald Duncan as a plan to extend in drama what had been done for music by the English Opera Group and eclectically backed by, among others, the Arts Council and a famous department store, with Mr Neville Blond as Maecenas, the project almost foundered in its first operative year. Future historians of the arts may be puzzled to learn that the turning point was a television excerpt from *Look Back in Anger*, which fanned that play into a financial success.

Televising whole plays from theatres is no longer possible or practicable. When there were thirty thousand sets it was a talking point, but no manager could afford to broadcast his play to thirty million. So a compromise was reached to televise excerpts, never including the last act, which would be inviolate. This has worked well. Some say it is a tease, some say it is a taste. Many West End plays have flourished after showing an excerpt.

Louis Verneuil's Americanized comedy *Affairs of State* was empty before the TV visit, which I arranged with Tom Arnold. After the relay the Alexandra palace announcer got confused and announced that it had been coming from the Comedy Theatre when it was in fact the Cambridge. This meant an abject apology by the announcer soon after which planted it firmly in the minds of viewers. Everyone flocked to see it. Tom Arnold became interested in the potential of television excerpts as a shot in the arm to the theatre and before production offered his coming comedy

"Mr Kettle and Mrs Moon" opening at the Duchess Theatre. After a discouraging tryout he was afraid the BBC would let him down and cancel the plans. But of course we did not and it was yet another Priestley success.

Peter Sellers in *Brouhaha* can only be described as 'Never a dull moment.' Sellers was a brilliant impressionist in variety, and in this play no one knew what he would do next, or say, nor exactly where he would come in. He was impatient of the nightly repetition of lines, he added and improved all the time. It was a hectic theatre visit and very funny.

Lindsay Anderson's production of *Billy Liar* was at the Cambridge Theatre and we had agreed to televise an excerpt. The TV producer got alarmed at the ruggedness of the language as Billy's father seemed to use the word 'bloody' every time he opened his mouth. It was proposed to cut this word everywhere, which would have watered it down but made it acceptable for 'family viewing' and almost impossible for the actor to remember.

Kenneth Adam, then Controller of Programmes, having agreed to the decision to cut the 'bloodys' stood firm. Suddenly Emile Littler, who owned the theatre himself, declared that he could veto the relay unless the 'bloodys' were restored. Kenneth Adam agreed suddenly in a 'publish and be damned' mood. Emile Littler told me years later he was worried that children might see it in emasculated form and be taken to see the whole play and find it quite different on normal nights. Be that as it may the bloodys came over in startling style, the bookings at once jumped to over £4,000 a week and Albert Finney and Tom Courtenay between them starred in it for two years.

The Bride and the Bachelor opened to terrible press notices. I suggested to Peter Saunders that he should wait for a television visit before taking it off. He agreed, and also stipulated that he should supply the audience himself on the night. They were the best laughers I have ever heard, I believe all from Woolwich. So startled were Cicely Courtneidge, Naunton Wayne and Robertson Hare that they almost dropped all pretence of speaking lines to each other. They turned music hall fashion, and spoke the lines to the audience, who loved every moment of it. Result, the laughs echoed all over the country and from the Duchess Theatre for eighteen months more.

David Tomlinson had faith in the French farce *Boeing, Boeing* and urged me to see it at Streatham Hill. Then many tribulations beset John Gale's management, it was too near Christmas, all theatres were booked and the production had to disband. However with cast changes it was reformed and redirected by Jack Minster. It opened at London's Apollo Theatre to a poor press which at once upset sensitive BBC. The relay was billed for only a few days after the London first night, indeed it was already in print in the Radio Times, classed as unalterable only next to the good book. "Can we get out of it?" was the idea. "What have you let us in for?" were the exact words. I suggested I be sacked for incompetence the day after the relay if we could have a truce till then. Meanwhile the play was an obvious success despite the critics. Of course on the TV night the result was a sensation, the play has run for thousands of performances, and nobody mentioned it again.

Another great theatre night was with Ruth Gordon, Sam Levene and Arthur Hill in Thornton Wilder's *The Matchmaker*. Originally called 'The Merchant of Yonkers,' with music it became the fabulously successful *Hello Dolly!*

There is, ludicrously, the other side of the coin. After broadcasting from one American comedy, *Olive Ogilvy*, based on a blonde film star, I phoned the theatre fully expecting to be told business was booming. Instead I heard that some seats booked had actually been cancelled.

Following my crusade for interdependence in the Arts, from television's resumption in 1946 to my departure from the BBC in 1964 one hundred and fifty London productions were televised in excerpts.

THIS WASN'T YOUR LIFE

If you are sensitive it is always worrying to be in possession of a secret and *This is Your Life* was genuinely kept a secret from the victims. Knowing the subjects planned for coming weeks made one instinctively move out of the way when you saw one coming, for fear of giving something away.

What's My Line? which ran for 13 years in Britain, and which I supervised for the last four, had a celebrity guest every week. This was, however, naturally known to the celebrity but had to be kept a general secret so that the very astute panellists should neither hear anything nor guess who it might be and so give the game away.

One weekend it had been arranged for Anna Neagle to be the celebrity of the Sunday *What's My Line?* and also to be the subject of the Monday *This is Your Life*. The first she knew about, the second she had no inkling of, though of course her husband Herbert Wilcox was part of the plot. As luck would have it Herbert Wilcox and Anna Neagle came to lunch at Television Centre the Wednesday before to discuss an entirely different project for Anna. I had arranged the lunch and was in on the project too, a possible telefilm series.

The lunch was therefore torture for me, to behave normally and yet give nothing away as the conversation seemed inevitably to turn to how various people had reacted and behaved confronted by an audience and the cameras of *This is Your Life*. To make things worse Herbert winked at me conspiratorially.

What's my Line? with Eamonn Andrews
as chairman began in 1951. A panel of four had to guess
the occupations of a number of challengers.
Team members in a June 1992 edition were (left to right)
Marghanita Laski, Jerry Desmond, Elizabeth Allen
and Gilbert Harding.

As Anna was getting into a taxi she suddenly turned to me and said "Cecil, what shall I wear for the television, a long dress or a short one?" Knowing the involved plans to trap her for *This is Your Life*, which was not my concern, on grounds of a spurious interview yet to be proposed to her for *Picture Parade*, which was my concern, it was on the tip of my tongue to say "Why don't you wear short for the one and long for the other?" Somehow I managed not to and mumbled something like that I was sure she would look fine in whatever she chose.

On the consecutive nights her *What's My Line?* was amusing and *This is Your Life* caused her so much emotion and shock she was in tears and caused quite a sensation.

Journalists even rushed to their typewriters to ask themselves whether *This is Your Life* was fair on the victims at all.

Of all the celebrities in hundreds of *What's My Line?* programmes the one who caused most chaos in an ordered studio was Seagoon Harry Secombe, irrepressible and delightful, always ready to dress up. One of the most natural was the Hollywood film actor John Wayne.

I persuaded Walt Disney to arrive on Sunday by air about 6:00 pm for a programme at 7:30 pm and to be booked as Mr Smith to avoid anyone reporting his name on the lists of passengers. And astute panellists like Isobel Barnett, Catherine Boyle, Polly Elwes, Dawn Addams, Barbara Kelly, David Nixon or Cyril Fletcher always did their homework very well, and their guesswork with eyes masked was always very accurate. So Richard Evens, the Director, and I had to resort to a lot of ingenuity to fool them and smuggle guests into the TV Theatre by secret doors, all the more difficult when sometimes, for planning convenience, one programme was performed live followed by another recorded in quick succession to the same audience for the following Sunday. This meant two celebrities to conceal at the same time.

Apparently the Producer of *This is Your Life*, T. Leslie Jackson, who had been studio manager for my productions in the old television days at Alexandra Palace, had conceived the idea of putting me on this hot spot and had gone to great lengths to bring this about. My spy system for my many programmes had always been very good and I thought I knew everything before it happened. An awful calm seemed to have settled over everybody, this worried me as people near to me were behaving in too exemplary a fashion. My secretary and my wife were both in the know. Certainly I wasn't. Until unfortunately a cable sent by the BBC's New York office to Broadcasting House was sent *en clair* instead of in code on a Sunday, and since the word Madden was mentioned an assiduous Duty Officer received it and phoned my flat. My wife was out, I answered the phone and took down the message. So I knew!

Then everything blew up and the programme was immediately cancelled. After the newspaper stories had died down a substitute programme was put on *A Tribute to John Logie Baird*, the great television engineer. In this I did take part as a television pioneer who knew him. However if my experience did nothing else it showed the public the programme was genuine. The producer later sent me the tape recording from Greer Garson as a souvenir.

I had been 31 years in the BBC, half my life to date, on a journey from radio to TV, back to radio for the war, back to TV for the peace and so on to 1964. I had been roughly 13 years a Producer, 7 as Executive in charge of almost every Department at one time, even Music, 11 years in the corridors of persuasion as Assistant to the Controller of TV Programmes - three Controllers to be exact, Cecil McGivern, Kenneth Adam and Stuart Hood and under Seven Directors General. It meant attending something like 1,600 Programme Board Meetings, as many post mortems. When Stuart Hood resigned from the BBC in 1964 and there was no controller to assist, the end of my time was nearing too. For me it has been a unique journey, often creative, sometimes frustrating, and with ever changing scenery. Perhaps the last open question can be Whither Television? The answer is everywhere.

1979
Cecil with eldest granddaughter Jennifer aged 12.

1981
Cecil at daughter Mardie's house with her husband Kernan,
brother Edward and children Caroline and Annabel.

1982
Cecil and his daughter Mardie discussing his 80th Birthday party
which was held in his flat in Chelsea on Sunday afternoon November 28th.
Birthday cards and all his plays and papers behind.

1983
Cecil on his 81st Birthday with youngest granddaughter
Annabel and his son Edward.

Cecil Madden
with granddaughters Jennifer and Caroline and Friend
Jill Fenson, who is holding his beloved dog Charlie. 1970.

POSTSCRIPT

Below is a copy of of his Obituary
from *THE TIMES*

Mr Cecil Madden, MBE, a pioneer of television production, died on May 27. He was 84.

Cecil Charles Madden was born in Morocco on November 29, 1902, the son of a consulate official. By the time he returned to this country, to go to school at Dover College, he was fluent in French and Spanish.

His introduction to 'showbusiness' came when working for Rio Tinto at one of their sulphur mines in Spain. They asked him to run a theatre, and he obliged by writing revues – in Spanish.

Back in London he penned a number of plays before being invited by the BBC in 1933 to produce radio talks. He moved to outside broadcasting and then became a senior producer in the Empire Service, which kept expatriates in touch with home. He took the service from strength to strength, laying the foundation for the vast expansion of external broadcasting in later years.

In the summer of 1936 Gerald Cock, the BBC's new Director of Television and a man given to bold initiatives, decided that the long delay in providing a television service could best be brought to an end by a burst of activity that would capture public attention.

It was decided to organize transmissions from Alexandra Palace to the Radiolympia Exhibition in August 1936. The programmes were planned by Madden, who by now had ample theatrical experience. He was given only ten days' notice to commission lyrics and music and to find stars and arrange films.

He was at the mercy not only of engineers but of what were known to be difficult reception conditions at Olympia. Yet, with every kind of technical difficulty to harass him, and Cock's two highly prized lady announcers – Jasmine Bligh and Elizabeth Cowell – both ill, Madden at last succeeded in presenting what one newspaper called 'real television'.

Between then and the official opening of the new service on November 2, 1936, he produced two further programmes – *Here's Looking at You* and the magazine *Picture Page*. Facilities were primitive and money scarce, but Madden delighted in the challenge and involved himself in every aspect of the new medium.

A whole series of programmes followed, among them *Picture Parade* and *The Gossip Hour*, the latter the forerunner of the ubiquitous 'chat' show. He was keen on drama and 'a play a day' was his slogan.

With television off the air for the duration of the war, Madden reverted to wireless broadcasting. During his wartime sound activities he put the Beverley Sisters and the George Mitchell Choir on the air for the first time.

He also produced the *Blitz Roundups*, *Variety Bandbox*, *Girl Friends of the Forces* and the *American Eagle in Britain* series. For D-Day he took charge of the

Cecil Madden
visited by The Beverley Sisters in his 80s.

integrated British-American-Canadian production for the Allied Expeditionary Forces Programme.

With the return of television in 1946, he was appointed chief planner of the service. Among programmes for which he was largely responsible were *This is Your Life* and *What's My Line?*

In 1950 he was made temporary head of children's television and set about transforming *Children's Hour* – until then a whimsy affair – into an intelligent and entertaining show.

His removal from the post six months later roused the ire of parents, not to mention the Televiewers' Association with its membership of 10,000 discerning children. But the BBC hierarchy turned a deaf ear to all their entreaties and Madden was forbidden to talk to the Press.

Instead, he was made assistant to the controller of television programmes. It was, perhaps, less than he deserved. In this post he remained until his retirement from the Corporation in 1964.

In retirement he founded the British Film and Television Academy. He was, at the time of his death, president of the British Puppet and Model Theatre Guild.

He wrote a number of plays over the years, usually with someone else. His published works include *Anywhere for a News Story*, *My Grimmest Nightmare* and *Not Long for this World*.

In the end, television outgrew Madden. But it owes much to his farsighted and devoted work during its infancy. Colleagues remember him as an enthusiastic and imaginative practitioner, and as a congenial companion.

He married, in 1932, Muriel Cochrane. She died in 1974. He is survived by their son and daughter.

POSTSCRIPT

Tributes to Cecil Madden, the first TV producer

ALTHOUGH the parentage of television may be a little vague, since it is impossible to pinpoint precisely who its father was, there is no doubt at all about the "midwife" who brought it into practical existence in 1936.

It was Cecil Charles Madden, who produced the very first television programme in the world.

Gerald Cock directed the new BBC service, but it was Cecil Madden who made it work and launched it as an entertainment medium.

There were no precedents to

By Stephen Williams, who worked alongside Cecil Madden at the Criterion Theatre throughout the war.

guide him in 1936. Only his own sense of theatre, his ingenuity and his genius for improvisation enabled him to do the job and so to lay the guidelines along which television production and production techniques have evolved ever since.

In sound broadcasting Cecil brought the same qualities to

bear, most successfully when called upon to launch and direct the programme output of three major BBC undertakings; the pre-war Empire Service; during the war the Overseas Light Entertainment Service, which was based in the underground Criterion theatre (off Piccadilly Circus); and from D-Day until victory, the Allied Expeditionary Forces Programme, in which the broadcasting organisations of the UK, the USA and Canada all co-operated.

For more than four years of the war Cecil literally lived in this Criterion theatre. His office was the star dressing room where four

secretaries were always in attendance known to the production staff as Mr Madden's Chorus. His bedroom was the Number 2 Dress Circle box, where he rarely got any real rest, for in addition to the bombs and gunfire outside there were programmes emanating from the Criterion stage all through the night as the Overseas transmitters swung from zone to zone of their world-embracing coverage.

According to Mrs Fenton, the theatre's housekeeper, Mr Madden must have lived in those days on milk — usually wartime powdered milk "reconstituted", for he hardly ever left the

building except for a breath of fresh air.

Yet in spite of the non-stop stress under which he existed, he never lost his calm, no matter how tired and haggard he came to look as the years went by.

Nor did he lose his enthusiasm for encouraging fresh talent, and among the dozens of artists of that period who have reason to be grateful to Cecil Madden are the Beverleys, Petula Clark, Moira Lister, George Mitchell, and Dorothy Squires.

He was a most dedicated broadcaster and a non-stop do-er, who loved every minute of his

work.

He was certainly a lot of fun to work with, and a great inspiration. He had the most infectious laugh in the entire Corporation, and he greeted everyone who came into his office by calling out his or her Christian name with that rising inflection which really did mean he was delighted to see the person concerned.

Cecil Madden's influence on a vast area of BBC activities was probably greater than any of his predecessors, contemporaries or successors. His name should always be remembered among the greats of British Broadcasting.

A pioneer who saw the potential of television

WHEN Gerald Cock, the BBC's first Director of Television, gave orders for a demonstration transmission of the new medium to be made from Alexandra Palace to the RadiOlympia exhibition in the summer of 1936, he called for Cecil Madden.

Up to then the BBC had followed

and supported the emerging technology, but now there was a need to present something in front of the cameras — programmes, and Gerald Cook appointed Cecil Madden, a senior producer in the Empire Radio Service and a man with a passion for theatre, to the task.

Cecil Madden had ten days in which to find artists and commission lyrics and

music. Against odds, it all came together, and was beamed across London to be seen by the thousands who visited the exhibition.

Variety

He moved straight ahead with preparations for the official opening of the BBC Television service, producing Here's Looking at You and the first Picture Page. At first it was regarded with scepticism by many in radio, and was seen by only the very few who had

television sets, but it blossomed as it caught on and techniques improved.

The service closed down during the war, but when it returned in 1946, he was appointed chief planner, and under his guidance many of Britain's best-known post-war programmes, and programme-makers were to emerge.

Cecil Madden, who later founded the British Academy of Film and Television Arts, first worked for the BBC in 1933, producing radio talks. He had written a

number of plays for the theatre, and he was able to indulge his interest in variety both in television and, where the service closed during the war, back in radio. Among the programmes he introduced was the forces' favourite, Variety Bandbox, and he uncovered a wealth of talent including the Beverley Sisters.

In his tribute, Television Managing Director Bill Cotton said: "In the oft played film of the inauguration of the BBC's Television Service on November 2 1936, there is a fleeting shot of Cecil Madden, hunched over a talk back microphone, directing the first production of the first regular television service in the world.

"If he had had time to think about it, it was for him a momentous experience, because amongst many doubters in the BBC, Cecil believed absolutely in the new medium, and could see its future potential.

Joy

"I am personally delighted that he was able to take part last year in the celebrations that surrounded the 50th anniversary of the BBC Television Service, and his joy in being asked to blow out the candles on the anniversary cake was plain for all to see.

"He will be missed by the many people whom he guided through the early days, but his reputation and his memory will remain as long as that little piece of film is shown."

●Left: In 1937, celebrating the 100th edition of Picture Page
●Right: In 1986, celebrating television's 50 years

Pictures record the Madden years

CECIL Madden was an avid collector of photographs, and during his years with the Corporation he compiled a series of photographic montages which reflect his interest in his work and provide a visual record of the personalities who came to the BBC.

He made a total of 19 montages for television and four for radio, and in addition he put together 30 "signature cards" to which almost every name in showbusiness contributed, says BBC research historian John Kane.

"He knew an extraordinary number of people. He was acquainted with almost everyone who was anyone, from Bing Crosby and Marlene Dietrich to Harry Secombe. He made a point of keeping up with events in showbusiness, and was a theatre-goer right up to the end of his life."

The montages and signature cards are dotted throughout the BBC, and John Kane has taken steps to trace them and in some cases, restore them.

"They make quite a collection," he said. "They and the dozens of albums and scrapbooks kept by Cecil provide an enormous amount of valuable information about the BBC."

Photomontages for 1950 (left) and 1959

Cecil Madden
Ariel Tribute
June 3, 1987.

315

ST. LUKE'S CHURCH

Chelsea

The Service is conducted by the
Rev. Derek Watson
Rector of St. Luke's, Chelsea
and the
Rev. David Winter
Head of Religious Broadcasting, BBC

CECIL MADDEN, M.B.E.

Organist: Barry Rose
Master of the Choirs, the Kings School, Canterbury

(1902 – 1987)

The RADA Singers conducted by Andrew Charity

The Martin Burgess String Quartet
(Royal Academy of Music)

THURSDAY 22nd OCTOBER 1987
11.30 am

ORDER OF SERVICE

ORGAN

Ciacono in E minor .... Dietrich Buxterhude

Three Preludes (Opus 105) ...   Charles Villiers-Stanford
    F major
    G minor
    E flat major

STRING QUARTET

String Quartet in C (K.465) "The Dissonance" .. Mozart
    Andante cantabile

RADA SINGERS

Music will calm thee .... Handel
                     arr. H.A. Chambers

THE BIDDING

The Rev. Derek Watson

HYMN

Praise, my soul, the King of heaven;
To his feet thy tribute bring.
Ransomed, healed, restored, forgiven,
Who like me his praise should sing?
Praise him! Praise him!
Praise the everlasting King.

Praise him for his grace and favour
To our fathers in distress;
Praise him still the same for ever,
Slow to chide and swift to bless.
Praise him! Praise him!
Glorious in his faithfulness.

Father-like, he tends and spares us;
Well our feeble frame he knows;
In his hands he gently bears us,
Rescues us from all our foes.
Praise him! Praise him!
Widely as his mercy flows.

Angels, help us to adore him;
Ye behold him face to face;
Sun and moon, bow down before him,
Dwellers all in time and space.
Praise him! Praise him!
Praise with us the God of grace.

John Goss (1800 – 80)
Formerly Organist at St. Luke's, Chelsea

READING

Lord Briggs

RADA SINGERS

Psalm 150: Praise the Lord

POEM

Valerie Hobson

Adieu! and Au Revoir .... John Oxenham

STRING QUARTET

String Quartet in D (Opus 64 No. 5) .... Haydn
Andante cantabile

ADDRESS

Bill Cotton, O.B.E.
Managing Director, BBC Television

Richard Todd	(Stage)
Joy Beverley	(Radio)
John Blundall	(Puppetry)
Cliff Michelmore	(Television)

RADA SINGERS

With Cheerful Notes .... Handel

PRAYERS

The Rev. David Winter

HYMN

LEAD us, heavenly Father, lead us
  O'er the world's tempestuous sea;
Guard us, guide us, keep us, feed us,
  For we have no help but thee;
Yet possessing every blessing
  If our God our Father be.

Saviour, breathe forgiveness o'er us;
  All our weakness thou dost know,
Thou didst tread this earth before us,
  Thou didst feel its keenest woe;
Lone and dreary, faint and weary,
  Through the desert thou didst go.

Spirit of our God descending,
  Fill our hearts with heavenly joy,
Love with every passion blending,
  Pleasure that can never cloy:
Thus provided, pardoned, guided,
  Nothing can our peace destroy.

James Edmeston (1791 – 1867)

THE BLESSING

The Rev. Derek Watson

ORGAN

Allabreve in D .... J.S. Bach

CECIL MADDEN, M.B.E.
1902–1987

C E C I L   M A D D E N.

Cecil Madden produced and directed the world's
first (high definition) television programme
at the BBC Alexandra Palace television studios
in August 1936. This was called HERE'S LOOKING
AT YOU.

During 31 years in Radio and Television he
created the following popular series:
VARIETY BANDBOX, SPORTSVIEW, STARLIGHT,
PICTURE PAGE, 100% BROADWAY, CABARET CARTOONS,
PICTURE PARADE, THE GOSSIP HOUR, STARS IN
THEIR COURSES, ANYWHERE FOR A NEWS STORY,
MEET THE DETECTIVE, AMERICAN EAGLE IN BRITAIN,
THE A.E.F. PROGRAMMES, NOW.

Among his stage plays, collaborations and
adaptations are: LOOPHOLE, INVESTIGATION,
THE HERO, CHELSEA REACH, CHATTERBOX, SATURDAY'S
CHILDREN, MAX AND MR MAX, SILENT WITNESS, THE
EQUATOR, PRESTIGE, THROUGH THE VEIL, THE
PRESIDENT'S DOUBLE, A TOUCH OF MAGIC.

Has also worked in the Spanish Theatre,
French Theatre and in Revue.

Cecil Madden is Founder of the British Film
and Television Academy. President of the British
Puppet and Model Theatre Guild. Honorary Life
Member of the Concert Artists Association.

Governor of Dulwich College Preparatory School
(30 years). Fellow of the Royal Society of
Arts. Member of The British Empire.

Jubilee Award Society of Film and TV Arts.
Honorary Founder Member British Film and
Television Academy. Freedom of the Police
Chiefs of U.S.A. Founder National Film School.
Governor Police Puppet Theatre.

Variety Club of Great Britain Awards Panel.

31 Years British Broadcasting Corporation.
Created Empire Service 1933-6.
Planner BBC Television Service 1936-9.
Childrens Television.
In charge - Allied Expeditionary Forces Programmes.
Producer 5 years American Eagle in Britain.
11 Years Assistant to three Controllers.
Head of Childrens Television 1950.
Vice Chairman Royal Academy of Dramatic Art Associates.
Member Society of Authors. Member Dramatists Guild of USA.

A typed copy of Cecil Madden's career.
Typed by him on his old huge typewriter

CECIL MADDEN

(1902–1987)

Acknowledgements
by
Mardie Madden Gorman

I have so many people to thank so, in no particular order, I would like to thank the Beverley Sisters not only for their help with reminiscences and photos but also for often going to visit him in later years always dressed alike and wonderful fun. My cousin Locker Madden and his daughter Eleanor for help with early family information. Jessica Sleath whose late husband Alan worked as a producer at the BBC for my father and who helped to organise his memorial service at St Luke's Church Chelsea in October 1987. I would like to thank Simon Vaughan the archivist of the Alexander Palace Television Society for his great help with checking information for Jennifer. Jill Fenson a good friend of Cecil. I would like to thank my friend Janet Marshall for her help editing the manuscript. Kathy Grade for all her kindness to Cecil over many years. Caroline Hurley, my daughter, for all her help and additional work.

Jennifer Lewis

Special thanks goes to all those who visited and read letters and newspapers to Cecil in later years after he lost centre vision in his seventies due to a deterioration of his retinas. This allowed him to send his early plays to repertory theatres and anyone interested. He had an old Roneo copier which you had to ink, to copy these plays. They were mostly by him though some were Spanish translations he had done, or collaborations. My mother always said she married him because he had a play on in the West End and his name was on the side of buses. I found a musical of Marie Lloyd with my illustrations in it from the 1960s. I have over thirty plays in my house now.

He loved the radio, and was always active and out and about, often with his second Yorkshire Terrier 'Astro' named by my children, and who came from the Battersea Dogs Home.

Finally I would like to thank my eldest daughter Jennifer Lewis for her time and energy taking the original manuscript which was typed on his 1930s' typewriter. She has shaped and edited it to what we have here. Jennifer is married and lives in the US with two children. She worked for the Museum of Television and Radio in New York as associate curator for several years and is now a published author of romance novels. Her website is www.jen-lewis.com.

For his 80th birthday we had an open house in his own flat in Chelsea (because of his eyes). So many stars coming and going. He had a birthday cake shaped like an old TV set which Petula Clark helped him to cut. When he died at 84 years old he had made lists for his 85th birthday party of who he wanted to be invited, we were planning it for October.

He was much loved by those who knew him and so very passionate about show business. We, the family that is, have heard these stories and more so many times but felt we had to put them into print.

MARDIE MADDEN GORMAN
London, 2007

VAUDEVILLE

THEATRE, Strand, W.C.2 Proprietors & Managers **J. & R. GATTI**

TEMPLE BAR 4871-2

In association with J. & R. GATTI
ARCHIBALD DE BEAR presents

MAX AND MR MAX

A Comedy in Three Acts
By CECIL MADDEN
From the Spanish of JOSE LOPEZ RUBIO & EDUARDO UGARTE

WITH

NICHOLAS HANNEN

EDMUND GWENN

KATHLEEN O'REGAN

D. A. CLARKE-SMITH

The Play Produced by NICHOLAS HANNEN

NIGHTLY at 8.30. MATS.: MON. & SAT. at 2.30

JOHN WADDINGTON LTD., LONDON AND LEEDS

Pictures record the Madden years

CECIL Madden was an avid collector of photographs, and during his years with the Corporation be compiled a series of photographic montages which reflect his interest in his work and provide a visual record of the personalities who came to the BBC.

He made a total of 19 montages for television and four for radio, and in addition he put together 30 "signature cards" to which almost every name in showbusiness contributed, says BBC research historian John Kane.

"He knew an extraordinary number of people. He was acquainted with almost everyone who was anyone,

from Bing Crosby and Marlene Dietrich to Harry Secombe. He made a point of keeping up with events in showbusiness, and was a theatre-goer right up to the end of his life."

The montages and signature cards are dotted throughout the BBC, and John Kane has taken steps to trace them and in some cases, restore them. "They make quite a collection," he said. "They and the dozens of albums and scrapbooks kept by Cecil provide an enormous amount of valuable information about the BBC."

CECIL MADDEN ARIEL TRIBUTE JUNE 3, 1987.